THE MAKING OF THE FIRST WORLD WAR

IAN F. W. BECKETT

THE MAKING OF THE FIRST WORLD WAR

YALE UNIVERSITY PRESS
NEW HAVEN AND LONDON

For information about this and other Yale University Press publications, please contact:
U.S. Office: sales.press@yale.edu   www.yalebooks.com
Europe Office: sales @yaleup.co.uk   www.yalebooks.co.uk

Set in Minion Pro by IDSUK (DataConnection) Ltd
Printed in Great Britain by TJ International, Padstow, Cornwall

Library of Congress Cataloging-in-Publication Data

Beckett, I.F.W. (Ian Frederick William)
    The making of the First World War/Ian F. W. Beckett.
       p. cm.
    Includes bibliographical references.
    ISBN 978-0-300-16202-8 (cl : alk. paper)
1. World War, 1914–1918.   2. World War, 1914–1918—Influence.   I. Title.
    D521.B377 2012
    940.3—dc23

                                                        2012017209

A catalogue record for this book is available from the British Library.

10 9 8 7 6 5 4 3 2 1

For Trina, who alone knows how much this book is her creation

CONTENTS

ILLUSTRATIONS

1 Exhausted Belgian soldiers from a dog-drawn machine gun section pictured at Louvain during the retreat to Antwerp, 20 August 1914 (IWM Q53207).
2 Enver Pasha meeting Kaiser Wilhelm II on the former German battle cruiser, *Goeben*, in Constantinople, October 1917 (IWM Q 23732).
3 The scene at Anzac Cove at about 0800 hours on 25 April 1915, the Australian 4th Battalion coming ashore together with the mules of the 26th Indian Mountain Battery (IWM Q112876).
4 The Ministry of Munitions' National Shell Filling Factory No. 6 at Chilwell, Nottinghamshire, 1916 (IWM Q30018).
5 Geoffrey Malins films British and French leaders leaving Beauquesne Chateau on 12 August 1916 (IWM Q950).
6 The funeral procession of Emperor Franz Joseph in Vienna, 30 November 1916 (IWM HU94385).
7 Torpedoes being loaded onto a German U-boat at Bruges, 1917 (IWM HU107214).
8 An apprehensive crowd outside the Winter Place in St Petersburg, 29 July 1914, the day before announcement of full Russian mobilisation (IWM Q828180).
9 London as photographed from a Gotha bomber on 7 July 1917 (IWM Q108954).

All photographs courtesy of the Imperial War Museum.

ACKNOWLEDGEMENTS

QUOTATIONS FROM Crown copyright material in the National Archives appear by permission of Her Majesty's Stationery Office. I also wish to acknowledge my thanks to the following for allowing me to consult and quote from archives in their possession and/or copyright: The Trustees of the Imperial War Museum; the Churchill Archives Centre, Churchill College, Cambridge; the National Library of Wales; and the National Maritime Museum.

My thanks also go to Heather McCallum of Yale University Press for her original encouragement to undertake this book after a discussion on Philip Bell's work on *Twelve Turning Points of the Second World War*, and also for her patience when the manuscript was delayed. My thanks for editorial support also go to Rachael Lonsdale and Tami Halliday. Two anonymous readers provided thoughtful feedback on the original proposal, and two more on the draft manuscript. I have also had the opportunity to test out various chapters on the students of the University of Kent.

My greatest thanks go to my wife, Trina, for her sterling work in helping me to lighten my usual literary style.

ABBREVIATIONS

AEF   American Expeditionary Force
AIF   Australian Imperial Force
ANZAC   Australian and New Zealand Army Corps
AWM   Australian War Memorial
BEF   British Expeditionary Force
CID   Committee of Imperial Defence
CUP   Committee of Union and Progress (Turkey)
GQG   *Grand Quartier Général* (French General Headquarters)
GHQ   General Headquarters
GPO   General Post Office
IWM   Imperial War Museum
LADA   London Air Defence Area
LCC   London County Council
NCO   Non-Commissioned Officer
OHL   *Oberste Heeresleitung* (German General Headquarters)
RAF   Royal Air Force
RFC   Royal Flying Corps
RNAS   Royal Naval Air Service
RSSILA   Returned Sailors' and Soldiers' Imperial League of Australia.
SPD   *Sozialdemokratische Partei Deutschlands* (German Social Democratic Party)

TNA	The National Archives
TsVPK	*Tsentral'nyi Voenno-Promyshlennyi Komitet* (Russian Central War Industries Committee)
VPK	*Voenno-Promyshlennya Komitet* (Russian War Industries Committee)

INTRODUCTION

At first sight, Nieuport on the Belgian coast is hardly inspiring. It seems to sum up one French general's description of Flanders in 1914 as a monotonous countryside with an air of melancholic sadness melting almost imperceptibly into the grey waters of the North Sea.[1] Two shipping channels, three drainage canals and the river Yser merge together at the 'Goosefoot'. It is hard to imagine that one of the most significant events of the First World War took place here. Two small monuments begin to suggest the importance of this desolate spot: one to a Belgian engineer, the other to a veteran waterman characterised as the hero of the 'flooding'. It might be thought that this celebrates saving the countryside in the manner of the apocryphal Dutch boy and the dyke. In reality, it is a celebration of flooding the Belgian countryside in October 1914.

The story is little known outside Belgium. In Britain the story of 1914 is one of the British army's initial retreat from Mons in August, the advance to the Aisne, and then its battles around Ypres in October and November 1914, of a thin line of depleted and bone-weary units clinging on desperately in the face of mass German assaults. In France, it is the story of the great losses during the battles of the frontiers in August, and the 'miracle' of the Marne in September as the Germans began to retreat when almost in sight of Paris. An abiding image for the French is the despatch of troops to the Marne front in Paris taxicabs. For the Germans, it is the failure of the opening offensive and the time of the *Kindermord* – the 'slaughter of the innocents' – the loss of the supposed schoolboy corps committed to the attempts to break through the British lines at Ypres. This had a profound impact on the young Adolf Hitler, serving in the 16th (Bavarian) Reserve Infantry Regiment. Yet it is the inundation of the Belgian countryside between Nieuport and Dixmude that was one of the major turning points of the war. The Germans had seized Antwerp, Ostend and Zeebrugge, and were poised to break through to the Channel ports of Calais and Dunkirk. Had they done so, it would have had the same result as in 1940, spelling the imminent defeat of Belgium and France, forcing the evacuation of the British Expeditionary Force (BEF), leaving Britain isolated, and heralding the possibility of a German invasion of Britain. Instead, it was the start of four years of deadlock on the Western Front.

In a war usually characterised as one of enormous casualties resulting from the massive application of modern technology, the impact of a 'silent conqueror' seems unlikely. Inevitably, it is the dramatic battles and the extraordinary loss of life that will occur to many as the most significant episodes of the First World War. But, as the flooding of the Belgian countryside illustrates, great battles may not be the most decisive events in a war. Even what seemed momentous political decisions at the time may not mean that much in the longer term. What, then, does constitute a pivotal point in war?

The most momentous changes that occurred as a result of the global conflict between 1914 and 1918 may not only have been less obvious to those who experienced them, but also remain effectively hidden from those who focus later only on the immediate consequences of the war. In the context of war, consideration of significant turning points should embrace all aspects of conflict, whether military, political, socio-economic, or cultural. A longer-term perspective will identify moments of far more historical significance than the immediate circumstances pertaining to a specific event. Emphatically, what matters in the shorter or longer term may not be simply those events assumed to have affected the actual course of a war. In that sense, the study of the First World War yields examples of both relatively well-known and readily accepted contemporary decision points, and also those longer-term consequences of events that may not be as well recognised. This book, then, is intended to provoke debate on the wider consequences of war by suggesting alternate ways of identifying key moments in a conflict. The familiar and conventional ways of looking at the war's most significant events are deliberately contrasted with less familiar episodes that also changed the course of history in the shorter or longer term. Even the familiar event, however, can yield a new interpretation.

War has an undoubted capacity to bring about long-term as well as short-term historical change. The First World War as a whole was a pivotal event globally that shaped the twentieth century through its unexpected scale, intensity, character, and dislocation of peoples. In Britain, for example, those who spoke of a 'Great War' in 1913 would have meant the struggle against Revolutionary and Napoleonic France a century before. Both the Seven Years War (1756–63) and the French Revolutionary and Napoleonic Wars (1792–1815) were global conflicts, but their longer-term legacies were not as great as those of events between 1914 and 1918. This new global conflict destroyed four empires – those of Imperial Germany, Austria-Hungary, Tsarist Russia and Ottoman Turkey. While that of Germany was a recent construct, the others were of long standing. The consequences were profound, not least in the Middle East, whose politics today remain conditioned by events between 1914 and 1918. The war gravely weakened Europe's influence generally, even if the United States chose to wield its new-found power in financial rather than military or diplomatic terms. Without the First World War, communism would probably not have triumphed in Russia, or fascism been given its opportunity in Germany and Italy. In that sense, the world as shaped by the Great War endured until the collapse of communism in Russia and Eastern Europe between 1989 and 1991. The Second World War further shaped global development, but along similar lines. But is it conceivable to contemplate the Second World War occurring without the First?

It was a global event of unquestionable importance. Naturally, global war will always have a greater impact than more limited conflicts, though the second most destructive war in history after the Second World War was the Taiping Rebellion, an internal civil war in China between 1851 and 1866 that cost perhaps 20 million lives.[2] Longer-term evolutionary and structural trends in history clearly need to be borne in mind alongside the immediate changes resulting from decisions made at a particular time, and pure contingency, in assessing the degree to which war either accelerated or, conceivably, hindered changes that would have occurred anyway over the course of time. Demography, for example, appears almost immune to the effects of war. There were approximately 10 million war dead in the First World War. Neither this, nor the estimated 21 million deaths from the influenza pandemic of 1918–19, which had little connection with the war, had any discernible impact on the long-term demographic trend. Similarly, the estimated 57 million war dead of the Second World War were of little account in the long-term. The global population was about a billion by 1850; it had doubled by 1930; has since doubled again; and probably doubled again by the end of the first decade of this century. Scientific and technological development, or industrialisation and urbanisation, will also promote change whether stimulated by war or otherwise. Ideology has, too, played a significant part in shaping the modern world. The most dramatic long-term change will be more apparent in states that are defeated, occupied or newly created as a result of war. Through accidents of location, some states are likely to suffer far more disruption than others. States that emerge victorious also have less inclination to change, and are more likely to revert to pre-war practices.[3]

What, then, of the great moments of decision or significance within a global conflict? 'Decisive' battle provides a ready metaphor. In the past, war has generally been interpreted in the light of contemporary events. Many British historians writing in the nineteenth century regarded the British system of liberal parliamentary democracy as the ideal form of government. They interpreted British history as an inevitable progression towards this particular end. In terms of military history, Sir Edward Creasy's *Fifteen Decisive Battles of the World*, published in 1851, exemplifies the same approach.[4] Such ideas still play a major, if unwitting, part in 'popular' military history that depicts combatants either improving or declining over time, being technologically advanced or retarded, or one side learning the supposedly clear lessons of the past while the other either ignores or misreads them.

Of course, there are military turning points in any conflict. Given that the popular image of the First World War in Britain remains one of mindless futility, it is perhaps inevitable that dramatic battles and the extraordinary loss of life involved – as on the Somme and at Verdun in 1916, or at Passchendaele in 1917 – will occur to many as the most significant events.

But great battles may not be the most decisive events. Despite the British obsession with the first day of the battle of the Somme on 1 July 1916, it was hardly a turning point in a military sense. Some of those historians who now look for a British 'learning curve' in France and Flanders between 1914 and 1918 have identified the Somme as marking its beginning. Some, too, have seen the de facto attrition strategy adopted on the Somme as significant in determining eventual victory. Such arguments are unconvincing.[5]

By contrast, given its undoubted continued impact on the British psyche, 1 July 1916 can be seen as a cultural turning point, but for the fact that it is a relatively recently developed memory of the war. In the 1920s and 1930s, it was Passchendaele that aroused more controversy as a representation of all that was deemed wrong with the British conduct of the war on the Western Front. The Somme only re-emerged into the collective memory in the 1960s.[6] While the first day of a major offensive has often caught the imagination, this is hardly true of the last day as continuing operations inevitably petered out. On the other hand, another military fiasco such as the landing of the Anzacs – the Australian and New Zealand Army Corps – at Gallipoli in April 1915 was a much more significant *contemporary* cultural turning point. It established a real sense of antipodean identity with lasting cultural and political implications. Gallipoli would have been a different kind of turning point had the campaign succeeded. Even after the now much vaunted British achievements of the 'Hundred Days' between August and November 1918 – driving the German army back from the territory it had occupied since 1914 – the front line was still continuous.[7]

There can be few more decisive battles than Tannenberg on the Eastern Front in August 1914. Yet it had no wider strategic meaning for the war as a whole other than in establishing the military reputation of the German commanders, Paul von Hindenburg and Erich Ludendorff. Their influence on the German conduct of the war was certainly to become pernicious. Equally, the battle of Sarikamish in the Caucasus in December 1914 not only proved a decisive Russian victory over the Turks, but also ended any prospect of the Turkish leadership fulfilling its pan-Islamic aims. It confirmed the image of Ottoman decline throughout Central Asia.[8]

The first battle of the Marne in September 1914 and the first battle of Ypres in October and November 1914 clearly ended Germany's expectation of a short victorious war. First Ypres certainly marked the moment of transition for the British from war as it had been to war as it would become. But an improvised defence had no relevance for the future conduct of the offensive from a fixed trench system. There was a more poisonous legacy in the British conviction that ground held at such cost should not be surrendered lightly, and in Sir Douglas Haig's belief that the Germans had failed at Ypres by ending their operations prematurely.[9] Thus, in closing the last gap in what was to become a continuous trench line from Switzerland to the sea, it was the Belgian opening of the sluices in October 1914 that really shaped the next four years of conflict.

So why was Germany defeated? In military terms, the 1918 German spring offensives in the west and the subsequent allied counter-attack have given rise to contrasting claims. Fritz von Lossberg, the chief of staff of the German Fourth Army, identified the slowing of one German advance during the Second Battle of the Marne on 18 July 1918 as 'the precise turning point in the conduct of the war'. It was a judgement echoed by officers of the German Seventh Army.[10] Lossberg saw it as such through the failure of the German High Command, and especially Ludendorff, to understand the state of the army by this time. Others have taken their cue from Ludendorff himself and interpret the British offensive at Amiens on 8 August 1918 – characterised by Ludendorff as the 'Black Day of the German Army' – as the crucial moment. Whatever the arguments concerning the sheer weight of materiel available to the Entente by the summer of 1918, Ludendorff's strategic and tactical decisions were the key to Germany's fortunes. One historian has identified Ludendorff's switching of the German operational objective towards Arras on 28 March 1918 as 'one of the decisive days of the Great War'.[11] But it was the decision to commit the German army to the second of the series of offensives – that on the Lys on 9 April 1918 – that best illustrated Ludendorff's strategic short-comings, and condemned Germany to defeat.

The introduction of a new weapon may mark a potential turning point in war. While that may be so over the longer term, it does not necessarily mean that such a weapon had any significant impact on the war in which it was first introduced. Clearly, the introduction of gas warfare had a significant initial impact at least at Second Ypres on the Western Front in April–May 1915, if not upon its first appearance, at Bolimov on the Eastern

Front in January 1915. In the longer term, gas was a military dead end. At most a 'force multiplier', it was a weapon against which troops were better protected than any other by 1918.[12] The introduction of the tank tells a similar story, albeit the tank was to prove considerably more decisive than gas in the future conduct of war. After its first use on the Somme in September 1916, the tank was deployed in large numbers at both Cambrai in November–December 1917 and at Amiens in August 1918. Whatever the initial impact on 20 November 1917 or 8 August 1918, the tank's chronic technological unreliability limited its utility beyond the first few days of any offensive.[13] In the longer term, the tank was a weapon with only a limited window of success between 1939 and 1941, before anti-tank guns, anti-tank mines, rocket-firing aircraft and defence in depth neutralised it.

Two other weapons first given extensive trials in the First World War – the submarine and the bomber – had limited impact at that time. Unrestricted submarine warfare certainly posed a very significant challenge to British shipping in both world wars, but the U-boats were defeated in both conflicts through a combination of an old solution for protecting commerce – convoys – and technological advances. Equally, strategic bombing failed to destroy civilian morale not only in both world wars, but also in Vietnam between 1965 and 1973, though continuing technological advances have rendered 'stand-off' aerial bombardment more militarily effective in more recent conflicts.[14] Yet the German return to unrestricted warfare in February 1917 was assuredly a turning point in contributing significantly to American entry into the war, with all that it implied for Germany's prospects of victory. Similarly, the greatest impact deriving from the first German use of heavy bombers – as opposed to airships – against London in June 1917 heralded the beginnings of the psychological fear of the bomber that marked the interwar years, with detrimental effects upon policymakers.

Decisions made by military or political leaderships not only raise the impact of personality and contingency,[15] but also suggest the significance of political and diplomatic events. Like those of military commanders, politicians' decisions can have far-reaching implications. A distinguished biographer of President Woodrow Wilson has suggested that the period from 1 May 1916 to 1 February 1917 is 'one of the fateful turning points of modern history, because the decisions that the leaders of the great powers made during this brief period determined the future of mankind for generations to come'.[16] By this, he meant not just the German decision to conduct unrestricted submarine warfare, but also the collective failure to find agreement on a negotiated settlement, and the adoption of far-reaching war aims. Only Romania (August 1916) was a new entrant to the war during that particular period. But while decisions to enter the war might be seemingly of relatively short-term moment, others had the potential to shape events over the longer term. Arguably Romanian entry or that of Italy in May 1915, while turning points for Romania and Italy, were of little real consequence beyond opening new fronts and further complicating the tangled web of conflicting war aims and promises. If American entry to the war in April 1917 ensured victory for the Entente, that of Japan in August 1914 carried significant consequences in the longer term. The entry of Ottoman Turkey in November 1914 not only widened and arguably prolonged the war, but had the most profound consequences for the future. It ensured the ultimate collapse of the Ottoman Empire with lasting legacies still evident to this day in terms of the Armenian genocide of 1915, the division of the Middle East between Britain and France, and the immediate post-war conflict between Greece and Turkey.

What added materially to the troubled legacy of the war in the Middle East was another political decision, namely the Balfour Declaration of November 1917 that gave recognition to aspirations for a Jewish national home in Palestine in contradiction to separate promises made to the Arabs within the Ottoman Empire. Similarly, an overtly political act – Woodrow Wilson's outlining of his 'Fourteen Points' for a peace settlement in January 1918 – had special significance. This was not only for the post-war deliberations at the Paris peace conferences, but also in terms of Wilson's unrealistic utopian vision of a new world order, and the subsequent bitter legacy of unfulfilled expectations.

Purely domestic political events might have consequences only for the particular state in which they were taken and, therefore, they might rank as a turning point only for that state. Britain's adoption of military conscription in January 1916 was a turning point only in terms of its own prosecution of the war, and of the previously long tradition of eschewing such continental practices. There was a reversion to voluntary enlistment after the war. Following the adoption of conscription in 1939 and its extension as national service, voluntary enlistment was adopted once more in 1963. The same could be said for the introduction of British Summer Time in May 1916 albeit that it is still with us. A turning point for Britain may well not reflect those in and for France, Russia or Poland. The German despatch back to Russia of Lenin in the 'sealed train' in April 1917 was a turning point in the history of Russia, of the Soviet Union, and even of history itself. However, it was not a turning point of the First World War, because the collapse of the Tsarist government and the abdication of the Tsar in March 1917 had already changed the whole course of the war.

On the other hand, domestic political events might prove of great consequence. The fall of the Tsar is one example, as is the coming to supreme political power of Hindenburg and Ludendorff in Germany in August 1916. The death of the aged Emperor Franz Joseph of Austria-Hungary in November 1916 equally proved symbolic of the wider collapse of his empire under the challenges of war. The ascent to political authority of David Lloyd George in Britain in December 1916, or Georges Clemenceau in France in November 1917, was less significant. While it ensured the greater and more effective mobilisation of their respective states' war effort, it did not materially alter the outcome of the war or leave any particular legacy. Aspects of such mobilisation, however, were potentially much more significant both in establishing an effective war machine but also in demonstrating the long-term growth of the state. The creation of the British Ministry of Munitions in May 1915 was certainly a turning point in this regard, pre-dating similar creations elsewhere.

The mobilisation of all of a state's resources also implied socio-economic and cultural turning points. Clearly, the First World War had a lasting impact on the position of organised labour and of women, as well as the relationship between the individual and the state, though it is difficult to isolate one particular turning point in this regard. Generic turning points may be part of a general cycle of development, but may occur at different times depending on the particular state. It is tempting to describe as turning points the extension of the franchise to women in Britain in 1918, or in the United States by the Nineteenth Amendment to the Constitution that same year, though the latter was not ratified until 1920. But advances in the working conditions of women during wartime were invariably set back after the war despite the fact, for example, that women had attained the vote in Scandinavia and Australasia before the war.

The Anzac experience of Gallipoli is an example of a cultural turning point that had a significant bearing on the formulation of national identity. The First World War also had a lasting impact on the ways in which war was memorialised. It illustrated the cultural discontinuity between older traditional values and the 'modern', though the origins of modernism and similar artistic movements lay in the pre-war decades. Cinema, too, had made its appearance before the war, but the ability to manipulate the medium for propaganda purposes was newly realised. The premiere of the first real documentary, *The Battle of the Somme*, in July 1916 was a contemporary sensation. It also created a powerful and unforgettable vision of the war on the Western Front that has stamped an indelible image on public consciousness ever since.

In many ways the First World War was a transitional conflict. It saw the emergence of much that was dramatically new in military, political, socioeconomic and cultural terms, but also witnessed much that was traditional. The sheer scale meant that it was likely to produce more potential turning points than would more limited conflicts. Those other long-term evolutionary forces that had helped to create the modern world also ensured that the turning points of the First World War would have a far greater impact than those of earlier conflicts. The way in which the First World War then shaped the modern world equally ensured that even a second global conflict would represent merely a continuation of those developments already set in train. The seeds of the Second World War were categorically in the First.

The moments here chosen do not represent a counter-factor exercise for it is not my purpose to suggest how events may have developed differently. It is what actually occurred that matters. As the poet John Dryden phrased it in one of his translations from Horace's *Odes*, 'what has been, has been'. Each moment, indicated by the chapter subtitles, represents a major event within the broad spectrum suggested by the main titles. Each illustrates the interplay of both long-term factors and the element of chance. How such pivotal moments came about has its own intrinsic interest. I have consciously chosen episodes that mix the familiar with lesser-known events in order to demonstrate the complexity of war's impact. We have, then, a war that changed the course of history as whole, but also some events within it that determined its course, and others that shaped particular histories for states, societies, institutions and individuals. After almost a century, the influence of the First World War is with us still.

CHAPTER 1

THE SILENT CONQUEROR

The Flooding of the Yser, 21 October 1914

THE DEFINING characteristic of the First World War in the popular imagination is the deadlock on the Western Front, that continuous line of trenches from Switzerland to the sea that was never broken from its establishment in the autumn of 1914 until the armistice in November 1918. Mention of the Somme, Verdun or Passchendaele instantly conjures up a featureless moonscape of villages and farms reduced to ruins, woods reduced to mere stumps, men struggling up to their waists in mud, in a theatre of unrelieved terror and disillusionment. Since the 1960s this mythic version of the Western Front has persisted despite the best efforts of historians. It should not be surprising, then, that the origins of the deadlock in the autumn of 1914 should be equally misunderstood.

The war's military turning points are sometimes interpreted in terms of the introduction of new weapons systems such as gas, first used on the Western Front in April 1915, or the tank, which made its debut in September 1916. Alternatively, it is tempting to emphasise the opening (but invariably not the closing) of great offensives such as Verdun in February 1916, the Somme in July 1916, and Third Ypres or Passchendaele in July 1917. Dramatic battles and extraordinary loss of life will occur to many as the most significant episodes of the war. Clearly, while related to pre-war military developments, the battles of 1914 ensured that the war would not be 'over by Christmas'. Inevitably, the story of the campaigns in the west in 1914 unfolds differently depending upon the particular national perspective, though it begins with a uniform narrative of the failure of the German 'Schlieffen Plan'. As suggested in the introduction, the familiar story of 1914 in Britain differs from that in France and Germany. The Marne most certainly ended the initial German hopes for a swift victory in the west irrespective of whether Paris was or was not an operational objective. It forced the Germans to retreat towards the Aisne but it did not end the German expectation of further offensive operations in the west, nor of victory. That was to be ended by the events in Flanders.

Missing from the usually accepted narrative is the fourth army that was engaged in Flanders in 1914, namely the Belgians. Perhaps the neglect of the Belgians stems partly from the idea that, at the time, British soldiers found them less welcoming than might have been expected given that the defence of Belgian neutrality had brought Britain into the war in the first place. Similarly, the initial sympathy for Belgian refugees soon palled in Britain itself. The young King Albert I of the Belgians – only 39 in 1914 – was a prickly ally of the British and French. Technically, he was not an ally at all for, throughout the war, Albert maintained the fiction that Belgium remained a neutral country defending its territory as an 'associated' rather than an allied power. Thus, the Belgians officially referred to the British and French forces as armies of the 'guaranteeing powers' as they were guarantors of Belgian neutrality under the 1839 Treaty of London. To give him his due, Albert did not hesitate for a moment in rejecting the German demand on the evening of 2 August 1914 that they be allowed free passage through Belgium. Tall and reserved yet autocratic by nature and jealous of his extensive political prerogatives, Albert tended to equate his own rigid ideas with Belgium's national interest, frequently taking a different line from his ministers, who were inclined to be Francophiles. By contrast, Albert was always deeply suspicious of French motives and increasingly grew equally disillusioned with the British. Not unnaturally, once deadlock was apparent, Albert took exception to the idea that major offensives should be conducted on Belgian soil, and he wished both to achieve liberation by diplomacy and to preserve his army to ensure a voice at the post-war peace conference.

In the wake of the criticism of the French diplomatic position following the 9/11 attacks on the United States in 2001, indeed, one Flemish journalist, Paul Belien, pointedly cast Albert and the Belgians as the real

'surrender monkeys' of the Great War in an article in the *Spectator* on
31 July 2004. While owing much to the acute divisions between the Flemish
and Walloon inhabitants of Belgium, evident in the clandestine organisation established by Flemish separatists in the Belgian army during the war
itself, there is an element of truth. Albert was prepared to contemplate
separate negotiations with the Germans in 1915, 1916 and early 1918,
seeking territorial compensation from them in exchange for the abandonment of the neutrality he still claimed. Yet, the Belgian flooding of the
countryside between Nieuport on the Flanders coast and the railway
embankment running from Nieuport to Dixmude between 21 and
31 October 1914 was one of the major turning points of the war. In a
conflict usually characterised as one of enormous casualties resulting
from the massive application of modern technology, the impact of a 'silent
conqueror' resulting from the opening of weir gates and sluices seems
unlikely. As suggested in the introduction, the Germans had already seized
the port of Antwerp and were poised to break through to the Channel
coast. This heralded the possibility of a German invasion of Britain. It
should be remembered that two regular divisions were initially kept back
in Britain to guard against such a possibility in August 1914, and that many
of the Territorial and even New Army formations were initially stationed
in East Anglia. Preparations were begun on 7 October to remove livestock,
vehicles and petrol supplies from eastern counties, and an invasion attempt
was anticipated around 20 November 1914 when tide and winds were
favourable. It is true that the Germans had ruled out any such attempt
before the war, but the symbolic capture of Calais and Dunkirk would still
have posed significant political problems for the British government. It
might be argued that the speed of infantry advance in 1914 was relatively
slow and that the German troops had already been exhausted by their
earlier endeavours to maintain an unrealistic marching timetable to victory
beyond the effective range of available (and mostly horsed) supply transport. In October 1914, however, the BEF had reconnoitred last-ditch positions should the Germans break through at Ypres, and I Corps came very
close to ordering such a withdrawal on 31 October 1914. No one had any
doubt that such a breakthrough would have been disastrous.

Instead the man-created lagoon – between 18 and 21 miles long, between
1¾ and 2½ miles wide, and 3 to 4 feet deep – not only prevented the

German army from breaking through, but also effectively rendered the frontline in the west a continuous one from Switzerland to the sea. It was the true beginning of four years of deadlock on the Western Front.

As noted also in the introduction, the key location of Nieuport does not stimulate the senses for the casual visitor any more than the Flanders coast did for contemporaries.[1] Two canalised shipping channels – the Bruges and Furnes canals, three drainage sluices – the Nieuwbedelf, Nieuwendamme and the North Vaart, and the canalised river Yser merge together. The equestrian monument to King Albert erected in 1938 dominates the scene. But it is the two small monuments that are significant. One is to a Belgian military engineering company; the other to the veteran waterman, Hendrik Geeraert, remembered as the hero of the 'flooding'. Geeraert, however, is only one of an extraordinary collection of characters involved in a story that remains all but unknown.

As both sides endeavoured to move to the north in search of an open flank following the first allied encounters with German entrenchments on the Aisne – the so-called 'race to the sea' – the position of the Belgian army in its 'national redoubt' at Antwerp appeared ever more problematic. While Antwerp was the largest port in mainland Europe, its choice as a national centre of resistance owed most to its being suitably equidistant between France and Germany as a symbol of Belgian neutrality. The plan had also been originally adopted in the 1850s when France was the most likely enemy and the most likely direction of invasion was from the south. It certainly made little military sense, lying as it did 50 miles from the sea up the notoriously difficult waterway of the Scheldt, the mouth of which was Dutch territory. Commanded by General Hans von Beseler, the German III Reserve Corps began to bombard the city on 28 September 1914. Heavy German artillery had already demonstrated its potential, smashing supposedly modern Belgian fortifications at Liège in August, and then French defences at Mauberge in early September. The obsolete fortifications of Antwerp presented little obstacle to the formidable array of guns available to Beseler and, under the punishing artillery fire, the Belgians made early preparations for a retreat to Ostend. The British ambassador, Sir Francis Villiers, and his French counterpart were warned on 30 September that a German breach of the line of the outer forts would precipitate withdrawal. In the hope of at least prolonging the defence until the BEF was deployed to the north and might mount a relief, the British Cabinet agreed on 1 October to send the 7th Division if the French commander-in-chief, Joseph Joffre, also provided a regular division. Despite the French Minister of War, Alexandre Millerand, impressing on Joffre the political necessity of supporting the Belgians, Joffre promised only the 87th Territorial Division and a marine fusilier brigade.

Joffre felt the enterprise doomed from the outset, but the British intention to put in troops exerted pressure. Accordingly, Joffre sent General Paul Pau to report on the situation, in the hope that Pau – elderly, likeable and persuasive – could get the young Belgian monarch to release his field army from the city for operations in conjunction with the French and British to the south. Insisting on 7 October that the real purpose should be to facilitate a junction of the allied armies, Joffre limited the 87th Territorial Division to the Poperinghe area some 70 miles southwest of Antwerp and sent only the marine fusiliers into the city itself. As far as Joffre was concerned, the British desire to save Antwerp to keep the city out of hostile hands was merely 'traditional dogma'.[2] Moreover, having shut itself up in Antwerp when superior in numbers to its opponents, the Belgian army had forfeited any role commensurate with its strength. Napoleon had once suggested that Antwerp was 'a pistol, pointed at Great Britain',[3] and from the mouth of the Scheldt it was only 60 miles to England's east coast. But, in some respects Joffre was justified, for Antwerp could only have been realistically maintained if the allies had supplied it by sea and thus violated Dutch neutrality. The Dutch had declared the Scheldt neutral on 6 August, though Churchill was quite ready to force its passage.

With the German assault on Antwerp intensifying, the Belgian government was evacuated from the city though no decision was actually taken with regard to the Belgian field army. On 3 October, however, the field army withdrew to a second defensive line, between Termonde and the Nèthe. Albert, who was his own commander-in-chief, was determined to stay to the last and share the fate of the garrison. His prime minister (technically Chief of Cabinet), Baron Charles de Broqueville, and the king's private secretary, Jules Inglenbleek, tried to persuade Albert otherwise. De Broqueville, who doubled as war minister, apparently told Villiers that the army would begin its withdrawal from the city on 3 October, though this was entirely false. While Joffre welcomed the apparent news of a Belgian withdrawal as a means of uniting the allied armies in the field, the reaction in London was very different for no one had seriously expected such a situation to arise so quickly. With the Prime Minister, Herbert Asquith, absent fulfilling a political engagement at Cardiff, a hasty meeting between the First Lord of the Admiralty, Winston Churchill, the Secretary of State for War, Field Marshal Lord Kitchener, the Foreign Secretary, Sir Edward Grey, and the First Sea Lord, Prince Louis of Battenberg, decided to send immediate reinforcements to Antwerp, with Churchill himself also going there. The First Lord had been on his way for a weekend inspection visit to Dunkirk when recalled to London, and appears to have decided on his mission despite the advice of Grey and Kitchener to the contrary. Indeed, it was suggested at the time that even Villiers was not informed of Churchill's mission, and had begun burning his files. Churchill had been concerned about Antwerp and the Channel ports for some weeks, having raised the possibility of sending British Territorials to reinforce the Belgians, and even making the improbable suggestion to transport Russian troops there from Archangel. In early September, however, like the rest of the Cabinet, he had rejected a Belgian request for 25,000 men to be sent to keep open a land corridor into Antwerp, though some heavy naval guns had been supplied to the Belgians.

On arrival at Antwerp, Churchill made an arrangement with De Broqueville. The defence of the city would be prolonged for at least ten days. But, if the British government could not state definitely what steps they would undertake to relieve the city within three days, the Belgians were free to evacuate it, upon which British troops would be sent to Ghent to cover the withdrawal. Having been sent briefly to Ostend by Churchill in late August, a Royal Marine Brigade – many of them aged reservists or new recruits – and the Queen's Own Oxfordshire Hussars, the first Territorial Force unit to see active service, had been landed at Dunkirk in early September. On 28 September one of the marine battalions had been sent forward to Lille with the remainder pushing forward to Cassel two days later. Patrols were sent out in buses and on bicycles. The Royal Naval Air Service armoured cars of Commander Charles Samson motored further afield, engaging advanced German cavalry patrols with buccaneering if amateurish enthusiasm. The marines would now be sent to Antwerp with the addition of two naval brigades. The latter would be taken from the newly constituted Royal Naval Division – Churchill's 'Sea-dogs' as the former First Sea Lord, Sir John ('Jackie') Fisher, called them[4] – drawn from those naval reservists surplus to manning ship requirements on mobilisation, supplemented by New Army volunteers. Unfortunately, they were only partially trained as infantrymen – many had never even fired a rifle – and lacked equipment of all kinds, including ammunition pouches, greatcoats and water bottles: some even reportedly had to slip bayonets through their belts or tie them on with string. Nor did they have any artillery, engineers or transport. Asquith himself considered it 'idle butchery' to send the marines to Antwerp, but this did not apparently lead him to make any objection, possibly because he was wrongly informed by Churchill that all recruits would be left behind and only 'seasoned reservists' taken.[5]

The British 7th Division and the 3rd Cavalry Division were to land at Ostend. The French would also provide the territorial division and marine brigade they had previously pledged. In all, some 53,700 men and 75 guns would be available once all had arrived, the French providing 23,500 men and 40 guns and the British the remainder. In typically extravagant style, Churchill sent a telegram to Asquith on 5 October offering his resignation as First Lord in order to take personal command of the British forces at Antwerp. Asquith indicated he must return to the Admiralty, despite Kitchener's apparent willingness to make Churchill a lieutenant general. Indeed, when Churchill's telegram was read in Cabinet, it produced merely 'a Homeric laugh'.[6] Instead, Lieutenant General Sir Henry Rawlinson was ordered to take command of the British forces at Antwerp and Ostend. With the three days stipulated in Churchill's agreement with the Belgians expiring on 6 October, and without any British troops having thus far reached Ghent, the Belgians began to withdraw to the left bank of the Scheldt. Before leaving Antwerp for Ostend that day, Churchill directed Brigadier General Archibald Paris, acting commander of the Royal Naval Division, that he must not be caught in any capitulation of the city.

Meanwhile, Major General Thompson Capper's 7th Division was disembarking at Zeebrugge. Most recently Inspector of Infantry, Tommy Capper was the epitome of the 'offensive spirit'. Almost ludicrously brave – he was to be killed at Loos in September 1915 – Capper was certainly not the easiest of superiors, spectacularly falling out with his chief of staff, Hugo

Montgomery, in November 1914 and demanding his removal after having already threatened to remove all his three brigade commanders in October. Mindful of his orders not to get shut up in Antwerp, Capper declined to entrain immediately for the city, as the Belgian authorities in Zeebrugge wished. In any case, he soon received Rawlinson's instructions to proceed to Bruges, King Albert having requested that the British secure Ghent and the Belgian line of retreat. No other allied troops had yet appeared. Joffre had the French 87th Territorial Division landed at Dunkirk and then sent it to Poperinghe to cover the Belgian field army's retirement, rather than to relieve Antwerp.

On 8 October, Paris concluded that the defence of Antwerp could not be carried on much longer, and informed the Belgians that, in compliance with his instructions, he would withdraw. Churchill, whom Paris contacted personally by telephone, was furious with the decision, which effectively forced the hand of the senior Belgian commander in Antwerp, General Victor Deguise. Kitchener had already made a similar deduction to Paris and his orders for the withdrawal of the Royal Naval Division crossed with Paris's call to London. Unfortunately, three battalions of the 1st Naval Brigade totalling 1,479 men lost contact with the remainder of the force and, rather than surrender to the Germans, marched into internment across the Dutch frontier. Part of the rearguard battalion of the Royal Marine Brigade was also forced to surrender on 9 October, some 936 marines and seamen as a whole falling into German hands. Antwerp city with 26,000 Belgian troops was formally surrendered on 10 October, freeing Beseler to march on Zeebrugge and Ostend, the latter being occupied on 15 October. Beseler's first attempt to force the Belgian positions on the Yser failed on 18 October. Nieuport, with the vital locks and sluices that controlled the drainage of the low-lying area next to the sea, thus remained in Belgian hands.

To the southeast, Dixmude, not much more than a large village, was held by the French marine fusilier brigade commanded by Rear Admiral Pierre Ronarc'h. Ronarc'h was a short and sturdy 49-year-old Breton, who had seen land-based service in the China Relief Expedition of 1900 and was the youngest general officer in the navy. Composed of some 6,000 surplus seamen – mostly Breton reservists – rather than trained marines, and hastily put together in just two weeks, the brigade had previously been intended for the defence of Antwerp but, as with the French Territorials, Joffre had had no intention of committing it to a relief operation. According to one contemporary French author, Dixmude was to become a 'raft of suffering at the entrance to the delta of marshes, watched over by ancient windmills with shattered wings'.[7]

King Albert, who had been persuaded finally not to stay in the city by his Bavarian-born Queen, Elisabeth, left Antwerp on horseback in the company of Pau. He had decided to lead his army towards the coast since there were clearly German forces between the Scheldt and the Lys. Albert also distrusted the French and preferred to keep in touch with the British, though he and his military adviser, Captain Commandant Emile Galet, had placed too much faith in the British ability to sustain the defence of Antwerp. Above all, Albert believed it vital to remain on Belgian soil. His small army, however, was close to collapse.

Prior to 1909 the Belgian army had been a professional one of long-service volunteers, conscription only being used to maintain a strength of some 40,000 men. The Flemish Catholics who had dominated government for much of the period since 1870 had been anti-militarist and opposed to allowing Catholic youths to mix with Walloons, who might be tainted with socialism. Growing European tensions resulted in an increase in the size of the army in 1902 and, just a few days before his death in 1909, Albert's uncle, King Leopold II, had signed a new conscription law. Further legislation in 1913 then extended the reach of conscription. The intention was to raise the strength of the army progressively to about 100,000 men in peacetime, with a field army upon mobilisation of 150,000; a garrison army for the key fortresses of Antwerp, Liège and Namur of 130,000; and an available reserve of 60,000 men. In the event, the Belgian field army in August 1914 comprised 117,000 men in six infantry divisions and a cavalry division, and some 130,000 garrison troops. The verdict of the French military attaché in 1909 was that the Belgian army would prove 'if not inoffensive, at least of little danger to the invaders'. Three years later, his view was unchanged. In July 1914 his successor also reported that the army was 'not capable of doing much', and that the Belgian people themselves did not have the necessary 'feeling of abnegation and of sacrifice' to make a fight of it.[8]

The uncertain state of relations with France as well as Germany, and the failure of pre-war negotiations even with Britain, resulted in the army's divisions being widely scattered immediately before the German invasion. Thus, in August 1914, despite the representations of the army's chief of staff, 1st Division watched the coast from Ghent, 2nd Division was at Antwerp, 3rd Division facing the German frontier at Liège, 4th and 5th Divisions were covering the French frontier from Namur and Mons, and 6th Division and the cavalry covering Brussels. These seven divisions had been confronted by 34 divisions from the German First and Second Armies. The last fort at Liège fell on 17 August – the Germans had actually expected to take it in just 48 hours – and the last fort at Namur on 25 August, but most of the field army had managed to make it back to Antwerp by 20 August. With the refusal of the British to send troops to keep open the land corridor from Antwerp south of the Scheldt to the sea, the Belgians had been compelled to detach the 4th and 6th Divisions from the Antwerp defences for the purpose. Attempted sorties from the city then led to heavy casualties and declining morale. The bombardment only added to the defenders' woes, one describing 'a distant rumbling' swelling into a roar and ending 'with a frightful detonation which moved and shook the whole fort'. He continued, 'We went through this moment of indescribable agony regularly every seven minutes, and every time each of us asked himself whether the shell that was coming was the one that was going to crush him to death.'[9] The Germans penetrated the Nèthe line on 5 October, leaving no intact line of defence apart from the old inner ring of forts. Two days later, they were across the Scheldt at Schoonaerde, severely restricting the corridor by which the Belgians could escape the city. Significantly, when Deguise surrendered to a German colonel at Fort Sainte-Marie on 10 October, only the commandant of the fort, an NCO and a private accompanied him. The Germans asked where the rest of the expected 400-strong garrison were, and when Deguise pointed to the only two who had remained with him, the colonel 'very politely refrained from any comment'.[10]

On 9 October, General Pau presented a demand from Joffre that the Belgian troops should not retreat to the coast. Rawlinson, De Broqueville and the Belgian deputy chief of staff, Lieutenant Colonel Maximilien Wielemans, attended a meeting at Ostend on the following day. Pau attempted to persuade King Albert to give up personal command of his army and send it into France to operate between Calais and St Omer with

Boulogne as its base. Formerly head of De Broqueville's military cabinet, the Francophile Wielemans had effectively been appointed head of the Belgian General Staff on 6 September, when De Broqueville managed to persuade Albert to remove both the existing chief of staff, Lieutenant General Antoine de Selliers de Moranville, and his deputy, Baron Louis de Ryckel. When rebuffed, Pau insisted that the Belgians mount an offensive towards the line Poperinghe–Ypres–Poelcapelle after 48 hours' rest. This Albert also resisted, despite De Broqueville's support for the French general, on the grounds that the army was incapable of offensive operations without more rest. By this time, too, Albert, who already enjoyed a stormy relationship with De Broqueville, had taken a violent dislike to the French military attaché at his headquarters, Eugène Génie, whom he described as an untrustworthy dog. Génie's predecessor, Colonel Aldebert, had resigned when Albert had declined to follow his advice and had retired with his army into Antwerp. At least the Belgian ministers did agree to ask the French government to extend their hospitality to them by allowing them to instal a government in exile at Le Havre, whence they proceeded without Albert on 13 October.

Albert had agreed, on 12 October, to accept general directions from the French High Command, or Grand Quartier Général (GQG), on the same basis as did the BEF, namely the right to retain independence if it was considered that national interests were at stake. On the same day as his ministers left Ostend, Albert issued a proclamation to his army, indicating that anyone who spoke of retreat would be considered a traitor to his country. On 15 October, when his army reached the line of the Yser, Albert also met every divisional commander to warn that they would be dismissed if they abandoned their positions. The following day, Albert proclaimed that anyone fleeing would be shot, any officers claiming sickness would be court martialled and all staff officers would be sent to the front. Had the worst come to the worst, however, Albert envisaged withdrawing the remnants of his army, now down to only 82,000 effectives, to Britain rather than to France.

There was then a meeting at Furnes on 16 October between Albert and Ferdinand Foch, newly tasked by Joffre with co-ordinating the allied armies in the north. Buzzing with his customary energy and theatricality, the 62-year-old Foch had already berated Wielemans and other Belgian staff officers for continuing to retreat, before he went to see the king: Foch's own officers heard him repeatedly shouting 'Attaque, attaque'. According to Albert's account of the subsequent meeting, Foch asked whether the Belgians would continue to resist, to which the king replied that they would, but that a major effort was not possible and that help was needed. Foch, who insisted the German forces in the area were second-class formations, promised help within forty-eight hours though it was not until 23 October that the 42nd Division actually arrived. Even then Albert did not believe his own army capable of an offensive and he deplored the continuing French commitment to such a course of action. Nonetheless, Foch found Albert far more resolute than any of his subordinates though he wrote to Joffre that it would be best to have some French troops on the left of the Belgians, hence Joffre's readiness to despatch the 42nd Division under a taciturn and imperturbable Corsican, Paul Grossetti. On one occasion, indeed, Grossetti was to be found during the subsequent battle on the Yser calmly directing his men while sitting on a chair in the middle of a crossroads under fire. According to the account of the only Frenchman present with Foch when he met the king, Lieutenant Colonel Brécard, Albert expressed his high regard for Foch, but an account by Galet suggests Albert had a less laudatory opinion of the Frenchman and his demands.

In the meantime, Rawlinson's two divisions – now formally constituted as the British IV Corps – were ordered to hold Ghent and Bruges for as long as possible, then retire on the line St Omer–Dunkirk. With the Belgian field army that had escaped Antwerp beginning to reconcentrate around Ostend and Dixmude, then retiring on the line Dixmude–Furnes with its base at Dunkirk, Rawlinson began to pull back from Ghent, as there was at least a 10-mile gap between him and the Belgians. His subsequent orders from the commander-in-chief of the BEF, Field Marshal Sir John French, to advance to Ypres, which he reached on 14 October, to link with Lieutenant General Edmund Allenby's cavalry arriving from the Aisne in advance of the rest of the British forces, then opened a new gap. With the BEF now set to advance to the northeast in the hope of driving a wedge between Beseler and the rest of the German army, the Belgians completed their withdrawal behind the Yser.

The Germans, too, were redeploying to the north and there was increasing contact as the BEF pushed eastwards from Ypres. On 23 October the Chief of the German General Staff, Erich von Falkenhayn, demanded greater efforts from his principal commanders in the north, Duke Albrecht of Württemberg of the German Fourth Army and Crown Prince Rupprecht of Bavaria of the German Sixth Army, who happened to be the Belgian queen's uncle. Falkenhayn viewed their gains thus far as purely tactical. Prompted by his chief of staff, Albrecht concluded that, while opportunities should still be taken to seize significant ground, the offensive in front of Ypres should be halted, with the effort now directed further north against the Belgians and French. Both German army commanders were aware that losses among trained officers and NCOs were still reducing the effectiveness of their reserve formations. Accordingly, the Fourth Army made a major assault on Dixmude on the evening of 24 October. Ronarc'h held on, repulsing some fifteen separate attacks over a period of five hours. He doubted whether his men could hold out for much more than twenty-four hours given his losses and his men's fatigue. The Belgians, too, were at the limit of their moral and physical resistance and there were no reserves available: by 31 October, the Belgian army had declined to just 34,161 effectives, a loss in just twelve days of a third of those who had escaped from Antwerp.

Another effort was being made by Beseler further north on the Yser. He had been attempting to cross the river since 18 October. A relatively narrow and sluggish stream, the Yser had only low banks, though the one on the western side was higher than that on the eastern bank and there were only eight places where it was bridged. The German effort was hampered by fire from Royal Navy monitors, which persuaded Beseler that it was not possible to cross the river at Nieuport. Elements of the XXII Reserve Corps had therefore been brought up to assist Beseler at Dixmude. On 24 October, however, having previously been restricted to operating at Nieuport, Grossetti's French 42nd Division reinforced the Belgians, with instructions to hold 'with or without the Belgian army'.[11] Beseler was checked, though not before he had got across the Yser. On the following day, however, the 43rd Reserve Division broke into Dixmude in a flurry of street fighting, some 20 to 30 shells a minute falling on the defenders. According to one Belgian account reproduced in the German semi-official history of the battle for Ypres, the Germans had attacked 'with the howls of wild beasts; lusting to massacre, they tread the wounded under foot and stumble over the dead: and, though shot down in hundreds, they keep coming on. Then follow isolated fights with bayonets and the butts of rifles: some are impaled, others strangled or have their skulls bashed in.'[12] There were a number of documented atrocities, with at least 161 Belgian civilians slaughtered out of hand in Dixmude: the episode was reminiscent of the many earlier German atrocities committed during the original invasion of Belgium.

The ground, impeded by wide dykes and thick hedges, was generally between the high and low water level and extremely swampy, hindering the German attempt to bring up ammunition and supplies, and they were driven out of Dixmude. The Belgians, however, had taken heavy losses and the Dixmude–Nieuport railway embankment was now seen as the last possible position that could be held. As a result, preparations were made to break the locks and allow the sea to flood the approaches to Nieuport. Foch later claimed that he had suggested the line of the embankment for a last stand, and also that he had prevented the Belgians from retreating even farther. King Albert countered that such a retreat had never received his agreement.

There are various versions of the origins of the inundation policy. Foch was one who claimed the initiative, allegedly suggesting it to the Belgians on 25 October and seeking Joffre's authorisation on the following evening. Foch had certainly previously recommended flooding the area in front of Dunkirk, orders for which were suspended when the Belgians objected and it was felt too difficult to evacuate civilians. Matters were already in hand, however, before Foch's intervention, which actually was confined to mentioning the plans for Dunkirk. The chief lockmaster in Nieuport, Gerard Dingens, had supposedly raised the possibility on 19 October, while a young Belgian officer, Commandant Delarmoy, was also credited with suggesting the scheme earlier. By contrast, Albert's military adviser, Galet, credited the idea to Captain Commandant Prudent Armand Nuyten of the Belgian General Staff, formerly a professor of military administration and law at the Belgian military academy, who also selected the railway embankment as a suitable last line of defence. It should also be noted that the Belgians had released floodwater earlier in defence of Antwerp and also of the town of Berlaere.

A naturalised Belgian born in the Netherlands, the 65-year-old Dingens comes across from the contacts he had with British and Belgian officers as somewhat self-important. There is no doubt that he was a prominent and well-connected citizen in Nieuport. His attitude towards those who questioned him about inundating the countryside was invariably one of its impossibility, perhaps because he did not wish to be held responsible for destroying farmland. The Flemish-speaking Nuyten initially met Dingens on 13 October to ask some questions about the locks, but without apparently revealing any notion of opening them. As it happened, unidentified British officers from Rawlinson's staff had also questioned Dingens at Nieuport, as early as 10 October, about the possibility of flooding the area south of the Bruges Canal, as a means of isolating Ostend. One of these officers was almost certainly Colonel Tom Bridges, who had been acting as a liaison officer between the BEF and the Belgians. Three days later, Bridges raised the idea of flooding the low-lying polders around the Yser in a meeting with Rawlinson and his Belgian liaison officer, Captain Commandant de Lannoy. Significantly, Bridges suggested that Nuyten be asked to examine the problem. Rawlinson then formally proposed it on 15 October. On 17 October a Belgian engineer tasked with the defence of the lower Yser, Captain Robert Thys, similarly suggested flooding the area east of the Yser as a means of preventing a German advance. The son of a railway entrepreneur who had made a fortune in the Congo, Thys had earlier resigned his active commission to join his father's firm and supervise hydroelectric projects in the Congo: he had then immediately returned to the Colours when the Belgian army was mobilised on 31 July 1914. Wielemans was certainly also shown papers by a magistrate in Furnes, Emeric Feys, on the flooding of the area in the 1793–94 campaign during the French Revolutionary Wars, but this was only after the decision had already been taken. As it happens, the Dutch rebels had frequently flooded parts of the Low Countries to prevent the advance of the Spanish army during the Eighty Years War (1568–1648). While the Belgian decision in 1914 might be seen, therefore, as another measure of the increasing totality of warfare, there was particular historical precedent for extreme measures in the region.

The first actual initiative was that of the headquarters of 2nd Division on 21 October, prompted by Thys and his fellow divisional engineers, to flood the area between the Bruges Canal and the Yser by opening the sluices on the Nieuwendamme. The operation was a hazardous one, for the Germans were so close to the Goosefoot that Dingens had been forced to evacuate his staff on 20 October. Dingens had also apparently removed the special-ised tools, handles and keys necessary to open the sluices. Fortunately, a Belgian corporal had made the acquaintance of an experienced waterman and tugboat operator, 51-year-old Hendrik Geeraert, who could operate the sluices and knew where to find sufficient tools to do the job. In a wartime photograph later used as the basis for his portrait on a Belgian 1,000 franc note in circulation from 1950 to 1958, Geeraert stands with his arms determinedly folded, wearing a loose shirt and an old cap, his trouser waistband carelessly turned over. The weather-beaten face, with an impres-sive walrus moustache, gazes away from the camera, hinting at a casual disdain for authority. The lock doors of the Nieuwendamme were success-fully opened late on the evening of 21 October. Orders were issued to accelerate the flooding on 24 October by opening the locks on the canal-ised Yser, the idea being to drain the river on several ebb tides, then to raise the water level on subsequent rising tides to create a flood. Geeraert again assisted the Belgian engineers. (It should be explained that, as well as regulating water levels in the canals, the locks were used to allow the low-lying ground to shed water when they were closed at high tide, and they were opened at ebb tide to release the excess out to sea.)

Meanwhile, it was realised that the French plans to flood the approaches to Dunkirk risked cutting off the Belgian army by inundating the area behind it. Accordingly, Nuyten was despatched to find a solution on 25 October and was put in touch with the 59-year-old supervisor of the water authority in Furnes, Karel Cogge. Nuyten wanted to ensure the floodwater stayed east of the vital railway embankment being held by the Belgians to keep German artillery at bay. Rather like Dingens, Cogge was inclined to doubt the viability of utilising the so-called Spanish lock on a disused branch of the Furnes Canal to flood the area, at the same time closing all the culverts through the railway embankment, which had never been designed to contain water. Despite suffering from bronchitis, Cogge agreed to accompany Captain Commandant Victor Jamotte on a hasty survey of the terrain and watercourses between Furnes and Dixmude on 26 October. The military situation continued to deteriorate and, though the Belgians were well aware of the potential environmental impact, there seemed little alternative to inundation. Indeed, on 26 October, King

Albert, accompanied by Galet, visited the British General Headquarters to ask for reinforcements. The volatile Sir John French displayed what the Belgians characterised as 'phlegmatic solidarity', but had none to give.[13] As a result, Thys was ordered to open the old Spanish lock that night. Cogge's wife was reluctant to allow her husband to go with Thys but relented when Thys was able to offer 2,000 francs and a decoration. As with the earlier operation at the Nieuwendamme, several tides would be required to build up a sufficient flood and Cogge and Thys were out again on the nights of 27 and 28 October. 'French' water was added by opening a temporary dam that the French had erected three days earlier when flooding the eastern approaches to Dunkirk and blowing the levee between the Furnes Canal and the North Vaart.

Worried by the slow rise in the water level, and on their own initiative, Geeraert and Captain Commandant Borlon wanted to open the lock gates on the North Vaart on the night of 28 October, but Thys vetoed this on the grounds that it seemed likely the Germans now controlled the Goosefoot, and if any of the party were captured the secret would be out. In reality, the Germans were unaware that Nieuport had been abandoned by the French troops sent to secure it and, in any case, were preparing for an attack on the Belgian position at Ramscappelle to the south. In the event, caution was abandoned due to the lack of progress of the floodwater and, on the following night, Geeraert and Captain Fernand Umé successfully opened the North Vaart gate without attracting German attention. They repeated the operation on the next two nights.

Now at last the water was rising, 'a silent conqueror at first scarcely visible'.[14] The flood had reached between Pervyse and Dixmude by 28 October, and got to Pervyse on 31 October. The German forces in front of the Belgians were already suffering shortages of supplies. A diary found on the body of an officer from the 202nd Reserve Regiment on 27 October had recorded three days earlier: 'For several days we have had no hot food. The bread, etc., is hardly sufficient. The emergency rations are exhausted. The water is very bad, quite green, but it is drunk, as no other is obtainable. Man is reduced to the state of a beast.' Indeed, the officer in question, describing himself as in a 'shocking plight', was relying on what little could be shared with his men.[15] Initially, the Germans seem to have attributed the rising water to recent rainfall and did not realise what the Belgians had done. It is also conceivable that the Germans did not grasp that the Belgian maps, with which they had been issued, measured the average tidal heights differently: there was a difference of over six feet between the Belgian calculation of the average height of the spring ebb tide and the German calculation of the summer high tide.

Beseler attempted to continue his offensive, briefly taking Ramscappelle south of Nieuport on 30 October, until it became apparent that the water might actually cut off the leading divisions of III Reserve Corps. According to the German official history of First Ypres: 'On the morning of the 30th the advancing troops had been up to their ankles in water; then it had gradually risen until they were now wading up to their knees, and they could scarcely drag their feet out of the clayey soil.' Indeed, when the Germans looked behind them, 'the green meadows were covered with dirty, yellow water, and the general line of the roads was only indicated by the houses and the rows of partly covered trees'.[16] Though the Germans did capture Dixmude on 10 November, their effort on the Yser effectively ceased on 30 October. It had cost the Belgians some 18,000 casualties, and the Germans at least 9,500 casualties. The Belgians continued to hold the Yser line for the rest of the war.

The inundations had secured the allied left but, equally, rendered the German right secure, and they were able to deploy their forces further south to the evolving battle around Ypres. Nonetheless, the events along the Yser effectively completed the continuous trench line of the Western Front. The Germans remained in possession of the high ground, of most of Belgium and much of the more industrially valuable part of France. They could afford to stand on the defensive and allow the Western allies to try to solve the problem of deadlock. It was bad enough that Ostend and Zeebrugge were in German hands, the threat to British interests sufficient to justify the Passchendaele offensive in 1917. While German access to the Channel was to be blocked by the Dover Barrage of anti-submarine nets and mines, this was to be put in place from February 1915 onwards precisely because of the loss of Ostend and Zeebrugge. The loss of Calais and Dunkirk in 1914 would have made the laying of the barrage more hazardous, and the supply of the BEF in France and Flanders potentially far more difficult. It would also have opened two more ports to German vessels with concomitant consequences for the imposition of the allied blockade on the Central Powers. In short, the loss of the Channel ports would have been absolutely catastrophic for the allies.

As for those who had played a role in the inundation, Thys returned to the Congo after the war. Umé became professor of electricity at the Belgian military academy and Nuyten eventually became Belgian chief of staff. Dingens returned to his work at the Nieuport locks and died in 1926. Cogge, who received the Order of Leopold, simply retired. Geeraert was drafted into the Belgian army's corps of engineers but, sadly, died in an asylum in 1925. King Albert, whose single-minded determination had preserved his army and his country against the odds, died while climbing alone in the Ardennes in 1934.

CHAPTER 2

THE WIDENING OF
THE WAR

Turkey's Entry into the War, 29 October 1914

ONE OF the star attractions of Vienna's Heeresgeschichtliches (Military History) Museum is the motorcar in which Archduke Franz Ferdinand was assassinated by a gunman in Sarajevo on 28 June 1914. A 1910 open-top Austrian-built Gräf und Stift 'Double Phaeton', it is a vehicle that seems suitably grand for the occasion it represents. The only hint of its part in such a dramatic event, however, is a neat hole at the top of the rear offside passenger seat, through which passed the bullet that accounted for Franz Ferdinand's wife, Sophie. There is another car in the equivalent Turkish Military museum (Askeri Müze) in Istanbul, this one a rather more old-fashioned-looking 1909 French-built Laffly S20 TL. By no means as impressive a vehicle, it is riddled with bullet holes and, a trifle melodramatically, contains a wax dummy of the victim, the Ottoman Grand Vizier (First Minister) and Minister of War, Mahmud Şevket Pasha, assassinated by gunmen on 11 June 1913. While Franz Ferdinand had died when his car was brought to a halt by the driver taking a wrong turn in Sarajevo, Şevket's car had been stopped by road repairs as it passed through Bayezid Square in Constantinople: at least five assassins fired ten shots from another car. In its way, this was just as significant a murder as that of Franz Ferdinand. It is by no means clear who killed Şevket. It may well have been opponents of the İttihad ve Terakki Cemiyeti (Committee of Union and Progress, or CUP) that had dominated Turkish politics since the revolution of the so-called 'Young Turks' in July 1908, and had increased their power by a military coup in January 1913. On that occasion, a group of ten army officers had stormed the previous Grand Vizier's office, shooting dead the then Minister of War, and forcing the resignation of the Ottoman Cabinet. Şevket, formerly commander of the Turkish III Corps, was installed as the new Grand Vizier. While sympathetic towards the CUP, Şevket had only loose connections to the movement, and there were only three CUP ministers in his government. His murder allowed the CUP to suppress the Liberal Party and the hard-line elements to marginalise its own liberal wing.

The effect of Şevket's assassination was to consolidate the CUP's influence. One of the three CUP ministers, former Foreign Minister Prince Mehmed Said Halim Pasha, replaced Şevket as Grand Vizier, and other prominent CUP figures joined the government for the first time. On 4 January 1914, Enver İsmail Pasha, who had led the attack on the Grand Vizier's office a year earlier, became Minister of War. It was Enver who would play a crucial role in bringing Turkey into the war in October 1914.

The war had become a global conflict immediately, by virtue of the participation from the beginning of the overseas colonial empires of Britain, France, Germany and Belgium. The war would widen further through the subsequent entry of other powers. Clearly, at the very least, the entry of any new belligerent would have potential diplomatic and political implications for the course of the war, even if it did not necessarily have any immediate or even longer-term military impact. Any choice to remain neutral had similarly potential political, diplomatic and economic significance. Thus, the entry of Japan (August 1914), Italy (May 1915) and, ultimately, the United States (April 1917) all had important consequences. The entry of other states such as Thailand and Liberia (both 1917), and a raft of Central American states, including Guatemala, Costa Rica and Honduras (all 1918), had far fewer consequences: the declaration of war on Germany by the Onondaga American Indian nation (July 1918) merely amuses.

Arguably, the most momentous turning point of all in these terms, however, was the entry to the war of the Ottoman Empire. David Lloyd George and Erich Ludendorff alike were to claim that Turkish entry prolonged the war by at least two years. In the short term, it meant new theatres of military operations. Apart from the disastrous Dardanelles expedition (April 1915–January 1916), by which the British and French hoped to knock Turkey out of the war, Turkish entry also brought an unsuccessful Turkish advance towards Egypt in February 1915. There was, too, the campaign waged by the government of India in Mesopotamia from November 1914 to the fall of Baghdad in March 1917; the British advance into Palestine in early 1916, culminating in the fall of Jerusalem in November 1917 and of Damascus in October 1918; and British promotion of the 'Arab Revolt', normally dated as beginning on 7 June 1916.

The CUP's ambitions to restore the Ottoman Empire as a great power also resulted in its ready acquiescence in what has been characterised as a German global strategy of subversion, intended to stimulate nationalism in India, Afghanistan, Egypt, the Sudan, Morocco, and among the Turkomans of Persia: 140 million Muslims were ruled by Britain, France and Russia. In the event, the German and Turkish strategy was ineffective, but the consequences of the campaigns in the Middle East were profound. Turkish defeat, and the collapse of the Ottoman Empire, saw the partition of the Middle East between the British and French. The results, and the contradictory promises made during the war to Arabs and Jews, remain evident to this day. Imposition of the allied peace settlement helped forge the modern secular Turkish state, but also led to the Greco-Turkish war of 1920–22, with its own enduring legacy of uprooted peoples and mutual hatreds. At the same time, Turkish entry to the war opened a new front for the Russians in the Caucasus, and cut Russia's lifeline from the Black Sea to the Mediterranean. This arguably increased economic pressure on the Tsarist government and hastened its collapse. The war in the Caucasus also led directly to the genocide of the Armenian people, yet another lasting source of dispute in one of the world's most turbulent regions.

Turkish entry was a result of a protracted internal political struggle within the CUP or 'Unionists'. The Unionists had first come to prominence as one of a number of reformist 'Young Turk' groups opposed to the conservative and repressive policies of Sultan Abdülhamid II. Their strength grew especially among young army officers in the Turkish II Corps and III Corps, based respectively at Monastir (now Bitola) and Salonika (now Thessaloniki). On the back of what was effectively a military revolt at Salonika, on 24 July 1908 the CUP forced the Sultan to concede the restitution of the liberal constitution of 1876. It created in effect a constitutional monarchy. In the newly elected Chamber of Deputies that met in December 1908, the CUP had the greatest number of seats, but it preferred influence to actual power. Following a supposed counter-revolution by a single battalion in Constantinople in April 1909, quickly put down by troops from the II Corps and III Corps, the Sultan was compelled to abdicate. The Sultan's First Eunuch was hanged from the city's Galata Bridge, but the Second Eunuch survived by wisely showing the CUP's leaders how to access the treasury in the Yildiz Palace. Abdülhamid was succeeded by his brother, Reşad, who was installed as Sultan Mehmed V. Unionist influence over the government fluctuated thereafter, with some of its nationalist policies provoking revolt among the empire's ethnic minorities. During the course of the Italo-Turkish War of 1911–12, when the Italians seized Libya and the Dodecanese islands, the CUP's power weakened temporarily despite its elaborate organisational network throughout the empire and its administration, and its strong support amongst army officers. Territorial concessions to the Balkan powers that attacked Turkey in October 1912, thereby initiating the First Balkan War, had then undermined the new government. Accordingly, Enver and his colleagues had launched their coup on 23 January 1913. Their objective was a progressive, secular, modernised and Westernised state, but also one free of the European political and economic control imposed on the Ottoman Empire since the late nineteenth century. It would be a relationship of equality rather than subordination.

Tsar Nicholas I had characterised the Ottoman Empire as the 'sick man of Europe' back in 1853. Greece had already won its independence in the 1820s, Serbia, Romania, and Montenegro became so in 1878, and Bulgaria effectively so, though the Turks continued to claim sovereignty until 1908. Bosnia and Herzegovina were occupied by Austria-Hungary and then annexed in 1908. Cyprus and Egypt were effectively lost to Britain in 1878 and 1882 respectively, and Tunisia to the French in 1881. Crete passed under international protection in 1898. Ottoman public debt had been placed under European control in 1881 and, under the so-called Capitulations, foreign nationals enjoyed immunity from Turkish taxation and justice, and changes in customs duties required the consent of the great powers.

The CUP had then seen the influence of the Ottoman Empire further eroded during the First Balkan War, as the forces of Serbia, Bulgaria, Greece and Montenegro pushed the Ottomans out of Macedonia, Albania,

Epirus, most of Thrace and various Aegean islands. The Turks managed to hold the so-called Chatalja line just 30 miles from Constantinople, but it left just a tiny remnant of the former Ottoman possessions in Europe: 55,000 square miles of territory had been lost, representing 80 per cent of Turkey's remaining European territory, and equating to an area almost as large as England and Wales. Some 4 million people inhabited the lost territories. The victors soon fell out over the spoils, with Serbia and Greece fighting Bulgaria in the Second Balkan War of 1913–14, during which Enver managed to recapture Edirne (formerly known as Adrianople) in eastern Thrace from the Bulgarians in a lightning raid in June 1913. Serbia emerged as the greatest victor from the Balkan Wars, its territory doubling in size, and its population increasing by 1.5 million, but it was actually Greece and Bulgaria that most threatened remaining Turkish territory in Europe. Tsarist Russia appeared to retain its long-term interest in controlling the straits of the Dardanelles and the Bosphorus, thus attaining free access to the Mediterranean. How then could the CUP attain its own objectives?

Between 1912 and 1914 some of the CUP leadership favoured long-term defensive alliance with one of the great powers as a means of advancing their aims, while others wished to reach accommodation with all the powers. Still others, of whom the most prominent was Enver, wished to overthrow the whole post-Balkan Wars settlement, though this would also require an ally. Just 32 years old when he became Minister of War, Enver was simultaneously promoted from colonel to brigadier general, though this was also partly in recognition of his achievement at Edirne. Shortly after assuming office, he married a niece of the Sultan. It was a rapid rise for someone of humble beginnings. Born at Adana near Turkey's Black Sea coast in 1881, Enver was largely brought up at Monastir, where his father was either a bridge-keeper or a minor railway official. Enver's mother was an ethnic Albanian of peasant origin, who, it was later said, earned a living from laying out the dead. Graduating from the military academy as a lieutenant in 1899, Enver was serving at Salonika when recruited into the CUP in 1906. Two years later, he was prominent in the revolt at Salonika that triggered the overthrow of Abdülhamid. After two years as military attaché in Berlin, Enver returned to fight against the Italians in Libya, distinguishing himself there as well as in the First Balkan War.

It has been suggested that Enver's leadership of the coup in January 1913 was born of frustration rather than personal ambition, but there is no doubt that he greatly profited from it in terms both of power and wealth. Winston Churchill, who had met Enver before the war, described him as a 'charming fellow – vy good looking & thoroughly capable'.[1] The American ambassador to Constantinople, Henry Morgenthau, noted Enver's almost feminine appearance, the pale face, and the delicate hands and the long tapering fingers. He characterised Enver as a 'matinee idol'. Certainly Enver, who neither drank nor smoked and was regarded as having an impeccable private life, cut a dapper figure. Nonetheless, while the Austro-Hungarian ambassador described Enver as a dilettante, Morgenthau remarked on Enver's audacity, cold-blooded determination and remorseless lack of pity.[2] Notably vain, Enver clearly believed himself a 'man of destiny', and had developed a distinct manner while in Berlin, often striking consciously Napoleonic poses. Certainly, in April 1915, the American chargé d'affaires in Constantinople, Lewis Einstein, contrasted the relatively modest young man he had first met in 1908 with the altogether more ambitious figure seated behind a desk, with photographs of Napoleon and Frederick the Great on either side, something also mentioned by Morgenthau.[3] But for his small stature, of which he was always conscious, Enver's Napoleonic pretensions were to prove greatly misplaced.

As Minister of War, Enver immediately set out to purge the officer corps of potential rivals, though, to be fair, he also continued essential military reforms originally started by Şevket. Enver's familiarity with many German officers from his time in Berlin further strengthened his hand, for key military appointments were gifted to officers from the German military training mission led by Otto Liman von Sanders, which had been appointed in October 1913. Liman was originally supposed to command the Turkish I Corps at Constantinople but, in the face of Russian objections, this was converted to a wider yet less threatening advisory role.

Whatever Enver's precise role in the decision to enter the war, it should be borne in mind that the CUP leadership was a collective one. The wealthy and Egyptian-born Said Halim was something of a figurehead as Grand Vizier. Born in 1865, he was a nephew of a former Khedive of Egypt, and had been privately educated, speaking both English and French well. Foreign diplomats, however, had found him somewhat uncommunicative as Foreign Minister. Einstein described him as a 'rather pompous little man who speaks as if he ruled the Empire, where he is only a figurehead, ignores business, and takes orders from Talaat'.[4] The latter, Mehmed Talât Bey, was one of two further key figures, the other being Major General Ahmed Cemal Pasha. A former postal clerk, Talât was alongside Enver during the January 1913 coup, and became Interior Minister at the age of 39. Talât enjoyed considerable sway over the CUP committees and branches. The 42-year-old Cemal was first appointed Minister of Public Works, then Navy Minister in March 1914. Like Enver he had support in the army, and was somewhat resentful of the number of posts occupied by the Germans

Talât, born in 1874, was originally from Edirne, northwestern Turkey, his father an examining magistrate. British diplomats thought the black hair, heavy black eyebrows, swarthy complexion and beaked nose betrayed what was generally supposed to be his mother's gypsy roots. He was power- fully built – Morgenthau recalled that he had 'rocky biceps' and 'gigantic wrists' – but was famously glutinous and paunchy as a result.[5] To such foreign observers, Talât appeared more Turkish than his CUP colleagues, a 'bold and hearty' peasant, not without spontaneous good humour, but with an evidently cruel streak. One British diplomat, who had known him well before the war, recalled, after his death, that Talât was an 'engaging villain'.[6] Another noted that Talât had 'a light in his eyes, rarely seen in men but sometimes in animals at dusk'.[7]

Cemal had been born in 1872 on Mytilene in the Aegean. A serious rival to Enver, their relationship was one of mutual loathing. Highly ambitious, ruthless and opportunistic, Cemal was just as vain as Enver, though less popular. Morgenthau found even his laugh 'unpleasant', leaving a memorable pen portrait of a stumpy and stoop-shouldered figure, whose eyes – 'black and piercing, their sharpness, the rapidity and keenness with which they darted from one object to another, taking in apparently everything with a few lightning-like glances' – suggested 'cunning, remorselessness, and selfishness to an extreme degree'.[8]

Others, however, also had some influence within the CUP. The speaker of the lower chamber of deputies, the genial Halil Bey, had gained great respect among CUP's parliamentary deputies for his integrity. Known later in life as Halil Menteşe, he had been born at Milas on Turkey's Aegean coast in 1874. The expertise of the independently minded, bespectacled 39-year-old Finance Minister, Medmed Cavid Bey, a former economics teacher, was also widely recognised. Born in Salonika in 1875, Cavid's background was a particularly interesting one, for he was said to be of a sect commonly called Dönmeh (literally 'turncoat') by Turks, but Ma'min ('faithful') by its members. Originally Jews expelled from medieval Spain in the late sixteenth century, the Dönmeh had largely followed their messianic leader in converting to Islam in the mid-seventeenth century. Many had remained covert Jews in their private religious practice for a considerable period. Having been assimilated over time, the majority subscribed, by the late nineteenth century, to a kind of mystical Islam with a distinctive Judaic element. The sect was especially strong in Salonika, and had identified readily with the radicalism of the CUP. In theory, no minister could act without majority support in the CUP's central committee, but in practice a great deal was decided by small groups meeting wholly informally behind closed doors. Broadly speaking, Said Halim and Talât leant towards forging an alliance with Germany and Austria-Hungary, but were not averse to reaching an accommodation with Britain, France or Russia. Cemal appeared to favour the British and French, while the Francophile, but essentially neutralist, Cavid wanted none of either alliance. As already indicated, Enver clearly favoured Germany.

Enver has often been associated with the 'Pan-Turanian' idea that Russia's Turkic territories in the Caucasus and Turkestan might be won for the Ottoman Empire with the support of Germany and Austria-Hungary. In addition, Enver, Talât and Cemal all associated themselves primarily with areas now lost to Turkey. Talât and Cemal, of course, had been born in the lost territories, while Enver had been brought up there. Equally, some of the party's main ideologues were from territories within the Tsarist Empire; another, Ziya Gökalp, was actually a Kurd. In many respects, however, it was a resurgent Turkish nationalism that most appealed to the CUP leadership as a whole. They desired to consolidate the Turkish state on its heartland in Anatolia, which could be suitably purged of alien elements to ensure greater ethnic homogeneity. Ethnic minorities generally were viewed with suspicion as posing a threat of foreign-backed unrest. Some exchange of population had already taken place in the Balkans through mutual expulsion. 'Turkification' also accorded with the prevailing intellectual climate, newspapers and periodicals fuelling a wider public mood of revisionism. Islam offered a degree of shared identity in this vision, but it was actually the Germans who were to prove keenest on a 'Pan-Islamic' war. Enver and his colleagues, therefore, were more interested in their own national identity than a wider Islamic identity. Enver, indeed, was careful to counsel the Germans against the proclamation of a general jihad (or holy war) that would apply to all infidels, including Germans, offering instead a call for Muslims under Entente rule to rise in rebellion. It was in this sense, therefore, that jihad was promulgated in November 1914.

Germany had no apparent territorial ambitions in Turkey, and had been more sympathetic to resurgent Turkish nationalism than the other great powers, seeing the advantage of opening markets in the Ottoman Empire for German goods. Germany had secured the contract for building a new railway line to Baghdad in 1903. In turn, the CUP had willingly sought the German military mission's help in reforming the army, though it should be noted that the gendarmerie remained under the command of a French officer, and the Ottoman navy had been under the command of a British officer, Rear Admiral Sir Arthur Limpus, since 1908. In 1914, indeed, two new battleships, the *Reşadiye* and the *Sultan Osman*, were being completed for the Turkish navy in British yards. It was also the case that France held 62.9 per cent of Turkey's foreign debt, and that Britain was the next largest overseas investor, holding 22 per cent of the foreign debt. Any approach to Turkey by the Entente, however, was hampered by Anglo-French indifference, coupled with Russian ambitions. The Turks were also mindful of the possibility that their neutrality in any confrontation between the great powers might give Russia the pretext to seize the straits. Nevertheless, some agreements were concluded with Britain, France and Russia on outstanding disputes, at a moment when the Germans seemed to be cooling towards an alliance with Turkey based on an assessment of Ottoman military weakness that was generally shared by all the great powers. In any case, the CUP leadership was more concerned with an escalating confrontation with Greece over two of the Aegean islands – Chios and Mytilene – which the Greeks had seized in the First Balkan War. The CUP even pursued the possibility of an alliance with Bulgaria, notwithstanding Bulgarian occupation of Thrace, in recognition of the new hostility between Greece and Bulgaria.

As Europe lurched towards war in July 1914, it appeared the opportunity might arise to revisit the Balkan Wars settlement, especially as Bulgaria had grown closer to Germany through acceptance of a large German financial loan. The imminent delivery of the new battleships would give Turkey naval supremacy over Greece. In addition, the public mood favoured revision of the existing status quo, and would be further mobilised behind the government if it succeeded in challenging foreign financial and legal immunities such as the despised Capitulations. In mid-July, therefore, Said Halim, Enver and Talât approached the German and Austro-Hungarian ambassadors in Constantinople, seeking their support for a Turkish alliance with Bulgaria. Neither Liman, nor the German ambassador, Baron Hans von Wangenheim, believed the Turks were unlikely to prove anything other than a liability as an ally. As recently as March 1914, the Chief of the German General Staff, Helmuth von Moltke, had described the Ottoman Empire as 'militarily a nonentity' and dying rather than sick.[9] Nevertheless, Kaiser Wilhelm II insisted upon a favourable response, for he had long been attracted to the idea of posing as a liberator of Muslim populations under British, French and Russian rule. Said Halim proposed a formal alliance on 27 July outlining the conditions upon which Turkey would enter a war between Germany and Russia. Enver then met Wangenheim and Liman on 1 August to discuss a war strategy, it being agreed that the Turkish army would mass on the Russian frontier while remaining dependent upon Bulgarian and Romanian actions. Said Halim and Wangenheim signed the secret treaty of alliance on 2 August 1914. It was concluded with the knowledge of only a handful of Unionist leaders: Cavid and Cemal were not informed. Meanwhile, all factions were then satisfied by the simultaneous decision on 3 August to mobilise and to declare neutrality, the latter being publicly declared on 5 August. The alliance was concluded on the assumption by at least Said Halim that the war would be over quickly, that both Bulgaria and Romania would join the Central Powers of Germany and Austria-Hungary, and that Turkey could fight a war with Bulgarian assistance only against Greece and Serbia. In fact, Bulgaria did not enter the war until October 1915.

Wangenheim himself was far from sanguine at Turkish readiness for war, and urged on Berlin the benefits of keeping the Turks as benevolent neutrals. A tall, burly man, Wangenheim was physically imposing, but, according to Lewis Einstein, lacked sufficient diplomatic dignity for he was 'far too nervous, mercurial, and journalistic in his methods'.[10] For his part, Enver, who became deputy commander-in-chief on 2 August – the Sultan was nominally commander-in-chief – kept repeating his promise to enter the war as soon as possible. On 3 August he ordered mines laid at the entrances of the Straits. Enver, though, was not quite the hawk usually depicted, for he also held out against actually initiating action for some time in anticipation of reaping the full benefits of a German alliance without risking war. His own estimation back in February 1914 had been that the Turkish army would not be ready for a war for five years, and by that he meant only a localised war in the Balkans.

The Germans were certainly anxious to bring the Turks into the war against Russia as soon as possible. Part of the requirement for a successful war against Russia was naval supremacy in the Black Sea, but on 3 August the British government had unilaterally seized for the Royal Navy all foreign warships being built in British yards, though financial compensation was promised: the Reşadiye and the Sultan Osman became respectively HMS Erin and HMS Agincourt. Limpus had been expecting to sail out to greet the two ships in late July, and arrangements had been made for a week of celebration. The posting of British guards over the vessels on 29 July then alerted the Turks to the British seizure of their vessels in advance, and the Turkish ambassador had been told two days later that they would be detained temporarily. On 1 August, therefore, when Enver offered the Sultan Osman to the Germans as additional enticement, it was in the knowledge that the offer was worthless. With the apparent knowledge of only Said Halim, Enver had already invited the Germans and Austro-Hungarians on the same day to send their own warships through the Straits in clear violation of international law, which prohibited neutral powers from harbouring belligerent warships. On 3 August the German Admiralty accepted the invitation for two warships under the command of Rear Admiral Wilhelm Souchon, the battlecruiser Goeben, and the light cruiser Breslau, which had been cruising in the Mediterranean. Souchon was described as 'a droop-jawed determined little man in a long, ill-fitting frock-coat, looking more like a parson than an admiral'.[11]

Despite appearances, Souchon proved an energetic and skilful seaman. The German ships were sighted by British battlecruisers off the North

African coast the following morning, before a state of war formally existed between Britain and Germany. Despite failing boilers in the *Goeben* – four seamen were scalded to death and many others collapsed from exhaustion – Souchon outpaced the shadowing British ships. His force was sighted again off the straits of Messina on 6 August, but Rear Admiral Troubridge felt unable to risk engaging the two German ships with inferior armoured cruisers, and Admiral Sir Berkley Milne, sailing with his battle-cruisers, concluded that watching the Austro-Hungarian fleet was a greater priority and, in any case, fully expected Souchon to double back to the western Mediterranean. Souchon passed the Straits on 10 August, after Enver personally authorised their admittance to Turkish waters. Milne was never employed again. Though Troubridge was acquitted by the court martial he had demanded, he did not command at sea thereafter, eventually commanding naval guns landed in support of the Serbian army.

The arrival of the two German ships brought considerable internal debate, Said Halim having previously told Wangenheim that they would not be permitted to enter the Straits. Meanwhile Cavid and Cemal had raised their objections to the secret treaty of alliance of which they were now aware. On 4 August, therefore, Said Halim and Talât had proposed a revision to its terms, tying Turkish entry to the war to that of Bulgaria, and to Romanian neutrality. Germany would also be required to support abolition of the Capitulations; to support Turkey's attempts to conclude agreements with Bulgaria and Romania; to guarantee the return to Turkey of the Aegean islands if Greece came into the war; to redraw the Balkan frontiers; to restore the 1878 frontiers in the Caucasus; to forswear any separate peace while any Turkish territory lost during a war remained in enemy hands; and to provide a post-war indemnity. In return, the *Goeben* and *Breslau* would be admitted through the Straits. Wangenheim agreed on 6 August, since the Germans anticipated that the arrival of their ships would accelerate Turkish entry to the war and, as he informed Berlin, most of the provisions were dependent upon a decisive German victory. As soon as the ships arrived, Enver certainly pressed to unleash them against Russian targets, but his colleagues would not act while Bulgaria remained neutral. On 9 August the Turkish Cabinet had also agreed to maintain neutrality until the course of events elsewhere became clearer. Wangenheim was also informed that, to maintain the pretence of neutrality, there should be an immediate (but fictional) announcement that the *Goeben* and *Breslau* had been purchased by Turkey. It was announced by the Turks that the purchase had taken place for 80 million marks on 11 August, before the Germans had actually agreed to it: *Goeben* became the *Yavuz Sultan Selim*, and *Breslau* the *Midilli*. The British and French were informed that the German crews would be replaced as soon they could be replaced, an assurance accepted by the British prime minister, Asquith, who was content that 'Turkish sailors cannot navigate her [the *Goeben*] – except on to rocks or mines'.[12] In reality, Souchon and his crews simply put on fezzes, but Asquith proved partly right in the long run. The German ships did not emerge into the Mediterranean again until 1918, when they might have made a significant difference to the naval balance had they joined the Austro-Hungarian navy in the Adriatic. Meanwhile, the German Military Mission extended its control over the Turkish army, and began preparations for campaigns against Egypt, and against Odessa on Russia's Black Sea coast. Wangenheim was told, however, that the *Goeben* and *Breslau* must stay within the straits until an alliance was concluded with Bulgaria.

To a greater or lesser extent, Said Halim, Cemal and Talât were now all happy to delay matters for the foreseeable future, though Talât and Halil were sent to open negotiations with Bulgaria, Romania and even the Greeks. Bulgaria finally signed a treaty of alliance with Turkey on 19 August, but one without any obligation to enter the war. It was also clear that Bulgaria would not act without a guarantee of Romanian neutrality. Increasingly, Said Halim was inclined towards Cavid's preference for strict neutrality, to which Cemal also appeared attracted. Cavid and Cemal, indeed, opened discussions with the British, French and Russian ambassadors, seeking various guarantees for the future integrity of the Ottoman Empire, and for the return of territory lost to Bulgaria should the latter join Germany. The Entente powers were prepared to guarantee Turkish territorial integrity if Turkey remained neutral, but the CUP leadership felt this an empty promise given Russian ambitions. Enver, however, was now pushing ahead with his own preparations for war regardless, but Souchon counselled caution until more war supplies were received from Germany, and until the outer defences of the Dardanelles had been strengthened.

The initial German military successes, which had encouraged Enver to pressure his colleagues into intervention, looked less impressive by early

September 1914, with the Germans retreating from the Marne and the Austro-Hungarians suffering defeat against the Russians in Galicia. Though Talât had now swung his support behind Enver, the other CUP leaders believed that greater concessions could be won from the British, French and Russians. On 9 September, therefore, to increase leverage on the Entente powers, the Turkish leadership unilaterally abrogated the Capitulations, and raised customs duties. Wangenheim and his Austro-Hungarian opposite number publicly joined the ambassadors of Britain, France and Russia in their formal protest. Wangenheim in particular believed it simply a further ruse to delay Ottoman entry to the war, but was also worried about the position of Europeans in Turkey without the former legal safeguards. There was little he could do, however, and he was forced to indicate, albeit in private, that the issue would not be pressed. It had the desired effect, with the Entente ambassadors all indicating a willingness to negotiate. In turn, the Germans now upped the pressure, Wangenheim and Souchon both urging that the fleet be allowed to enter the Black Sea. Their expectation, of course, was that Souchon would be able to manufacture a suitable incident at sea with the Russians to force war. A game of cat and mouse ensued within the CUP leadership, with Enver authorising a naval foray on 14 September, but being forced to cancel it when Said Halim threatened to resign as Grand Vizier. Cemal had also reacted violently to the authorisation. A furious Souchon threatened to go ahead on 19 September on his own authority. On Berlin's instructions, Wangenheim then reluctantly ordered Souchon to make a brief excursion on the following day, on the grounds that Germany was entitled to use its own ships as it pleased: so much for the fiction that they were Turkish. Enver and Talât argued that sending the ships into the Black Sea would deter Romania from joining the Entente, a patently absurd suggestion. On 21 September, Souchon then did take the *Breslau* briefly into the Black Sea, despite an equally absurd threat by Cavid and Cemal that the forts guarding the Bosphorus would be ordered to fire on it.

The near panic that followed enabled Enver to persuade his colleagues that Souchon should be allowed to take *Goeben* and *Breslau* into the Black Sea in pursuit of German interests, provided he did not provoke war. Paradoxically, he also managed to persuade them that, if Souchon formally accepted command of the Ottoman navy, then he could take the whole fleet. Limpus had resigned the appointment as soon as the German vessels had passed the Dardanelles, and, not surprisingly, Souchon accepted the invitation on 24 September. The British promptly withdrew the remainder of their naval mission and, on 26 September, indicated that Ottoman ships passing into the Mediterranean would now be regarded as hostile. In retaliation, on 29 September, Enver declared the Straits closed to shipping. Characteristically, he did not consult his colleagues. Meeting Said Halim after a Cabinet meeting at which Enver's decision had been reported, Henry Morgenthau described the Grand Vizier as white faced and trembling, 'a picture of abject helplessness and fear'.[13] Enver's colleagues, however, still had sufficient resolve to refuse to allow him to despatch Souchon's fleet into the Black Sea, and even elements within the army were questioning whether war preparations should continue. Touchy and short-fused at the best of times, Liman had been pressing for Turkish entry to the war for some time: he had even threatened at one point to withdraw the German military mission unilaterally if the Turks did not act. The German war minister, Erich von Falkenhayn, had also lost patience, having refused on 10 September to send any more war supplies to Turkey until the promise to enter the war had been honoured. It was increasingly clear that Turkey could no longer avoid commitment without risking abandonment by Germany.

Enver and Talât resolved to break the deadlock within the CUP leadership by securing a German financial loan. Cavid did not expect the Germans to respond but, on 6 October, the Germans duly offered a loan of the equivalent of 5 million Turkish pounds in bullion. Initially, the Germans had insisted that 95 per cent could not be released until Turkey actually entered the war, but Wangenheim was persuaded on 11 October that at least 40 per cent should be advanced. Halil had now been won over by Enver and Talât. Cemal was also brought on side on 9 October, possibly by the promise of command of the proposed advance on Egypt and the Suez Canal, since he harboured ambitions to rule a conquered Egypt, an ambition he shared with Said Halim. The German gold arrived in two instalments, on 16 and 21 October, being routed through Austria-Hungary, Romania and Bulgaria by special train. On 22 October, Enver notified the Germans of his intention to attack Russia at sea without declaration of war, and to attack into both the Caucasus and Egypt. Souchon was also given sealed orders to proceed to attack the Russian fleet, to be opened upon receipt of a radio message from Enver, once the Cabinet had finally agreed on war. Talât and Halil seem to have had second thoughts, but Enver and Cemal were resolved on action. Apparently without the knowledge of Said Halim and Cavid, Souchon went to sea on 27 October.

In fact, no message was received from Enver, and Souchon resolved to act himself. As he described it, Souchon went to sea in anticipation that he 'would not, so to speak, prevent the canons from discharging by themselves' if he met the Russians.[14] He was meant to provoke a Russian reaction but, instead, two days later, he bombarded Sebastopol, Odessa and two other Russian Black Sea ports, laid mines and sank some merchant ships, claiming that the Russians had attacked him first. Said Halim and Cavid staged a rearguard action to try to avoid war, and a conciliatory note was sent to Russia on 1 November. It was too late. Russia formally declared war on Turkey on 2 November, followed by Britain and France on 5 November. Cavid resigned that same day, as did three further ministers, though Said Halim and two others were persuaded to remain. Within the CUP Central Committee, the vote for war had been 17 to 10. The formal Turkish counter-declaration on 11 November 1914 duly invoked a jihad against the infidel.

To some extent, Enver had embraced German plans for Pan-Islamic war as early as 6 August 1914. As suggested before, he and his colleagues were motivated primarily by nationalism, and much the same nationalism motivated other ostensibly Islamic groups in the Middle East and Central Asia. Consequently, Pan-Islam had little real unifying potential. The aims of the Turkish *Teskilâti Mahsusa* (Special Organisation), which Enver had created, therefore, were not the same as those of the Germans, who stressed Islamic nationalism more than Pan-Turkism, since the extension of Ottoman rule was unwelcome to many nationalities. Indeed, the Turks actively suppressed non-Turkic minorities, the most obvious example being the Armenians though other Christian minorities were also targeted. The strategy had only mixed success. In the case of Persia, the Germans secured a treaty in 1915, and control over the Swedish-officered gendarmerie, but this sparked an Anglo-Russian occupation in response. Some German influence, through the Sikh Ghadarite movement, was apparent in the short-lived mutiny of an Indian battalion in Singapore in February

1915. The Turks supported the Senussi in Libya, who were not suppressed by the British until March 1916, and also a revolt by the Sultan of Darfur in the Sudan in 1916. Neither the revolt in Libya nor that in the Sudan, however, threatened the stability of the Entente.

Ill prepared for war, the Turks had no domestic capacity for armaments manufacturing, and an inadequate transport infrastructure. By 1916, large areas of Lebanon, Syria and eastern Anatolia were also facing famine conditions: an estimated 500,000 people died in Lebanon and Syria alone as a result. Nonetheless the Turks proved doughty opponents in defence, as both the Gallipoli and Mesopotamian campaigns illustrated. Where they took the offensive, however, they failed. The Turkish advance on Egypt and the Suez Canal, directed by Cemal, was easily repulsed in February 1915. Enver regarded an offensive into the Caucasus as more significant, in the expectation of inspiring revolt among Russia's Islamic peoples. Therefore, he commanded the operation himself. The peoples of the region, however, had their own nationalist aspirations, not least the Kurds, many of whom deserted to the Russians. The Russians also raised a division among Christian Armenians. The latter were regarded by the Turks as Russian puppets and had suffered previous Turkish repression. Consequently, the role of Armenian troops in the repulse of the Turkish offensive in December 1914 and January 1915 – the Turks lost between 75,000 and 90,000 men around Sarikamish – and the subsequent declaration of a provisional Armenian government in April 1915, provoked genocide by the Turkish authorities. A local response by the Turkish Third Army quickly evolved into a general policy. An estimated 1.3 to 2.1 million Armenians died in both Anatolia and Transcaucasia as a result of massacre, deportation to the Mesopotamian desert, starvation and disease, the majority by September 1915. Both Enver and Talât were directly implicated in these policies. It was not just Armenians who suffered at Turkish hands. Other similarly suspect minorities such as Greeks were deported from Cilicia and the Bosphorus. Cemal, who became governor of Syria in 1915, was equally implicated there in the bloody repression of Christians, Syrians and Lebanese.

After Russia's collapse in 1917, the Turks weakened their forces in Palestine and Mesopotamia to advance once more into the Caucasus in February 1918. They took Baku in November 1918, but were then forced to withdraw. The British had already advanced into Syria in September

1918: Damascus fell on 1 October and Aleppo on 26 October. On the Mesopotamian front, too, the British were advancing up the Tigris towards Mosul. The Turks opened negotiations on 26 October, and concluded an armistice at Mudros in the Aegean on 30 October 1918, by which the Entente occupied the Dardanelles and Bosphorus. The peace settlement partitioned Turkey's Middle Eastern possessions between Britain and France, and granted independence to Armenia, and autonomy for the Kurds. It was not the intention to reverse the verdict of the Balkan Wars with respect to Macedonia, which remained Bulgarian. Britain, France and the United States, however, all supported Greek territorial claims in some measure. Ultimately, Greek occupation of Smyrna (now Izmir) gave added impetus to Mustafa Kemal's nationalist revolt against Sultan Mehmed VI, who had succeeded as Sultan on the death of his brother in July 1918. Only peripherally involved in the pre-war Young Turk conspiracies, Kemal had made his military reputation at Gallipoli in 1915–16. He not only suppressed attempted independence on the part of Armenia, but also defeated the Greek attempts to annexe Thrace and Anatolia between June 1920 and August 1922. Kemal's victory brought the Turks into a new confrontation with the British occupation forces in the 'neutral zone' at Chanak (now Cannakale) near Constantinople, from which Britain was forced to back down through the lack of support from the French, Italians and the Dominions, apart from New Zealand and Newfoundland. The Sultan fled, and the Sultanate was abolished in November 1922. The Treaty of Lausanne in July 1923 revised the original terms of the Treaty of Sèvres in August 1920 to Turkey's advantage, in terms of the restoration of Armenia, eastern Thrace, Smyrna and Anatolia. It led to a mass exchange of Greek and Turkish populations: 1.5 million Greeks left Anatolia and 400,000 Muslims left Greek territory.

In many respects, the reform programme of Mustafa Kemal fulfilled the aspirations of the Young Turks to secularise, modernise and Westernise Turkey. Ironically, therefore, it was out of defeat rather than victory that the kind of new Turkey, concentrated on the Anatolian heartland and envisaged by the CUP, emerged, albeit shorn of any wider ambitions of rekindling the greater glories of the Ottoman Empire. Like the CUP's vision, Kemal's also had little room for ethnic diversity. The CUP leadership, however, had already paid for its own failures. In July 1919 the Sultan's new Turkish government tried the absent leaders of the CUP, many of whom had slipped away after the armistice. Enver, Talât and Cemal were sentenced to death in absentia, and Cavid to fifteen years' hard labour. Said Halim, who had been ousted as Grand Vizier in 1917 and replaced by Talât, was one of a number exiled to Malta. In December 1921 an Armenian assassinated him while he was visiting Rome. Talât had fled to Berlin at the end of the war, and had been assassinated there by another Armenian in March 1921. Cemal had also fled to Germany, but was assassinated in Tbilisi by yet another Armenian in July 1922. Cavid, who had returned to office as Finance Minister in 1917, initially fled to Switzerland, but returned to Turkey in 1921. Seen as a rival by Kemal, he was executed in 1926 for alleged sedition. Halil, who had become Foreign Minister in 1915 and Minister of Justice in 1917, was another of those exiled to Malta. He returned to Turkey in 1922, re-entering politics and serving as a parliamentary deputy between 1931 and 1946. Surviving supposed implication in the plot against Kemal that had cost Cavid his life, Halil died in 1948.

As for Enver, he also initially went to Berlin, transported there with Talât and Cemal on a German submarine. He then accepted an invitation from the Bolsheviks to visit Moscow in 1919. Disillusioned with apparent Bolshevik support for Kemal, Enver appears to have convinced Lenin that he could unite the so-called Basmachi and turn them against British rule in India. Derived from the Turkish word *basmak*, meaning to plunder or violate, the term was used to describe the insurgents in a widespread popular Islamic uprising against the Bolsheviks that had followed their dissolution of the autonomous government in Turkestan in January 1918. Reaching Bukhara in November 1921, Enver promptly defected to the Basmachi, proclaiming himself Emir of Turkestan and commander-in-chief of all the Armies of Islam. Enver managed to bring about a temporary unity between the disparate groups fighting the Bolsheviks, but any lingering Pan-Turanian dream was extinguished when he was killed in a skirmish with Bolshevik cavalry near Bol'dzhura in Turkestan on 4 August 1922.

CHAPTER 3

THE MAKING OF A NATION

Australia's Coming of Age at Gallipoli, 25 April 1915

Planned as Australia's new capital city in 1908 but only really constructed in the 1920s, it has to be said that Canberra rather lacks character. The buildings seem generally to try too hard to impress. There is one vista, however, that does make an impact. Looking up the broad expanse of Anzac Parade from Old Parliament House, used by the Australian Parliament from 1927 to 1988, the eye is instantly drawn to the towering Byzantine-like dome of the Australian War Memorial (AWM) below the forested slopes of Mount Ainslie. The memorial's design was conceived in 1926, and it was completed in November 1941. Opened on 25 April 1965, Anzac Parade has a series of national monuments to Australia's armed forces, and to the wars in which they fought.

One of the closest to the AWM is the Kemal Atatürk Memorial, unveiled on 25 April 1985. It is emblazoned with the same words of reconciliation, of the then Mustafa Kemal in 1934, that are inscribed on a similar monument unveiled on the same day at Ari Burnu on Turkey's Gallipoli peninsula. Ari Burnu ('Bee Point' in Turkish) lies above, and at the northern end, of what has been known to Australians since 25 April 1915 as Anzac Cove. Having walked through the small war cemetery at Ari Burnu, the visitor can use a flight of steps to get down on to the pebbled shore. Turning to the left around the shallow headland of Ari Burnu itself, the astonishingly small area of Anzac Cove can be seen, arching gently away to the equally slight Hell Spit to the south. The modern road above the cove only marginally lessens the impact. The beach is somewhat less than half a mile long, and not much wider than the length of a cricket pitch. Yet, here, as testified by the whole atmosphere of the Australian War Memorial, and also by the very names of both Anzac Cove and Anzac Parade, a young nation's independent identity was seemingly forged from the experiences of the original Anzacs, the Australian and New Zealand Army Corps (ANZAC), albeit that independence was still seen as firmly within the orbit of the British Empire.

In reality, the Anzacs were only a minority of the forces deployed at Gallipoli. More Frenchmen than Australians died at Gallipoli, and 87 per cent of Australia's dead in the Great War were lost in other theatres of war. The Australian federation itself had also come into being in January 1901, during an earlier imperial war in South Africa, in which over 16,000 Australians (and just under 8,000 New Zealanders) had served overseas. Nonetheless, Anzac Cove became the supreme evocation of a new national identity seen as distinctive from that of the mother country. Other imperial and colonial subjects asserted their new-found national pride in similar ways, but the continuing relevance of Anzac Cove and Gallipoli for Australians and New Zealanders marks it as a significant turning point in imperial and colonial history. That little of the Anzac legend was actually true remains a testament not only to the power of founding myths of national identity, but also to the imagination of one man, more than any other, whose vision was encapsulated in the original AWM. This was Charles Bean, official war correspondent and, later, Australian official historian of the Great War.

Australia was in the midst of an election campaign when war broke out. The incumbent (and soon to be defeated) Liberal prime minister, Joseph Cook, and his Labor opponent, Andrew Fisher, vied to demonstrate imperial loyalty. It was Japan rather than Germany that was most feared but, legally, Australia had no choice but to follow Britain's lead. In any case, Australia's political and economic security were widely perceived as being ultimately dependent upon a British victory. The 52,561 men enlisted in Australia by the end of 1914 represented only 6.4 per cent of those eligible, but rigorous physical standards were applied to recruits for the Australian Imperial Force (AIF), as the Australian component of the Anzacs were officially designated. By 1918, however, between 412,000 and 416,000

Australians had enlisted, some 13.4 per cent of the white male population, of whom approximately 331,000 served overseas. This compares favourably with the 19.3 per cent of white males who enlisted in New Zealand, 13.4 per cent in Canada, 11.1 per cent in South Africa, and the 22.1 per cent of the British male population who served in the wartime army.

Expecting to go direct to France via England, the initial Anzac corps comprising the 1st Australian Division and the mixed New Zealand and Australian Division, was instead diverted to Egypt, largely because of the difficulties of adequately accommodating the corps on Salisbury Plain, where the Canadian Expeditionary Force had already suffered deaths from pneumonia and meningitis. The Anzacs were still training in Egypt, therefore, when the Dardanelles campaign was conceived. Resulting, of course, from the Turkish entry to the war, the campaign was the great might-have-been that seemingly promised so much as an alternative to the deadlock and slaughter on the Western Front. The expectation of success was invested at the time with a romanticised, classical and crusading imagery evocative of Troy and the Hellespont. One who evinced such literary allusion was the poet Rupert Brooke, who died of blood poisoning from an infected mosquito bite on 23 April 1915 while his troop transport was riding at anchor in Tris Boukes Bay off the island of Skyros. Another was the commander of the Mediterranean Expeditionary Force, Sir Ian Hamilton, a liberally minded soldier of some literary skill. Hamilton's memoir of the campaign is suffused with classical romanticism, as in his description of the 'enchanted background' of the Dardanelles: 'There, Hero trimmed her little lamp; yonder the amorous breath of Leander changed to soft sea form.'[1] Perhaps not surprisingly, in an address to his troops on the eve of the landing on 25 April he proclaimed, 'The difference between the spear of Achilles and our steel bullets will not be discernible in the sphere of the Gods.'[2] Quite what the ordinary regular soldiers of the 29th Division made of this is uncertain.

Unfortunately, the lack of any real governmental machinery in Britain for the adequate discussion of strategic options, compounded by the unwillingness and inability of the professional heads of the armed forces to offer any meaningful advice even when asked, left a vacuum in decision-making. The seemingly great diplomatic and military possibilities arising from knocking the Turks out of the war, based on a series of unproven assumptions about the reactions of the Turkish government and other states to a purely naval attack on the Dardanelles straits, seduced all into too easy an acceptance of success as a foregone conclusion. In the event, the initial naval operation to force a way through the straits, which began on 19 February 1915, was bedevilled by the problem of not being able to neutralise the Turkish shore batteries until the minefields had been cleared, and it being all but impossible to clear the mines until the shore batteries had been destroyed. An attempt to rush the fleet through on 18 March resulted in the loss of three battleships and the crippling of a fourth.

Reluctantly, it was resolved that the army would have to neutralise the forts by landing on the Gallipoli peninsula, though this would take time to organise. There had been little cooperation between army and navy prior to the war, however, and the landings had to be improvised in the absence of any specialised landing craft. Since artillery could not be landed immediately, fire support would depend on the navy, but naval delayed-action high-explosive shells were not ideal for such a task, given the high angles required in the difficult terrain. Nor was there any efficient means available for easy ship-to-shore communication or, for that matter, ship- or ground-to-air communication. In any case, there were no adequate maps to assist indirect fire from the ships, and too few aircraft available for reconnaissance. Once ashore, matters would be no better, for artillery was technically limited at this stage, and it would prove difficult to locate Turkish positions accurately. There remained the difficulty of coping with steep elevations. Indeed, it is hard to see how a similar deadlock to that on the Western Front could ever have been avoided, even given what Winston Churchill later bitterly characterised as a long chain of missed chances. At no point, indeed, did the British or imperial forces advance more than 4 miles inland as the campaign became a bitter struggle for the high ground.

The campaign was to give rise to more than its fair share of legends. The former collier, the *River Clyde*, deliberately run aground on V Beach at Cape Helles on 25 April, instantly called to mind the Trojan Horse. That same day, the 1st Battalion, The Lancashire Fusiliers won 'six VCs before breakfast' on W Beach, known thereafter as Lancashire Landing. Later, in August, according to supposed witnesses, the 'vanished battalion' – 1/5th Battalion, the Norfolk Regiment, including a company recruited from the king's Sandringham estate – disappeared into strange clouds, from which it never re-emerged. The most potent myth of all, however, was that of the Anzacs at Anzac Cove.

British forces landed at five beaches – S, X, V, W and Y – around Cape Helles on the southern tip of Gallipoli on 25 April 1915. The Anzac role was to land on Z Beach, also called Brighton Beach, some eight miles further to the north of Helles on the western side of the peninsula. Twice as long, and wider than Anzac Cove, and free of the steep and rugged terrain backing it, Z Beach offered relatively easy access to the heart of the peninsula at its narrowest point. The object was to cut off the main Turkish forces to the south, preventing any reinforcements reaching the Helles front. It was anticipated that there would be far more opposition at Cape Helles, hence the commitment there of the 29th Division. Landing in the pre-dawn darkness, without any preliminary naval bombardment, and where the Turks would not expect it, the 1st Australian Division and the New Zealand and Australian Division would be expected to achieve complete surprise. Yet, many of those within the Anzac command structure had serious misgivings about possible Turkish resistance to a landing, particularly from artillery positions known to be located on high ground at Gaba Tepe. There was a lack of clarity as to the precise point at which the landing was supposed to take place. It was originally believed that the difficulty of navigating steam pinnaces with packed cutters trailing behind, in darkness and in a strong current, brought the Anzacs ashore at Anzac Cove up to a mile and a half further north than intended. It would appear possible, however, that one of the midshipmen in charge of a leading tow chose to move further north in the belief that landing too close to Gaba Tepe would be too risky. Moreover, the Turks had become aware of the ships moving offshore at least half an hour before they opened fire on the approaching boats. Ironically, Turkish barbed wire and entrenchments on Z Beach would probably have led to just as many casualties, but landing in the wrong place caused instant confusion.

One of the most atmospheric accounts of the first tense minutes at Anzac as the first glimmering of light began to pierce the gloom is that of the British war correspondent, Ellis Ashmead-Bartlett: 'Every eye was fixed on that grim-looking line of hills in our front, so shapeless, yet so menacing in the gloom, the mysteries of which those in the boats, which looked so tiny and helpless, were about to solve.'[3] Initially, it seemed as if the Turks had been taken completely by surprise and there would be no opposition. Then the firing began: Bean calculated it started at 4.29 a.m.[4] Jumping into the water up to their waists and sometimes up to their armpits, the Anzacs struggled ashore. One recalled, 'Hell was loosed in all its furies . . . stopping to think meant certain Death . . . looking down at the bottom of the sea, you could see a carpet of dead men who were shot getting out of the boats.' Another wrote of 'sitting jammed together like sardines in the boats, while the Turks blazed away merrily at us from the top of a big hill just skirting the shore.'[5] Under the unexpectedly heavy fire, the Anzacs scrambled up the steep slopes to find themselves in a tangle of scrub-covered gullies, ravines, and dry watercourses. Contact between, and within, units was easily lost. Sergeant George Mitchell of the 10th (South Australia) Battalion in the Australian 3rd Brigade described the attempted advance as one of sudden spurts: 'A scramble, a rapid pounding of heavy boots and clattering equipment, a startled yell and a crumpling body which has to be leaped over, a succession of slithering thuds, and we are down in the bushes forty yards ahead.'[6] Some groups got about a mile and a half inland, but increasing Turkish resistance pushed them back. With cohesion breaking down by the afternoon, men – both wounded and unwounded – began to make their way back down to the beach. Charles Bean later challenged the conclusions about Australian morale drawn by the British official historian, Cecil Aspinall-Oglander, but there is overwhelming evidence of what was termed 'straggling' by inexperienced, disorganised and disoriented troops.

Commanding the Australian 3rd Brigade, Colonel Sinclair MacLagan also overcompensated for the troops landing too far to the north by ordering Colonel James McCay to direct his 2nd Brigade towards Gaba Tepe, leaving the Anzac centre and left weak in the face of counter-attacks mounted by Mustafa Kemal's Turkish 19th Division. MacLagan feared a Turkish attack from his right, but by focusing on the so-called '400 Plateau' (soon to be called Lone Pine) to the south, he diverted attention from what would prove to be the dominating heights of Sari Bair to the north. The latter was the very axis down which Mustafa Kemal directed the weight of his counter-attack, securing the high ground at Chunuk Bair and forcing the Anzacs off another key feature called 'Baby 700'. Though little field artillery was available, the situation was made worse by the guns being landed late, and then being ordered withdrawn by the commander of the 1st Australian Division, Major General William Bridges, for fear that they would be overrun as the situation continued to deteriorate.

Coming ashore at about 8.00 p.m. to consult with Bridges and Major General Alexander Godley of the New Zealand and Australian Division, the corps commander, Lieutenant General Sir William Birdwood, was told that the only course was to abandon the landing and re-embark. Birdwood sent a message to be relayed to Hamilton offshore in HMS *Queen Elizabeth* at about 8.45 p.m. It made stark reading:[7]

> Both my Divisional Generals and Brigadiers have represented to me that they fear their men are thoroughly demoralised by shrapnel fire to which they have been subjected all day after exhaustion and gallant work in the morning. Numbers have dribbled back from the firing line and cannot be collected in this difficult country. Even New Zealand Brigade which has been only recently engaged lost heavily and is somewhat demoralised. If troops are subjected to shell fire again tomorrow morning there is likely to be a fiasco, as I have no fresh troops with which to replace those in the firing line. I know my representation is most serious but if we are to re-embark it must be at once.

Convening with Birdwood again at about 10.00 p.m., Godley and Bridges did not want to wait for Hamilton's decision, but to evacuate immediately. Birdwood wanted to remain. Rear Admiral Thursby, who had supervised the landing, felt evacuation to be too risky. Thursby's opinion carried weight and at about 2.30 a.m. on 26 April, Hamilton sent Birdwood the famous exhortation that the Anzacs must 'dig, dig, dig, until you are safe'.[8] The Anzacs did, indeed, hang on, though Hamilton again contemplated withdrawal on 8 May, until dissuaded by Birdwood. It is not clear how many casualties were suffered on 25 April, but between the landing and 3 May, Bean's official history records some 8,100, including 2,300 killed: possibly 500 or so died on 25 April. By the time the campaign was abandoned, and the Anzacs were finally evacuated on the night of 18 December 1915, 8,141 Australians and 2,271 New Zealanders had been killed.

Gallipoli had a particular intensity for all its participants. Allied troops had their backs to the sea in small and heavily shelled enclaves. Unlike on the Western Front, there was no safe rear area. All supplies, including water, had to be brought on to the peninsula from the main bases established at Moudros Bay on the island of Limnos, landed from small boats, and then taken up to the front line under fire. In the summer heat, lice and flies were ever present. Dysentery and enteric was endemic, and the medical systems were unable to cope. By contrast, blizzards, thunderstorms and heavy snowfalls struck the peninsula in November 1915, causing at least 16,000 cases of frostbite, and hastening the desire to abandon a campaign that was going nowhere. For the Anzacs, the campaign revolved around such features as Quinn's Post, Shrapnel Valley, Plugge's Plateau, Russell's Top, Lone Pine and the Nek. For Australians, the latter became almost as evocative as Anzac Cove itself. In the early morning of 7 August, the 3rd Australian Light Horse Brigade took 472 casualties, including 298 dead, in a disastrous attempt to take it. In effect, since MacLagan had pushed the 1st Australian Division to the right on landing, the New Zealand and Australian Division was made responsible for the more critical left flank as it landed later in the morning of 25 April. In effect, the security of the Anzac position fell to the New Zealand and Australian Division, and the 1st Australian Division was a junior partner in the subsequent actions that determined success or failure. The attacks on Lone Pine and the Nek in August, therefore, were in support of primarily New Zealand offensives to the left. There was an increasing tendency to forget the contributions of the New Zealanders: as it happens the first use of the acronym 'Anzac' was by a New Zealander, and the nickname 'digger' was also first applied to New Zealanders.

From the very beginning, the story of the Anzacs was extensively reported. It was Ellis Ashmead-Bartlett who began to establish the legend in his despatches from the front. These fully confirmed the expectations of the Australian and New Zealand public that their men's exploits would rank with the bravest deeds of empire. The 34-year-old Ashmead-Bartlett was the son of a Conservative MP, Sir Ellis Ashmead-Bartlett, who had been a Civil Lord of the Admiralty in Salisbury's administration between 1886 and 1892. Educated at Marlborough College, which he had cordially hated, Ashmead-Bartlett had accompanied his father on a visit to the Turkish army during the Greco-Turkish War of 1897. He had served in the South African War as a subaltern in the Bedfordshire Regiment before

being invalided home. Ashmead-Bartlett had then become a war correspondent for the *Daily Telegraph*, covering the Russo-Japanese War, French
and Spanish campaigns in North Africa, and the two Balkan Wars. He had
also found time to stand unsuccessfully for two different seats in the January
and December 1910 general elections. In 1914 Ashmead-Bartlett was then
chosen by the Newspaper Proprietors' Association as the official representative for the London press with the Mediterranean Expeditionary Force.

Tall and fair, self-opinionated and conceited, Ashmead-Bartlett liked to
live well and invariably beyond his means: he was declared bankrupt in
December 1914, hence his readiness to accept the Gallipoli assignment
and its salary of £2,000. Henry Nevinson of the *Manchester Guardian*, who
represented the provincial press during the campaign, recalled that
Ashmead-Bartlett would 'issue from his elaborately furnished tent dressed
in a flowing robe of yellow silk with crimson, and call for breakfast as
though the Carlton [Club] were still his corporeal home'.[9] He had brought
out his own cook and his own supply of champagne. There may have been
what Nevinson regarded as an air of 'magnificence' about Ashmead-
Bartlett, but he appears to have been a man with a kind of inner rage,
always ready to rail against perceived slights. Compton Mackenzie, who
served on Hamilton's headquarters intelligence staff, was briefly mistaken
for Ashmead-Bartlett one day by a staff officer who wanted to avoid dining
with him: '"Oh, its you, Mackenzie!" he exclaimed. "We thought it was
Ashmead-Bartlett, and we didn't want to ask him to lunch." He shouted
jovially, and from other dug-outs all round emerged the relieved faces of
the Army Corps staff'.[10] Possibly influenced by his deteriorating relationship with Hamilton and his staff, to which his own difficult personality
had materially contributed, Ashmead-Bartlett became increasingly critical
of the conduct of the campaign.

Running into censorship problems, Ashmead-Bartlett persuaded Keith
Murdoch of the Melbourne *Age*, en route to London to run the United
Cable Service in August 1915, to carry a highly critical letter for him to
give to Prime Minister Asquith. Informed by Nevinson, the military
authorities detained Murdoch at Marseilles and seized the letter. In fact,
Ashmead-Bartlett had already voiced his criticisms to Asquith and many
others when briefly back in London in May 1915. Reaching London
himself, Murdoch also met Asquith and other ministers. In September he

wrote his own critical and greatly overstated letter to Fisher's Labor government in Australia, with which he was on close terms. Asquith also circulated Murdoch's letter to the Committee of Imperial Defence. Hamilton always believed the affair had played a significant role in his recall from the Gallipoli command in October. Succeeding Fisher as Australian prime minister that same month, William Morris Hughes was less willing to rock the imperial boat and requested that no other Australian journalists be allowed to visit the peninsula without his approval. Hughes, however, was a populist and not above exploiting the Anzac myth for his own ends, and was to employ Murdoch as a kind of unofficial cheerleader.

Ashmead-Bartlett was also sent home on 2 October 1915, subsequently undertaking public lecture tours in the United States and Australia in 1916, speaking on 'With the Anzacs at the Dardanelles'. He also showed film he had taken: this was later produced as the short feature, *With the Dardanelles Expedition: Heroes of Gallipoli*, with captions written by Bean. There had been considerable alarm on the part of the British and Australian governments at the prospect of the lecture tours and Ashmead-Bartlett was required to submit his text in advance. Short of money as always, however, Ashmead-Bartlett recognised the need to modify any criticism to maximise the commercial opportunity. He drew good crowds and took the opportunity to sell his Gallipoli diary to the Mitchell Library in Sydney. He also sold copies of the photographs he had taken on the peninsula to the public.

Whatever his faults, Ashmead-Bartlett undeniably wrote vivid and engaging prose. He did not venture as close to the front line as Bean. Therefore, his information was often second-hand but more analytical. Since transmission of Bean's first despatch was held up in Egypt, it was Ashmead-Bartlett's account of the Anzacs that was published first, on 7 May 1915. It made an instant impact. For its author, the Anzacs were 'the finest lot of men I have ever seen in any part of the world' and 'a race of giants'. These 'raw Colonial troops in those desperate hours proved themselves worthy to fight side by side with the heroes of Mons and the Aisne, Ypres, and Neuve Chapelle'.[11] Bean later acknowledged the importance of Ashmead-Bartlett's despatch, as the 'first to impress on the world the main facts of the landing and the impression is still there'.[12] Motivated by a sense of personal slight and economic necessity Ashmead-Bartlett, however, did not have any consciousness of creating a political and cultural legacy.

The publication of Ashmead-Bartlett's despatches in 1915 was soon followed by other similar paeans to Australian heroism. E. C. Buley completed his *Glorious Deeds of Australians in the Great War* in October 1915, and various participants' memoirs appeared in 1916. The first full narrative of the campaign was *Australia in Arms: A Narrative of the Australasian Imperial Force and Their Achievements at Anzac* by Philip Schuler of the Melbourne *Age*, who had visited Gallipoli in July 1915. Echoing Ashmead-Bartlett, Schuler proclaimed the landing as the moment when 'Australia attained nationhood by the heroism of her noble sons.'[13] Australian schoolchildren were also receiving as school prizes such titles as John Adcock's *Australasia Triumphant* in 1916. The perpetuation of the legend of Anzac, however, was to be principally the work of Charles Edwin Woodrow Bean.

Born at Bathurst in New South Wales in 1879, where his English father was headmaster of the college, Bean moved to England with his family upon his father's appointment as headmaster at Brentwood School in 1891. Educated at his father's *alma mater*, Clifton College, where Douglas Haig was also a pupil, Bean won a scholarship to Hertford College, Oxford. Returning to Australia in 1904, Bean briefly took up the law and teaching, before some articles he had written brought him a job with the *Sydney Morning Herald* in 1908. Bean represented the newspaper in London between 1910 and 1912, before returning to Sydney in 1913 as its leader-writer. In 1914 he narrowly won the ballot to be the official representative of the Australian Journalists' Association with the AIF: Murdoch was placed second. Bean went ashore at Anzac between 0930 and 1000 hours on 23 April and was the only journalist to be present on the Gallipoli peninsula throughout the campaign, despite being wounded in the leg in August. At the time of his appointment, Bean also secured an agreement from the Australian Defence Department that he would go on to write an official history of Australia's contribution to the war.

Bean was tall and thin, with his wire-framed spectacles adding a distinctly academic look, though this was offset to some extent by the wavy red hair. There was no doubting his courage, however, and he was recommended for the Military Cross at one point but could not receive any decoration as a civilian. He was always far closer to the front line than Ashmead-Bartlett, who suggested that Bean almost counted the bullets in any action he described. Stemming from Bean's earliest journalism on workers in the Australian wool trade, he was passionately interested in the individual. In many ways, Bean's writing can be characterised as micro-history and, in his subsequent official history, countless individuals were to be mentioned, with brief biographies appended as footnotes to the text.

Bean was also very much a product of his public-school upbringing, espousing the robust Social Darwinism exemplified by Sir Henry Newbolt's 1908 poem in praise of Bean's own school, 'The Island Race: Clifton Chapel'. Bean certainly subscribed to the kind of concerns about 'national efficiency', and the deterioration of the imperial race that had been voiced in Britain during and immediately after the South African War. This had stimulated the establishment of the Royal Commission on Physical Training in Scotland in 1902, the Inter-departmental Committee on Physical Deterioration in 1903, and investigation into the condition of the working class by Seebohm Rowntree and Charles Booth. For Bean, the physical products of a century of British industrialisation recruited into the British army in 1914 possessed 'neither the nerve, the physique, nor the spirit and self control to fit them for soldiers'.[14] By contrast, therefore, Australian soldiers represented the very best imperial stock, independent, enterprising and adventurous, '[b]y reason of open air life in the new climate. And of greater abundance of food, the people developed more fully the large frames which seem normal to Anglo-Saxons living under generous conditions.'[15]

Bean was aware that not all Australians were supermen. In any given action, perhaps 20 per cent of men would not want to go forward at all, and 80 per cent of the rest would not want to go on once they had started. The remaining 20 per cent of those who started did keep going. Bean felt, however, that a larger percentage of those prepared to go forward would be found in the ranks of Australians as opposed to other national units. As he saw it in September 1915, his role was to tell the story of those who went forward and not the 'weaker ones who retired through them at the same time'.[16] Moreover, the story of those who went forward would provide a suitable and dramatic testament to the role Australians had played for the first time on the world stage. The official history in particular would be a 'permanent memorial in writing', and a national history 'that will be read by my nation as long as it exists'.[17]

Clearly, to tell the story only of those who went forward required a process of selection. This was already apparent in Bean's despatches from Gallipoli. Indeed, he had learned from an adverse reaction to his despatches covering the training of the Anzacs in Egypt, in which he had reported on Australian indiscipline. Now there could be no admission of any Australian errors, and failure would be converted into heroism in the face of adversity. In terms of the landing at Anzac Cove on 25 April, there could be no question of men 'straggling'. Indeed, the Australian government was to be successful in having such references cut from the post-war British official history. The reality was that of '16,000 disorganised and inexperienced soldiers being held at bay for most of the day by five weak and widely spread Turkish battalions'.[18] Similarly, while Ashmead-Bartlett described the Light Horse's disastrous assault on the Nek as an 'utterly futile attack ... which the merest tyro could perceive had no possible chance of succeeding', for Bean it was 'sheer self-sacrificing heroism'.[19]

Compared to Ashmead-Bartlett, Bean's despatches were somewhat clinical and lacking in the kind of visual imagery that the Australian press wanted, to the extent that some newspapers contemplated dropping their publication in the autumn of 1915. The style, though, was plain and lucid, a series of individual stories, based on immediate post-action interviews, linked to become a narrative. What Bean wished to conceal was also evident in an even earlier venture, *The Anzac Book*, published in aid of patriotic charities in 1916. The idea was not Bean's but that of a British officer, Major Stephen Seymour Butler, who solicited contributions from Anzacs serving at Gallipoli in November and early December 1915 – when plans for evacuation were already advanced – with the intention of producing a kind of New Year magazine for the troops. With evacuation, therefore, it became more of a souvenir. Barely 150 contributions were received, and the resulting publication was very much Bean's production. He carefully edited the material for publication, omitting anything that smacked of fear, boredom, malingering, and even a longing for beer. Replete with classical allusions and redolent of the values of Bean's public-school background, *The Anzac Book* conformed precisely to Bean's vision of the Anzacs, selling over 104,000 copies by the end of 1916.

Bean urged the creation of the Australian War Records Section in 1917 to collect material for the post-war history, and revisited the peninsula in 1919 with the artist George Lambert and photographer Hubert Wilkins. Lambert was able to make sketches for two large paintings, depicting the landing at Anzac Cove, and the charge of the Light Horse at the Nek: both are in the AWM. The now familiar Bean style continued in the twelve main narrative volumes of the official history published between 1921 and 1943, six of which Bean wrote entirely himself. Unlike the rather collaborative nature of the British Official History, Bean's was written much more from a single individual perspective. Indeed, much was based on his diaries and papers, Bean having secured a guarantee that his work would not be censored by the Australian military authorities. As in his journalism, Bean carefully selected his evidence and chose simplification and generalisation over wider analysis. It was a chronicle more than a history, from which the higher perspective of strategy, and of higher command decisions, was largely absent, being incidental to his main purpose. Because Bean mixed socially with Anzac officers rather than the other ranks, he also tended to assume that the latter shared his generally favourable view of Australian officers. Australian faults were noted on occasion, but unsavoury behaviour was treated as far from serious and, invariably, the Anzacs were not to blame.

Bean, therefore, told only part of the truth about the character and conduct of the Anzacs. In fact, there was more resistance to initial recruitment efforts in Australia than is sometimes supposed. Some 22 per cent of the first cohort of the AIF were British-born as opposed to Australian-born. Moreover, Australia was one of the most urbanised societies in the world in 1914, only 14 per cent of wartime recruits being employed in agricultural occupations. Yet, the Anzac 'myth' was predicated upon a supposed 'bush ethos' deriving from ideas of 'mateship' and egalitarianism. It was certainly the case that Australian soldiers generally had a jaundiced view of the British army, and that the view that Australians were undisciplined was equally widespread amongst the British military leadership. Quite often, the Australians were poorly trained and badly led, with a considerable social gulf between officers and men. Indeed, the New Zealanders were arguably more efficient by 1918 with greater staying power, and certainly suffered from fewer disciplinary problems. Nonetheless, the AIF did have the advantage of maintaining rigorous physical standards, and of the reasonable familiarity with firearms resulting from the introduction of compulsory military training before the war.

Certainly, too, the AIF undoubtedly drew strength from a notion of being different from the British. In fact, command over the Australian corps became symbolic of independence of spirit, the Australian authorities also refusing the attempts by the British High Command to extend the death penalty for disciplinary offences to Australians on the same basis as applied to British troops. Ultimately, the Australian, Sir John Monash, was elevated to the command of the Australian Corps in May 1918: ironically, Monash was of German extraction and wrote letters home to his father in German.

Underlying divisions within Australian society deriving from class (defined by income), religion and national origin were to become even more pronounced during the subsequent referenda on conscription in October 1916 and December 1917. Those most likely to oppose its imposition were Labor voters, Catholics and those of Irish extraction; those most likely to support it were women, males of military age and recent migrants. On both occasions, conscription was rejected: by the narrow margin of 72,476 votes in a poll of 2.5 million in 1916, and by a larger margin of 166,588 in 1917. The controversy over the first referendum split the Labor Party, and Hughes was compelled to create a national coalition with the Liberals in January 1917. Ironically, the secretary of the Anti-Conscription League was John Curtin, who would introduce conscription as Labor prime minister in the Second World War. In some respects, opposition to the war and, later, to conscription was economic in character. It reflected the increase in unemployment and short-time working at the outbreak of war, and the subsequent fears that conscription would further denude the rural labour force. It did not, therefore, reflect anti-war feeling as such, and there was a certain belief that a just war would find its own recruits without compulsion.

Bolstered by the sense of the heroism of its soldiers, increasing dominion independence for Australia, New Zealand and Canada was recognised in part by the attendance on occasions of Hughes and his Canadian counterpart at Cabinet meetings when in London. The South African statesman Jan Smuts joined the War Cabinet itself. Australia, Canada and New Zealand all insisted on a place at the post-war peace conference, and were duly represented both within a British Empire Delegation and by their own delegates, as well as being recognised as separate signatories of the Versailles Treaty. Increasing refusal by the dominions to automatically follow the lead of the British government in foreign policy, as they had in

1914, was also soon to be demonstrated. During the Chanak crisis in September 1922, Australia and Canada both declined to support any war in the face of resurgent Turkish nationalism. Australia's interests were no longer necessarily those of Britain, even though this did not become abundantly clear until the Second World War.

The spirit of a new independent nationhood was also maintained in the recognition given to 'Anzac Day', first celebrated nationally on 25 April 1916: there had already been some 'Anzac Day' commemoration in South Australia in October 1915. Promoted by Hughes, Anzac Day was partly a recruiting device and partly intended to bolster Hughes's prestige: it was also celebrated in London on 25 April 1916, with a march of Anzacs through the capital to a service at Westminster Abbey in the presence of George V, and a suitably rousing speech by Hughes at the Hotel Cecil. Subsequently, Anzac Day became a particularly important event given the difficulty for relatives of visiting distant graves. Interest in Anzac Day was waning in some areas when it was revived in the mid-1920s as a popular patriotic pageant by the Returned Sailors' and Soldiers' Imperial League of Australia (RSSILA), which found it convenient to draw attention to veterans' issues. All Australian states had adopted Anzac Day by 1927 as an official public holiday, despite opposition from Labor activists and frequent debates as to whether public houses and places of gambling or entertainment should be closed. Distance added to the popularity of exhibitions of war relics in Australia, and Will Longstaff's painting, *The Menin Gate at Midnight*, was purchased for the AWM and Australia and widely seen on a national tour in 1928 and 1929. Australian pilgrimage to Gallipoli or further afield was beyond the means of most private individuals, and the RSSILA declined to participate in the 1928 British Empire Service League's trip to Europe in the belief that it was not sufficiently 'Australian'. An Imperial Ex-service Association then emerged concomitant with a 'Wattle Tribute' proposed by the press to decorate graves abroad. The first pilgrimage set out in June 1929 for Egypt and Gallipoli, with about one hundred people taking part. Some four hundred veterans attended the unveiling of the Australian memorial at Villers-Bretonneux in the even more distant France in July 1938.

With waning interest, Anzac Day lost its initial imperial and national meaning both in Australia and New Zealand. Following protests in the

1950s against the general prohibition on sport and entertainment when Anzac Day fell on a Saturday, the New Zealand 1966 Anzac Day Act permitted such activities in the afternoons. A controversial play critical of Anzac Day by Alan Seymour, *One Day of the Year*, was banned from the Adelaide Festival in 1960 though subsequently performed by an amateur group in the city, and by a professional company in Sydney in 1961. From the mid-1960s to the 1970s, Anzac Day became more of a symbol of disunity, an opportunity for protest in the name of disparate causes, not least opposition to Australia's involvement in the Vietnam War. There was then another revival of interest in Anzac Day in the 1980s. This was largely driven by growing popular cultural nationalism promoted subsequently by successive federal governments, though it also became simultaneously a focus for opposition by feminists and Aborigines since it was seen, by some, as a divisive white male symbol. By then, the memories of the last few Anzac veterans themselves had become inextricably entangled with the myth, part of the very fabric of their own recollections. The same popular impulse saw the burial of Australia's own 'unknown warrior', chosen from an unidentified Australian body from the Villers-Bretonneux war cemetery in France, at the AWM in November 1993, and the state funerals of the last original Anzac in December 1997, and of the last survivor of Gallipoli in May 2002. An estimated 28,000 people attended the Dawn Service – the idea of a dawn service had been initiated in Western Australia in 1923 – in Canberra on 25 April 2007, with crowds of up to 30,000 in both Perth and Melbourne.

Gallipoli has remained an annual and fashionable event for many young backpackers. Australian cricket teams en route to do battle for the Ashes have also stopped off there. By 2003, numbers at the annual Dawn Service at Anzac Cove had reached 14,000. The Australian prime minister, Bob Hawke, attended at Anzac Cove in April 1990, and both prime ministers John Howard of Australia and Helen Clark of New Zealand did so in 2000. Inevitably, motivations have changed, grief and the search for meaning having been replaced by nostalgia, wanderlust, a passion for family history, even a wish, as Bruce Scates has remarked, 'to be connected with an event so much larger than themselves'.[20] As it happens, the Gallipoli peninsula has become in part a contested space with the appearance of more and more Turkish memorials since 1945 reflecting a different national myth in terms of the role of Mustafa Kemal as Atatürk, the 'father of the Turks'.

The promotion of Australian cultural nationalism has also been witnessed in the perpetuation of the Anzac myth in the cinema, which has had its own major influence on the popular memory of a younger generation. Thus, in Peter Weir's popular and award-winning film, *Gallipoli* (1981), the hoary old canard that British troops paused in their advance to make tea at Suvla Bay, while the men of the Light Horse died at the Nek, is given full prominence. In the cinematic version, there is no room for the fact that the operation was in support of the New Zealand Brigade attack on Chunuk Bair, rather than the unrelated British landing at Suvla, and that it was a wholly Australian-generated disaster. No opportunity is lost to depict British incompetence. A British officer seemingly orders a further fruitless attack on the 'Nek', which forms the film's climax. In reality, it was an Australian – Colonel John Antill – who ordered the attack. Only the sharp-eyed will notice that the officer with the impeccable English accent in Weir's film does actually wear Australian collar badges, a sleight of hand enabling Weir to claim historical accuracy. Weir regarded his film as a war memorial in celluloid, but it is an entirely dishonest exercise in articulating the legend and not the facts in the interests of a post-imperial generation. Bean knew the importance of the national myth, but he did not see his conscious cultivation of it as incompatible with loyalty to empire. Though the emphasis is different, however, the memory of Gallipoli and of the Anzacs still contributes to Australian national identity.

Ashmead-Bartlett, who had begun the process of myth making, returned to working for the *Daily Telegraph* in 1919. He was elected Conservative MP for Hammersmith North in 1924, but renewed bankruptcy forced his resignation two years later. His polemic, *The Uncensored Dardanelles*, was published in 1928. He died in Lisbon while covering the Spanish revolution for the *Telegraph* in May 1931. Bean, who subsequently declined a knighthood, continued to work on his official history, and to promote the AWM. During the Second World War, he worked for the Department of Information. He became Chairman of the Commonwealth Archives Committee in 1942, and Chairman of the Board of the AWM in 1952. Between 1947 and 1958 he was also Chairman of the Promotions Appeals Board of the Australian Broadcasting Corporation. Respected throughout Australia, Bean died in August 1968.

CHAPTER 4

THE MAN AND THE HOUR

Lloyd George's Appointment as Minister of
Munitions, 26 May 1915

ON THE morning of Friday, 21 May 1915, there were shocking headlines in the *Daily Mail*: 'The Shells Scandal. Lord Kitchener's Tragic Blunder. Our Terrible Casualty Lists.' The accompanying story proclaimed that soldiers' lives were being sacrificed because the British army did not have enough artillery shells to fight the war effectively. Such was the iconic status of Kitchener as Secretary of State for War that a copy of the newspaper was promptly burned outside the Stock Exchange, subscriptions were cancelled, and sales nose-dived. As the newspaper's owner, Lord Northcliffe, confided to his fellow press baron Max Aitken, later Lord Beaverbrook, he had failed to 'realise the extent to which the War Secretary had retained his prestige with the man in the street'.[1] Northcliffe had wanted to force Kitchener from office, but the ramping up of press agitation in the 'Shells Scandal' followed rather than precipitated a major change in the government direction of the war. That change itself made Britain the first of those states at war to attempt any systematic reorganisation of industry geared to winning the war.

Certainly, Northcliffe had already laid the groundwork for a public campaign for change. On 7 April his other title, *The Times*, had suggested that there had been an 'extraordinary failure of the Government to take in hand in business-like fashion the provision of full and adequate supply of munitions'. Three days later, the newspaper opined that the government 'ought to have insisted on instant organisation of the whole of our national resources'.[2] Then, on 14 May, *The Times* printed a telegram from its military correspondent, Charles à Court Repington, directly attributing the failure of the British offensive at Aubers Ridge (9 May) to a lack of shells. In reality, it was a convenient excuse for the failures of Sir John French's over-ambitious expectations of a breakthrough, and French detested Kitchener: Repington had been staying with French and was fed his version of events.

On Saturday, 15 May, Admiral of the Fleet Lord Fisher resigned as First Sea Lord over his differences with the First Lord, Winston Churchill, and profound disillusionment with the Dardanelles campaign. Churchill, who had brought the 74-year-old Fisher back from retirement as First Lord in 1914, described him as a decayed and ruined castle keep, in which 'its imperious ruler dwelt only in the special apartments and corridors with which he had a lifelong familiarity'.[3] Fisher tired easily, but his mind remained vigorous, and his discontent with the erosion of naval strength in the North Sea for the sake of the Dardanelles worried him more and more. It might be added that he had not expressed his opposition openly, his silence in the counsels of war echoing that of the Chief of the General Staff, Sir James Wolfe Murray, memorably nicknamed 'Sheep' Murray by Churchill. When HMS *Goliath* was torpedoed off the Dardanelles on 12 May, Fisher demanded that HMS *Queen Elizabeth* be recalled. Churchill claimed that 'Jackie' Fisher had actually simply walked out of the Admiralty building and gone missing for several hours that Saturday morning. Fisher was tracked down to a room in the Charing Cross Hotel, when Asquith ordered him back to the Admiralty. Beaverbrook on the other hand said that Fisher, when meeting the Chancellor of the Exchequer, David Lloyd George, in the street, had told him he was resigning. Lloyd George then sent for Asquith and, though unable to persuade Fisher to stay in office, they did manage to get him to go back to the Admiralty building: Fisher had threatened to resign on at least eight occasions already. Either way, a petulant Fisher promptly locked himself in his office, and refused to answer the door until an old friend and former First Lord, Reginald McKenna, now Home Secretary, glimpsed him peering through the blinds. McKenna had no better luck persuading Fisher to remain, and he departed for Scotland. Subsequently, Fisher sent Asquith quite ludicrous demands for complete control of the navy as the price for returning to the Admiralty. It was an extraordinary way to leave office in the midst of war.

Alerted by a cryptic note from Fisher, the Unionist leader Andrew Bonar Law saw Lloyd George at the Treasury on the Monday morning, and went on to meet Asquith in Downing Street. He agreed to join a new coalition government. It has sometimes been suggested that the 62-year-old Asquith was temporarily unhinged by the unexpected news that his confidante, Venetia Stanley, the 26-year-old young woman with whom he was infatuated, had resolved to marry one of Asquith's own younger ministers, Edwin Montagu. Diffident and lethargic though he was as a war leader, Asquith was an astute party leader intent on clinging to office. He feared that he might lose the general election that would have been due ordinarily at the end of 1915. Bonar Law, too, was apprehensive of fighting an election on an out-of-date electoral register, and with local constituency organisations weakened by enlistment of party agents, and contacts between MPs and constituents also eroded by enlistment of MPs and constituents. He was also aware of the growing unrest among his own backbenchers at their leader sustaining a Liberal government through 'patriotic opposition'. It suited both men, therefore, to enter a coalition.

On Monday, 17 May, Asquith told his Cabinet that the combination of Fisher's resignation and the shell scandal 'would, if duly exploited (as they would have been) in the House of Commons at this moment, have had the most disastrous effect on the general political and strategic situation'.[4] Two days later, Asquith announced the intention to form the new government. That same day, Lloyd George penned a letter to Asquith indicating that he could not continue as chairman of a powerless Munitions of War Committee without executive authority functioning under the auspices of the War Office. Since Kitchener was too popular to replace at the War Office, the only solution appeared to Lloyd George to be seizing control of munitions production. Having been refused the Treasury by Asquith, Bonar Law was minded to seek the proposed Ministry of Munitions for himself, but was persuaded otherwise after meeting Lloyd George. In theory, Lloyd George was appointed only temporarily to the Ministry of Munitions – as a means of preventing Bonar Law from being appointed – when the new government was constituted on 26 May. He expected to return to the Treasury. Lloyd George's formal appointment by Royal Warrant came on 9 June, with the ministry itself coming into being on 2 July.

The establishment of the Ministry of Munitions meant an end to the old pre-war ways of doing things. It would demonstrate how the power of the state over the lives of ordinary citizens would be greatly increased, even in a liberal democracy. It would prove an extraordinary experiment in state intervention and state welfare, marking a real turning point in attitudes on the part of government and governed. In a modern industrialised war, in which it was now just as important to out-produce as to outfight an opponent, mobilisation meant not just military manpower, but also of all means of production. What drove the creation of a 'war economy' above all else was the demand for more and more munitions. Other belligerents were suffering similar shell shortages to those of the British by the spring of 1915, but it took them longer to undertake the same kind of centralisation of munitions production. The French appointed an Under-Secretary of War for Artillery and Munitions within the War Ministry on 18 May 1915, but no Ministry of Armament and War Production appeared until December 1916. Though striving to remedy potential deficiencies in raw materials as early as August 1914, the Germans did not establish the Weapons and Munitions Procurement Office until September 1916, shortly before both it, and a number of other agencies, merged in a new Supreme War Office in November 1916. Lloyd George's Ministry of Munitions, therefore, was a pioneering creation. Yet, ironically, as Chancellor, Lloyd George had announced on 4 August 1914 that, despite the outbreak of war, government policy would be 'to enable the traders of this country to carry on business as usual'.[5]

Most had expected the war to be short. It was recognised that some limited government intervention might be needed in food supply, transport, maritime insurance, and the money markets, but for only a few weeks. Little thought had been given to the need to increase munitions production. The Mowatt Committee had calculated future required reserves of ammunition in 1904 on the basis of the experience of the South African War. The lessons drawn from the Russo-Japanese War appeared to be the need to ensure fire economy rather than increase the ammunition available. Each of the British army's standard eighteen-pounder artillery pieces was allocated only 1,000 rounds for active service, with a further 300 rounds in reserve in Britain, and another 500 to be manufactured within the first six months of a war. This represented a stock in hand two and a half times greater than at the start of the South African War in 1899, but it was assumed that there would be no need to fire more than 10 rounds a day per gun. The reality was rather different.

Already by 24 October 1914, with the BEF now fully engaged around Ypres, there was an attempt at shell rationing. Eighteen-pounders were restricted to firing 30 rounds a day. The actual average daily expenditure at Ypres between 21 October and 22 November, however, was 50 rounds per gun, rising to 80 rounds at really critical periods, with some individual batteries recorded as firing 1,200 rounds within 24 hours. Despite all efforts to send out as many shells as possible, the stock of eighteen-pounder shells was still reported as very small, that of 4.5-inch howitzer shells 'hopeless', and the amount of 9.2-inch howitzer shells decreasing by the day.[6] Moreover, the British army was notably deficient in the heavier calibre artillery that was soon to prove necessary for the siege-like conditions that unfolded on the Western Front.

Other calculations were equally misplaced. By 24 September, the French had only fifteen days' supply of shells left based on the current expenditure in Flanders. French industry had produced 10,000–12,000 shells a day initially but the requirement was now judged to be 80,000–100,000 shells. Similarly, by September 1914, the Russian military headquarters, Stavka, was demanding the delivery of 1.5 million shells a month, or three times the pre-war estimate, a total soon amended to 3.5 million shells per month. Having entered the war with a large stock of some 4 million field-artillery shells in August 1914, the Germans, too, had fewer than 500,000 left by September.

The South African War had demonstrated that the output of Britain's state ordnance factories was inadequate, but the Murray Committee in 1907 had concluded that the private sector could supply any increased wartime needs. The number of firms envisaged as contributing in the event of war was small, and there was little incentive for those firms outside the charmed circle of preferred manufacturers to invest in new plant and equipment without any certainty of future government orders. Had the war been fought along the lines of pre-war assumptions, all might have been well, but the demands for shells in France, the increase in ammunition scales, and the need to equip Kitchener's 'New Armies' of volunteers including their expanded artillery support – over 1.1 million men had enlisted by December 1914 – outstripped all capacity. Shortfalls were the product of the extraordinary additional orders placed with private firms by the government without regard for capacity, rather than of unrealistic expectations on the part of industry itself. In a sense, the shortage was an artificial one, generated by a combination of slow deliveries, accumulating arrears and further orders. Many contractors both at home and abroad simply failed to meet promised targets. British manufacture had to be supplemented by orders placed in Canada, the United States and Japan. Shortfall in weapons-production targets by June 1915 ranged from 12 per cent in rifles to 55 per cent in machine guns and 92 per cent in high-explosive shells. By May 1915, of 29.9 million rounds of eighteen-pounder artillery ammunition ordered since August 1914, only 1.4 million rounds had been delivered.

The man ultimately responsible for munitions procurement was Kitchener. In August 1914 this great imperial proconsular figure had been on home leave from Egypt, where he wielded political and military authority as British Agent and Consul General. Having established his reputation by reconquering the Sudan between 1896 and 1898, Kitchener had been summoned to act as chief of staff to Field Marshal Lord Roberts in South Africa in December 1899. He succeeded Roberts in the South African command, and was then commander-in-chief in India, taking up his Egyptian appointment in 1911. The War Office had been vacant since March 1914 with Asquith temporarily exercising a watching brief. The opportunity to secure Kitchener's services was too good to miss and, on 5 August, he became the first serving soldier ever to act as Secretary of State for War.

Kitchener was a better strategist than is sometimes suggested: unlike most, he certainly expected hostilities to last at least three years. It was his intention to commit his 'New Armies' increasingly to the fray so that 'our Army should reach its full strength at the beginning of the third year of the War, just when France is getting into rather low water and Germany is beginning to feel the pinch'. As he also expressed it to MPs in June 1916, that would give Britain maximum strength 'at the conclusive period of the war'.[7] Subsequently, Kitchener recognised that the abiding responsibilities of coalition warfare made it impossible to stand aside from commitment to the struggle in France and Flanders, remarking of the British offensive at Loos in September 1915, 'unfortunately we had to make war as we must, and not as we should like to'.[8] That he was a great magnet for recruiting is undeniable, his appeal forever encapsulated by the arresting stare and pointing finger on Alfred Leete's iconic poster, first issued on 5 September 1914.

Being a magnificent poster was not quite the same as being a good war minister. Lloyd George likened Kitchener to 'one of those revolving lighthouses which radiate momentary gleams of revealing light far out into the surrounding gloom and then suddenly relapse into complete darkness'. More succinctly, the Conservative MP Leo Amery characterised him as 'a great improviser, but also a great disorganiser'.[9] Not having served in the home army since 1883, Kitchener knew little of any pre-war military arrangements. Grown increasingly autocratic in his overseas assignments, Kitchener had previously clashed with the British High Commissioner for South Africa, Lord Milner, and with the Viceroy of India, Lord Curzon. On both occasions, he had won the political argument. In Asquith's Cabinet, too, most deferred readily to Kitchener's professional judgement. Lloyd George suggested that his colleagues were intimidated by Kitchener's overwhelming presence: he was, after all, 6 feet 2 inches tall, solidly built, and had enormous prestige with the public. Taciturn, secretive and constitutionally unable to delegate, Kitchener felt no need to explain any of his decisions to the politicians. In a sense he had a point for, as he remarked in September 1915, the Cabinet was 'so leaky. . . If they will only all divorce their wives I will tell them everything.' According to Beaverbrook, he added on another occasion that, in the case of Lloyd George, it was more a matter of a minister telling other men's wives.[10]

Within the War Office, the Master General of the Ordnance, Sir Stanley von Donop, had made arrangements as early as 24 August 1914 for more munitions work to be placed with civilian subcontractors to the usual suppliers. There was at least some recognition that firms new to munitions production could hardly be expected to do more than manufacture simpler components. There was also an understandable caution with regard to the safety of munitions manufactured by untried firms. Generally, however, the War Office was slow to communicate with industry. Raw materials, machine tools and suitably skilled labour were also into short supply. Due to the failure to control the enlistment of skilled manpower into the armed forces, small-arms factories had lost 16 per cent of their employees by December 1914, and chemical and explosive works had lost 23 per cent.

Lloyd George had interested himself in munitions production from the start, and it would appear that, like Kitchener, he appreciated at an early stage that the war would not be over in the shorter term. He had criticised von Donop in October 1914 for still observing the peacetime cost controls he had already abolished, leading to the creation of the Cabinet Munitions Committee. Lloyd George never quite understood that civilian firms could not immediately acquire the knowledge necessary to produce shells, and was unjustly critical of Kitchener and von Donop's supposed incompetence. His own policy as Chancellor, of abandoning competitive tenders for munitions and simply encouraging manufacturers to lay down new plant by advancing cash for purchases, only led to increased inflation. As difficulties mounted, however, he did see that the question of labour distribution required urgent attention. On 22 February 1915, therefore, as part of a wider Cabinet paper on the conduct of the war, he took the opportunity of a worrying strike by skilled workers on Clydeside to urge that the government take upon itself full powers to appropriate all civil-engineering plants capable of manufacturing munitions, and to assume responsibility for compulsory arbitration in any labour dispute. Lloyd George pressed for the passing of a Defence of the Realm (Amendment No. 2) Act in March 1915, which gave the government the requisite powers over engineering: firms could now be forced to take government work if they had the necessary plant to do so. Lloyd George also advanced his campaign for government control of the liquor trade, having suggested melodramatically – and improbably – in February that drink was doing as much damage to the war effort as German submarines. State purchase of the trade was not implemented, but licensing laws were generally tightened, and licensed premises were taken over where they were close to munitions factories at Enfield Lock, Carlisle and Gretna.

The Shells and Fuses Agreement was also negotiated in March to introduce 'dilution', whereby a reorganisation of working practices enabled the unskilled to undertake part of the work previously fully carried out by skilled men: an eighteen-pounder shell, for example, contained 78 different components. Dilution, therefore, was not the same as substitution of the unskilled for the skilled. As it happened, on the initiative of the armaments firm of Vickers, a dilution agreement had been negotiated in November 1914 between unions and the Engineering Employers Federation. The

agreement in March, therefore, brought the government into the partnership. Later that month, too, the so-called Treasury Agreements were
reached with thirty-five unions to prevent workers taking advantage of
their strengthened position: these agreements outlawed strikes, introduced
more flexible working practices, permitted dilution on war work, and
referred industrial disputes to official arbitration. Under the first agreement, employers promised not to use dilution as a means of reducing
employment or wages after the war and, by the second, promised restraint
of business profits.

Believing yet more was needed, Lloyd George persuaded Asquith to
establish the Munitions of War Committee (also called the Treasury
Committee) on 23 March – chaired by himself – to take any steps necessary
to improve munitions supply, but only in cooperation with the War Office
and Admiralty. The War Office could veto decisions made by the Munitions
of War Committee, and Asquith did briefly contemplate creating an entirely
new office for Lloyd George as 'Director of War Contracts' or 'something of
the kind'.[11] Kitchener wanted men directed to existing manufacturers rather
than work spread wider through civil industry. In March he established his
own Armaments Output Committee chaired by the Liverpool shipowner
George Booth to bring more civilian labour into the existing munitions
plants. This led to Lloyd George's frustration and his seizure of the chance
offered by the shells scandal to move against Kitchener. In many ways, the
work of Booth's committee anticipated the policy of the Ministry of
Munitions. It was also orders placed by the War Office, rather than by the
Ministry of Munitions, that sustained the war effort until the spring of
1916. The shells resulting from the first orders placed by the ministry did
not arrive at the front until October 1915, and were often substandard. By
May 1915, every three days the War Office was already receiving the
amount of ammunition that would have taken a year to produce under
peacetime conditions. By December 1915, the production of small-arms
ammunition had increased tenfold and, compared to the 871,700 shells of
all kinds produced in 1914, 23.6 million had been produced in 1915, a
twenty-seven-fold increase. Thus, Lloyd George was able to take the credit
in many cases for improvements already undertaken.

The blue eyes, long hair, almost hypnotic charm and indiscreet conversation won Lloyd George admirers but, in many other quarters, he was

equally distrusted. Many found such an intensely political animal unscrupulous, Margot Asquith writing that Lloyd George 'couldn't see a belt
without hitting below it'.[12] Certainly, as long ago as 1885 he had written to
his future wife, 'My supreme idea is to get on. To this idea, I shall sacrifice
everything – except, I trust, honesty. I am prepared to thrust even love
itself under the wheel of my Juggernaut if it obstructs the way'.[13] The now
ardent enthusiast for a greater war effort had been a fierce opponent of the
war in South Africa, and a leading 'Pro-Boer'. In reality, there was some
ambiguity in his actual views towards both pacifism and imperialism,
nor did he wish to be regarded solely as steeped in radical Welsh
Nonconformism. Yet, the radicalism was always close to the surface. As
Chancellor he had provoked constitutional crisis with the 'People's Budget'
of 1909, and his oratory had been equally inflammatory in passing the
National Insurance Act in 1911. Lloyd George simply had little truck with
tradition or convention, the latter especially evident in his many sexual
indiscretions, and in his casual indifference to financial proprieties. He
had come close to political disaster through his involvement in the Marconi
scandal in 1912, buying shares in an American subsidiary of the Marconi
company in the knowledge that it was about to receive a lucrative British
government contract. That same year, with his wife and four surviving
children safely ensconced back in Wales, he also took up his long-standing
relationship with his secretary, Frances Stevenson.

As the press baron George Riddell noted, the supremely self-confident
Lloyd George was 'always ready to examine, scrap or revise established
theories and practices'. Prone to espousing grandiose schemes, however, he
was not interested in detail, being keener on picking others' brains than
reading his ministerial papers. He disliked routine, and was wholly unsystematic in his working methods. As Riddell also suggested, 'he has a flair
for spotting what is wrong and suggesting a remedy, but he never thinks
out the details of attempts to put his scheme into operation'.[14]

In foreign policy, as in other areas of his politics, Lloyd George's personal
position had changed by 1914, as he had applied his agile mind to the
realities of the situation. Quite what stance he would take was uncertain so
far as his colleagues were concerned. After all, he had opposed Churchill's
naval-building programme. There is no doubt he hoped that war might be
avoided but, once convinced of the dangers posed by German ambition,

the 52-year-old Lloyd George applied himself to the waging of the war with all the zeal of the religious convert. He was certainly not in awe of Kitchener. Indeed, he clashed with him over the issue of a proposed Welsh Army Corps, which attracted Kitchener's suspicion for the overt politicisation involved in officer appointments by the so-called Welsh National Executive Committee.

The outbreak of the war preserved Lloyd George's political position. At virtually every turn of his career, he had acquired new enemies. With little interest in social connections for the sheer sake of them, Lloyd George did not tend to accumulate close friends. Even when he did so, his abiding concentration on the work of the moment often resulted in him severing contacts with those who no longer served his immediate purpose. Cordially hated by most Unionists, he had nonetheless flirted with the idea of a coalition government in 1910 in the interests of 'national efficiency'. Now, he was also under pressure from among his Liberal colleagues.

Recent by-election defeats had been attributed to the National Insurance legislation, and the immediate pre-war Budget had run into opposition on proposed grants to local authorities as a means of offsetting a rise in income tax to pay for more Admiralty expenditure. The Speaker of the Commons had even ruled that it did not appear to be a 'money bill' as defined by the Parliament Act. Lloyd George was no longer necessarily an automatic choice as Asquith's likely successor and, as late as May 1915, he may well have been more intent on galvanising Asquith than on displacing him. In the country as a whole, however, Lloyd George remained popular. Churchill, when writing to his brother, Jack, after his demotion from the Admiralty to Chancellor of the Duchy of Lancaster, remarked of Lloyd George, 'His successive failures in the Anti-Marconi, Anti-Navy, Anti-War and Prohibition operations do not seem at all to have affected his prestige or morale.'[15] Lloyd George always prided himself on his ability to interpret and represent the people's will. Certainly, his eloquence and willingness to talk to anyone made him especially successful as a negotiator with employers and unions.

Facing what he saw as the 'surly, suspicious, and hostile' attitude of the War Office to the new creation, the Ministry of Munitions, Lloyd George himself later wrote that 'it was for me a wilderness of risks with no oasis in sight'.[16] Going to the building allocated to him, 6 Whitehall Gardens,

Lloyd George found just two tables and a chair. He managed to keep the chair and one of the tables when men from the Office of Works arrived to remove even these, as not belonging to the new department. According to Lloyd George, he would work on his papers for an hour or two before breakfast, which generally served as an opportunity for meeting important visitors. He would then arrive at Whitehall Gardens at about 0900 hours to deal with correspondence, and to see departmental heads before a working lunch. Afternoons and evenings would be given over to parliamentary business, though the Cabinet would also often meet in the morning. There were also the constant tours to meet manufacturers and labour representatives around the country. No one could accuse Lloyd George of a lack of energy. One of his first decisions at the new ministry was to undertake what amounted to a mandatory industrial census, some 45,000 forms being returned to Whitehall within a month.

Despite Lloyd George's lack of office furniture, a ministry did exist in embryonic form. It was a merger between the Armaments Output Committee, the Munitions of War Committee and the War Office's Munitions Supply Organisation, over which von Donop presided as Master General of the Ordnance. As a ministry, it lacked a staff. Accordingly, it was largely manned by Lloyd George's introduction of 'men of push and go' and 'hustlers' brought from business into administration. Lloyd George first used the phrase when speaking on the amended Defence of the Realm legislation on 9 March 1915. Kitchener had begun the process, hiring figures such as George Booth and the scientist Lord Moulton, who was asked to help develop new high explosives and propellants. Lloyd George made over ninety further appointments, a system extended throughout Whitehall when he became prime minister in December 1916. Given Lloyd George's unsystematic ways of doing business, Booth found it necessary to write down what Lloyd George said to him, and then get Lloyd George to sign his concurrence. In practice, since there were not enough civil servants available, most of the new ministry's regional and local functions were also devolved to businessmen with ten district headquarters' offices and over fifty local boards of management that could place contracts directly with manufacturers.

Not all such businessmen were efficient administrators, and some undoubtedly forgot that they were not acting as personal representatives of either their industries or their firms. Eric Geddes, brought in from the North-Eastern Railway Company as Deputy Director of Munitions Supply, was to prove particularly successful, going on to be Director General of Transportation for the BEF in 1916, and Controller of the Navy, and then First Lord of the Admiralty in 1917. Some able civil servants were also found for the ministry, including Sir Hubert Llewellyn Smith from the Board of Trade and William Beveridge. There was certainly resentment of businessmen from Whitehall insiders. In turn, business came to question the degree to which government appeared to bow to labour demands to keep production going.

The sheer size of the bureaucracy created some confusion, compounded by the failure both to keep more than rudimentary staff records and to grade staff adequately. Responsibility for labour relations was also partly vested in the Admiralty, the War Office and the Board of Trade, as well as the new Ministry of Labour after 1916. In some respects the War Office and the ministry continued to compete for manpower until a fully fledged manpower policy was finally – and belatedly – adopted in December 1917. As an administrative machine, the ministry also worked rather better under his successors than under Lloyd George himself, for he was as improvisational as his men of 'push and go'. Nevertheless, in the fifteen months Lloyd George was at its helm, the Ministry of Munitions developed a highly innovative approach in such areas as managerial organisation, cost accounting, pooling of industrial research, welfare provision, electrification, mass production techniques, machine tooling and automation. It encouraged a substantial increase in the number of more efficient arc furnaces within the iron and steel industry. It was responsible not just for ammunition and shells, but also for the production of weapons, and all those other commodities such as machine tools, mineral oils and building materials required for their production.

Science was harnessed for the war effort through the Munitions Inventions Department established by Lloyd George in August 1915. Some ideas proposed, such as training cormorants to peck away the mortar on the chimneys at the Krupps armaments factory in Essen, were patently ludicrous. Subsequently, more worthwhile scientific research was undertaken, largely in collaboration with private firms, though Lloyd George tended to take credit for work already initiated by the War Office. Although initially turned down, the successful Stokes trench mortar developed by Wilfred Stokes of Ransomes & Rapier Ltd was eventually ordered by the War Office in September 1915: Lloyd George then greatly increased the orders. A better instance of the ministry's initiative was its response to the loss of German imports of optical instruments. This seriously affected production of such vital equipment as rangefinders, prompting the ministry to provide British firms with capital investment, and scientific and technical assistance sufficient to boost production. The 4 tons of optical glass a month being produced by 1918 was equivalent to twice the world's peacetime consumption four years earlier. Whole industrial sectors such as the gas, coke and dye industries were effectively taken over by requisitioning their entire output for the duration of the war.

The ministry commandeered raw materials, centralised foreign purchases and dealt in the import market, bringing in Indian mica, Greek magnesite and Swedish ball bearings. The ministry's post-war official history proclaimed that it had become the 'largest buying and the largest selling concern in the world, with a turnover amounting to hundreds of millions yearly'.[17] There were eventually over 25,000 employees in 50 departments, the majority women. By 1918, the ministry directly managed 250 government factories and supervised another 20,000 'controlled' establishments, and it had spent £2 billion. New factories, specially constructed on newly acquired land, included fifteen National Projectile Factories, fifteen National Filling Factories and four National Cartridge Factories. Peaceful rural landscapes gave way to 'an extensive industrial blistering, showing itself in acres of corrugated iron, and the gathering together of great populations engaged, as was obvious from their hands and complexions, in chemical processes quite foreign to the genius loci'.[18] The National Filling Factory at Barnbow near Leeds alone covered over 400 acres, employed 16,000 workers and produced 6,000 shells a day.

Certainly, the need to find alternative sources of labour, and the resulting difficulties of dilution, meant that the restrictive practices of the pre-war skilled unions had to be tackled head on. Government determination of manpower policies, in turn, led to direct involvement in labour relations. War distorted the normal working of the labour market, restructuring it in complex ways, yet without changing pre-war labour cultures or organisations, and also exacerbating pre-war sources of militancy in areas such as industrial restructuring and the challenge to skills. The premium put on skilled manpower gave labour an increased bargaining position. The voluntary agreements of March 1915 were incorporated in the statutory provisions of the Munitions of War Act in June 1915, which effectively suspended trade-union rules and restrictive practices in the munitions industry for the duration. It tied workers to their place of employment, preventing them from working for six weeks unless they obtained a leaving certificate from an employer first. Trade-union leaderships were nominated as the means through which government would negotiate for dilution and changes in working practices. Strikes on war-related work were now deemed illegal, and arbitration made compulsory.

The new regulations were naturally more easily applied in the ministry's own national shell and filling factories. Ultimately, rising food prices, higher rents, restricted labour mobility and wartime profiteering all contributed to growing discontent on the factory floor. Employers were generally encouraged to buy their way out of difficulties in face of the increasing shop-floor collective action organised by shop stewards. Lloyd George readily conceded national pay bargaining to the leaders of South Wales miners, who went on strike in July 1915. In the case of unrest on the Clyde over the winter of 1915–16, the concession of rent control, in an area where labour migration had led to a housing shortage and forced up rents, isolated the Clyde Workers Committee (CWC). The fact that the Clyde engineers were widely perceived within the labour movement as an elite also helped the government break the committee by the arrest and deportation of ten of its leaders from the Clyde in March 1916. Visiting the Clyde over Christmas 1915, Lloyd George received a rowdy reception: the soon to be suppressed Independent Labour Party journal, *Forward*, described him as Britain's 'best paid munitions worker'.[19]

Unwelcome though it may have been to employers and labour, state intervention in industry was unavoidable, and the Ministry of Munitions led the way in that process. The government fought shy of labour conscription as opposed to military conscription, but the demands placed on labour, as much as those placed on those compelled to fight, required appropriate reward to strengthen the cohesion of the 'home front'. Here, too, the Ministry of Munitions pioneered the extension of the limited pre-war state and private welfare provision, while also bringing novel intrusions by the state into the lives of the working class as consumers, through such means as liquor control, rationing and rent control. The Factory Acts were waived for the duration of the war, but from September 1915 onwards the Health of Munitions Workers Committee of the Ministry of Munitions, chaired initially by the Quaker industrialist Seebohm Rowntree, was empowered to inspect working premises. Over 900 factory canteens were established from the proceeds of an excess profits tax. The ministry employed welfare supervisors, and also set up cloakrooms and washing facilities. There was a small number of day nurseries, since there was some ambivalence when it came to married women in work. The ministry provided facilities for its own employees, and spent some £4.3 million on housing, building 10,000 permanent homes on 38 sites such as the Well Hall estate in Woolwich, at Eltham, and at Gretna, since commercial builders had little incentive to provide low-cost housing. Women working in the production of TNT (trinitrotoluene) were provided with a free daily pint of milk in the (mistaken) belief that it nullified its toxicity.

Women clearly did run the risk of TNT poisoning, from which 109 died during the war. There were also industrial accidents such as the explosion at the National Filling Factory at Barnbow that killed thirty-five women on 5 December 1916. Another thirty-five women died in an explosion at Chilwell in July 1918. Some seventeen women were among the sixty-nine fatalities in a massive explosion at the Brunner Mond Chemical Works at Silvertown in East London in January 1917, though most of these were nearby residents since the explosion took place after the end of the working day. Over 1,000 people were injured, and the hot metal fragments strewn over a large area damaged an estimated 70,000 houses: it was said that the blast was heard as far away as Cambridge.

The increasing presence of women in the industrial workforce was itself also a result of the ministry's efforts. Before the war, the most common employment for women had been in domestic service, accounting for approximately a quarter of the female workforce. The majority of women who were employed were single and working class. Even among the working class, the expectation was that most women would cease employment upon marriage. The war did not immediately lead to an increase in the female workforce because the first recourse to employers, as men enlisted or war-related business expanded, was to unemployed males. Women were also worse hit than men by the initial increase in unemployment due to economic uncertainty, so that Mrs Emmeline Pankhurst organised a major 'Women's Right to Serve' demonstration in London on 17 July 1915 with some 30,000 participants behind banners proclaiming 'Women's Battle Cry is Work, Work, Work'. It was the Ministry of Munitions that then championed positive recruitment of women to meet labour shortages, particularly after the introduction of military conscription in January 1916. It became almost fashionable for even middle-class and upper-class women to contemplate becoming a 'munitionette', although they were very much in the minority. Much of the expansion of women's employment occurred in commerce rather than industrial occupations: perhaps only 800,000 women came into the latter. Women in munitions were not necessarily new to employment, but lured from more traditional employment by the better pay. At the Gretna national cordite factory, some 80 per cent of the female labour force had been previously employed, with 36 per cent having been in domestic service. At Armstrong Whitworth's on the Tyne, 71 per cent had previously been employed, 20 per cent in domestic service. The overall increase of between 1.4 and 1.6 million women in paid employment between 1914 and 1918 also partly reflected the return of married women to work.

Wartime work, therefore, was not a novel experience for many women. Nonetheless, the disquieting flight of women from domestic service, the increased purchasing power available to 'munitionettes', and their working-class origins resulted in accusations of selfishness and extravagance. Wartime propaganda – as reflected in the Women's War Work Collection initiated by the Ministry of Munitions and subsequently placed in the Imperial War Museum – also exaggerated the extent of dilution. Unions and employers alike resisted dilution, and women were employed for very specific functions. It was also more widespread in controlled rather than uncontrolled establishments. Only about 23 per cent of the women who came into the munitions industry were actually doing men's work. Munitions work certainly did not mean equal pay for women, which government and unions alike also resisted. However liberating for some individual women, their wartime work was always seen as a cheap source of easily exploitable labour, which could be dispensed with in peacetime. At the end of the war, therefore, the number of women in employment declined rapidly. Two-thirds of those who had entered employment during the war had left it by 1920.

In so many ways, as the pulsating heart of a war economy, the Ministry of Munitions had transformed the relationship between state and society. Like other wartime creations, it disappeared after the war, but many of its practical industrial innovations survived, as did the memory of its achievements: in the Second World War, Beaverbrook was to model the Ministry of Aircraft Production on the Ministry of Munitions. Nor could the legacy of 'big' government and state intervention be entirely forgotten, even though the government was forced to keep its pledges to the unions on post-war restoration of the status quo in labour relations. The ministry's creation had not solved all the difficulties of industrial mobilisation immediately, and inevitably Lloyd George claimed credit for much that he did not initiate himself. There was no denying the ministry's overall success. From a situation in which only 500,000 shells were produced in 1914, the British munitions industry produced 76.2 million shells in 1917. By 1916, the Ministry of Munitions could produce in just three weeks what had been a year's production of eighteen-pounder shells in 1914: a year's pre-war production of medium shells took eleven days and a year's pre-war production of heavy shells just four days. The shift in emphasis that Lloyd George had made towards the production of heavy artillery was also in itself of enormous significance in a war increasingly dominated by the guns. By 1918, 61 per cent of the entire male industrial labour force was employed on war work of some kind.

Above all, the Ministry of Munitions secured Lloyd George's reputation as a dynamic man of 'push and go' himself. In the spring of 1916 Asquith tasked him with trying to find a solution to the deteriorating situation in Ireland following the Easter Rising in Dublin. On 6 June 1916, Kitchener was drowned along with 643 crew members when the cruiser taking him on a diplomatic visit to Russia, HMS *Hampshire*, struck a mine off Marwick Head in the Orkneys. Having lost control of munitions, the Secretary of State for War had been further marginalised by the appointment of Sir William Robertson as Chief of the General Staff in December 1915, and as the Cabinet's principal strategic adviser. Asquith and his colleagues were more than happy to see a discredited Kitchener accept an invitation to visit Russia in June 1916. His successor at the War Office was Lloyd George. Six months later Asquith too had been displaced and Lloyd George was prime minister. As Lloyd George himself had remarked in the House of Commons in March 1915, 'Instead of business as usual, we want victory as usual.'[20]

CHAPTER 5

THE POWER OF IMAGE

The First Public Screening of *The Battle of the Somme*,
21 August 1916

IN THE public mind, the memory of modern war is now largely encapsulated in a series of visual references. A campaign, even an entire war, can be summed up in a single image. For Dunkirk, it is one of long lines of men snaking across the sand towards the sea; for the Battle of Britain, one of pilots scrambling for their Spitfires; for Iwo Jima, a handful of American marines raising the Stars and Stripes on Mount Suribachi. In the case of the Vietnam War, it is perhaps either the South Vietnamese police chief executing a Vietcong suspect with a shot to the head in Saigon during the communist 'Tet' offensive, or that of a badly burned nine-year-old girl running naked from a US napalm strike. This is not entirely a new phenomenon. Roger Fenton's photographs from the Crimean War (1854–56) aroused extraordinary interest in Britain, albeit they were mostly static scenes of groups or individuals. Alexander Gardner's photographs of bodies – often artfully arranged after death – on the American Civil War battlefield of Antietam (1862) had an even greater impact in the United States.

Photographs of the drama of war in the mid and late nineteenth century were powerful enough when most ordinary civilians had little awareness of its realities. Previously, the public had relied on the written word, drawings and paintings. Francisco de Goya's illustrations of the horrors of the guerrilla war in Spain between 1808 and 1814 were certainly realistic, but Victorian battle art, prints, illustrated periodicals and the increasingly popular postcard were more likely to have stereotypical views emphasising courage and gallantry. Moving images, even if silent apart from a pianist's accompaniment, were always going to have a much greater effect on people's perceptions.

Such was the impact of the first true war documentary, *The Battle of the Somme*, shown to the wider British cinema-going public for the first time on 21 August 1916, that its images have continued to define the popular vision of war on the Western Front. The same two seemingly obligatory images recur over and over again in television documentaries, and in any news feature on the Great War. In one, soldiers climb out of a shallow trench: two fall, the second sliding back down into the trench. In the other image, a group step off over some low wire entanglements into enveloping smoke, two again falling. Knowing observers of the second sequence in particular will always note that one of these 'dead' soldiers casually crosses his legs, while the other glances back at the camera. Plain common sense ought to suggest that any cameramen standing in the open, as must have been done to film these sequences, would have been riddled with bullets if these were real attacks. It is usually assumed that these scenes were added in an attempt to provide missing elements of human involvement. The two sequences are separated by a perfectly genuine brief piece of film, showing distant and indistinct figures in No Man's Land, that demonstrates all too clearly how difficult it was to capture live battle action in any meaningful way.

The fact that these two famous scenes were so clearly faked does not somehow ring any alarm bells for lazy producers. Soldiers going 'over the top' died in very large numbers on the first day of the Somme, 1 July 1916, therefore this is what it was truly like. Given the limitations of the cameras available, as Stephen Badsey has argued, perfectly genuine footage 'produced a . . . film record of monstrous guns and strange landscapes, the sinister "empty battlefield" of twentieth-century industrialised warfare, and in an unusually exaggerated form'. Indeed, the greater ease of filming behind the lines placed an undue emphasis on the dramatic scenes provided by heavy artillery firing at distant targets, a subject that followed a set routine, which could be filmed from different angles to make a more satisfying edited image. As Badsey has also noted, soldiers marching in high spirits to the front in the early part of the film were next seen 'collapsing with pain at a dressing station or fatigue at a rest camp'.[1]

Cinema had created a series of visual clichés, to which audiences became accustomed through constant repetition. War had become shapeless, and individuals helpless, in a mythic version of the conflict that the images fashioned and perpetuated.

Already by 1914, there were over 4,500 cinemas in Britain, with an estimated weekly audience of 7 million, legislation in 1909 having demanded separate projection rooms and encouraged purpose-built buildings to replace the earlier bioscope tents and 'penny gaffs'. Tickets were cheaper than for theatres or music halls, and cinema was already the most popular form of entertainment for the working class. There were more than 12,000 cinemas in the United States. The first motion pictures at the birth of cinema had consisted of simple films of ordinary people undertaking unstaged everyday activities. William Friese-Greene's first films in 1889 were of Londoners strolling in Hyde Park on a Sunday morning. On the continent, the Lumière brothers filmed German and Austrian cavalry exercises in 1896. In Britain, Bert Acres filmed the Boat Race in March 1895 and the Derby in June 1896. The latter was shown on the following night at the Alhambra theatre in London's Leicester Square, and Acres's collaborator, Robert Paul, began regular weekly programmes at the Alhambra. A number of companies such as the Biograph Company in Britain began producing so-called 'topicals' and, in 1910, two French newsreel companies, Pathé and Gaumont, began operations throughout much of Europe and the United States. Clearly, the cinema had enormous potential as a news medium although newsreels reached individual cinemas at different times, the smaller provincial towns coming well behind the larger towns in terms of the distribution cycle.

The drama of war was always likely to be a winning formula. The problem with real war, however, was that it often occurred in inconvenient places. Early cameras were also immensely cumbersome, with lenses and film stock unsuitable for work in poor light conditions or at long range. Setting up a hand-cranked camera on its tripod in a war zone was hardly feasible and, in any case, the camera could only cope with a few hundred feet of film at a time, which was little more than a few minutes' screen time. Faking events for the camera was not uncommon. In 1898 the French filmmaker, Francis Doublier, faked an entire film of the French officer, Alfred Dreyfus, supposedly being tried for treason, transported to Devil's Island and imprisoned there. Doublier cobbled together his film from a scene of a French army parade, a Paris street scene, a Finnish tug going out to meet a barge, and a shot of the Nile delta. Another Frenchman, Georges Méliès, made several fake newsreels, including one of the coronation of King Edward VII in 1902 shot long before the actual event, which was delayed by several months because of the king's illness.

James Williamson's *Attack on a Chinese Mission Station* in 1898, supposedly an episode in the ongoing Boxer Rebellion, was shot in his own backyard, while the Edison Company filmed *Capture of a Boer Battery by the British* in 1900 in New Jersey. In 1904 the Biograph Company shot *Battle of the Yalu*, supposedly about the Russo-Japanese War, on Long Island after a snowstorm. Some early film-makers, however, did journey to war zones. In the case of the Spanish-American War in 1898, a film was shot of the charge of Theodore Roosevelt's 'Rough Riders' up San Juan Hill in Cuba, but it was too distant to make out much and looked more like a slow walk. In the case of the South African War, William Dickson of the British Biograph Company was one of several cameramen who went out in 1899. He took a new experimental telephoto lens, but it proved inadequate to the dust and haze. As Dickson reported, it was difficult to cover action due to 'the enormous bulk of our apparatus which had to be dragged about in a Cape cart with two horses'.[2] Dickson staged scenes for the camera, but only actually faked the raising of the British flag over Pretoria when he arrived too late to capture it in person. The films were immensely popular, those produced by one of Dickson's rivals, the American-born Charles Urban, giving the Warwick Trading Company a 52 per cent increase in its profits in the first six months of 1900.

Those companies without representation in South Africa simply faked action scenes, mostly on Clapham Common. A trade journal cautioned in January 1900 that common sense should prevail when viewing an apparent hand-to-hand encounter between British soldiers and Boers. Thus, 'when one sees gentlemen with tall hats, accompanied by ladies, apparently looking on, common sense would at once pronounce the film of the sham order'.[3] In January 1914, Hollywood's Mutual Film Corporation signed a contract with the Mexican revolutionary Francisco 'Pancho' Villa for $25,000, permitting them sole rights to film coverage of his campaigns. Villa agreed to fight as far as possible in the hours of daylight, to delay his attacks until the cameras were ready to roll and also to postpone executions from dawn until 0700 hours to take advantage of the better light. Any action that went on beyond dusk would be re-enacted at some convenient later time. Unfortunately, Villa never quite got the hang of movie making for, when asked to ride slowly past the cameras, he persisted in galloping. Consequently, little of the footage was of any use.

When war broke out in Europe, it was not inevitable that thoughts would turn to utilising this infant medium for propaganda, for it was damned, as one War Office memorandum remarked, as an 'instrument for the amusement of the masses'.[4] When it was first suggested that the cinema could be employed for propaganda, the Secretary of the Board of Film Censors remarked, 'What, has the country come to this?'[5] There was recognition, however, that the maintenance of national morale was crucial. While liberal democracies like Britain entered the war with greater legitimacy in the eyes of their population than more coercive political systems, much still depended on astute manipulation of public opinion by political leaderships. Initially, there was more than sufficient support for the war, the appeal to patriotic nationalism being reinforced by the shared values, and political and cultural symbols and rituals, that underpinned the concept of nation and state. The national and provincial press were over-whelmingly hostile to Germany, and the general tendency of a patriotic press to play the game with respect to domestic news consumption meant that most British government propaganda was actually targeted at opinion overseas. The Germans themselves did much to make the work of British propagandists easier. Naturally, German atrocities in France and Belgium were heavily featured. On 12 October 1915 the Germans executed the British nurse Edith Cavell for helping allied servicemen to escape from Belgium to the Netherlands. On 27 July 1916 they executed Captain Charles Fryatt of the British steamer *Brussels* for having previously outrun one U-boat and attempting to ram another attacking his vessel. The issue by a German firm of a medal commemorating the sinking of the *Lusitania* in May 1915, intended as a satirical comment on British hypocrisy in allegedly carrying munitions on a liner, was equally turned against the Germans.

It is easy to exaggerate the impact of wartime propaganda, though most governments clearly believed it to be effective. As the war continued and casualties mounted, governments were increasingly concerned to maintain the national will to win. The targets of this more coordinated effort, which was often concentrated on the projection of war aims, were primarily domestic opponents of the war such as pacifists and socialists. Generally, the state sought to project ideals of duty, sacrifice and solidarity within the civilian population while, at the same time, dealing with perceived injustices undermining civilian resolve such as war profiteering and 'shirking'. Propaganda embraced the efforts of both official and unofficial groups and organisations, including churches and schools. It extended into virtually all aspects of ordinary life, including popular leisure, be it music hall, gramophone records, and even children's board games. It also capitalised on the thirst for war news, and for entertainment.

Though frivolity made many uncomfortable, and theatres trod a careful path, escapism had much to do with the determination to maintain leisure pursuits, and with the popularity of plays, concerts, musical revues and films. The weekly cinema audience increased dramatically to an estimated 21 million by 1917, embracing both middle- and upper-class audiences for the first time, though the imposition of new taxes upon places of entertainment in May 1916 had some effect. The additional halfpenny on cinema tickets up to 2d, and 1d on seats up to 6d, pushed the wealthier patrons into cheaper seats, pricing out many working-class patrons. The tax also closed about a thousand cinemas. Only a small proportion of the total films produced in wartime Britain, amounting perhaps to no more than 10 per cent, dealt directly with wartime themes. As elsewhere in Europe, escapism and entertainment were the order of the day: the German authorities classed such products as *Schundfilme* (trash films). In 1915 the National Union of Women Workers undertook a survey of London cinemas for the Commissioner of the Metropolitan Police due to fears that indecency was taking place in darkened auditoriums. While commenting mainly on lighting conditions, many of these impeccably middle-class ladies also remarked on the films being shown. Visiting the cinema at 53 The Strand, a Miss Hicks noted 'a hopelessly silly and vulgar American performance'.[6] Many of her colleagues especially disliked Charlie Chaplin's comedies, but Chaplin was altogether the greatest attraction at British wartime cinemas. His comedy, *Shoulder Arms*, opening just two weeks before the armistice in 1918, was immensely popular despite the risks involved in cinema going from the influenza pandemic, which led to widespread cinema closures.

The mobilisation of the cinema was the work of Charles Masterman's War Propaganda Bureau at Wellington House in London's Buckingham Gate, which had already turned to the talents of prominent writers such as Rudyard Kipling, Sir Arthur Conan Doyle, Thomas Hardy, Arnold Bennett, John Galsworthy and H.G. Wells. Similarly, Wellington House moved towards sponsoring official war artists, the first of whom was Muirhead Bone, a Scottish landscape artist, in July 1916. Technically, Masterman was Chancellor of the Duchy of Lancaster, but upon appointment to the Cabinet in February 1914 he had lost by twenty-four votes the by-election still then customary for those accepting government office. Failing to find another seat, he was to resign from the Cabinet in February 1915. Previously Financial Secretary to the Treasury, Masterman had also played a prominent role in the introduction of national insurance in 1911 and remained chairman of the National Health Insurance Commission, whose headquarters happened to be Wellington House. A Christian Socialist rather than a Liberal, Masterman was characterised by his own more forceful wife, Lucy Lyttleton, as a 'vivid, tormented man'.[7] Largely unfulfilled, he died from a combination of excessive alcohol and other ailments in 1927. There is no doubt, however, that his wartime work was invaluable.

Masterman perceived that it was precisely the cinema's appeal for the working class that made it so valuable. He was increasingly frustrated at the lack of photographs or film to use in attempts to influence British and neutral, especially American, public opinion. A number of film companies had attempted to get cameramen out to the Western Front in August 1914. F.W. Engholm of the Topical Film Company reached Belgium and managed to make eleven newsreels up to the fall of Antwerp to the Germans in October 1914. However, Kitchener, who had enjoyed a poor relationship with the press in his campaigns in the Sudan and South Africa, ordered all newsmen and photographers expelled from the Western Front in September 1914. The War Office even wanted to ban the export of any newsreel from Britain during the war on grounds of security. The French by contrast permitted filming at least in rear areas from May 1915 onwards, while the Germans had established a special film unit at the start. A suitably edited version of a German war newsreel was shown at the Scala cinema in London's Fitzroy Square in May 1916 in the absence of any British material.

Sir John French, however, believed that film could be a useful recruiting tool, and his GHQ Intelligence Section also wanted to give some publicity to the Indian Corps in view of fears of potential revolutionary subversion in India. Accordingly, a Canadian-born commercial travel photographer, who had covered both the Boxer Rebellion and the Russo-Japanese War, Hilton DeWitt Girdwood, was tasked in May 1915 with filming Indian troops in France. Girdwood, who hoped to turn a decent commercial profit from the resulting film, was in France between 22 July and 10 September 1915. He was frequently frustrated, however, by opposition from Sir Douglas Haig, in whose First Army the Indians were serving. Eventually, Girdwood managed to film in the front line under fire, though two 'attacks' he filmed were staged for him in rear areas. About 4,000 feet of film proved useable, but contractual problems meant that *With the Empire's Fighters* was not premiered until 11 September 1916, by which time *The Battle of the Somme* had stolen all the limelight. Though Girdwood was the first official cameraman in France, only provincial audiences saw his film, and it has been all but forgotten.

The problem Girdwood encountered was that Masterman had pressed ahead with his own scheme to get cameramen to France. The main press agencies would not cooperate with the restrictive conditions laid down by the War Office for any relaxation of the prohibition, so Masterman turned to the cinema newsreel firms. These had established a consortium known as the Topical Committee of the Kinematograph Manufacturers' Association in March 1915. The Topical Committee had already been in contact with the Permanent Secretary at the War Office, Sir Reginald Brade, and it would appear that the Army Council agreed to establish an official film unit sometime between March and July 1915. This would be paid for by the Topical Committee, but act under the direction of GHQ's Press Section, which provided news for the press. The War Office would retain censorship rights, and provide the captions for films produced, retaining copyright and taking a penny royalty out of the hiring charge to cinemas of 4½d per foot. In August, Distin Maddick, the proprietor of the Scala, was appointed Director of Kinema Operations to oversee filming in France. In deference to Girdwood, the contract finally signed between the War Office and the Topical Committee in October 1915 excluded the latter from marketing films in Egypt or India. Equally Girdwood was prevented from marketing his film in Britain, and it was only in May 1916 that he reached an agreement by which he could lecture and tour with just one print of his film in Britain.

Meanwhile the Topical Committee had begun work. Though a very early colour process was available, it was decided to film only in black and white. The veteran of films depicting the South African War, Charles Urban, now head of Kineto Films, and who had developed the rejected 'kinemacolor' process, began producing a series of films in October 1915. These were based on home military or naval subjects under the title of *Britain Prepared*. First shown on 27 December 1915, *Britain Prepared*, which ran for three hours, was uninspiring and had relatively limited appeal, not least for American audiences. When shown in Russia, it apparently had a rather different impact than intended, for Russian troops could see how much more equipment British troops possessed and how much better fed they were.

The Topical Committee then sent two cameramen, Geoffrey Malins and Edward 'Teddy' Tong, to France in November 1915 to begin making a series of newsreels behind the lines. Their first efforts duplicated Girdwood's film, *With the Indian Troops at the Front* being shown in January 1916. This proved an additional impediment to Girdwood when he eventually managed to show his own film nine months later. Tong, who worked for William Jury's Imperial Pictures, fell ill and was replaced by J.B. McDowell in June 1916. Malins was given the honorary rank of lieutenant while McDowell remained a civilian, though he later accepted a commission. Born at Hastings in 1886, Arthur Hebert Malins, as he was originally known, had been a portrait photographer before moving to the Clarendon Film Company and then joining British Gaumont. In 1914 he filmed Belgian and French troops in Flanders, and French troops in the Vosges, before being invited to become one of the Topical Committee's cameramen. Less is known about John Benjamin McDowell, but he had been born in Plumstead in 1878, and began work as an apprentice at Woolwich Arsenal before turning to cinematography. Before the war, he had gone into partnership with Albert Bloomfield to form the British and Colonial Kinematograph Company, which successfully recreated the Battle of Waterloo for the cinema in a Northamptonshire field in 1913.

Malins had an advanced sense of his own worth, later recording in his self-serving and unreliable memoir, *How I Filmed the War*, that 'I have always tried to remember that it was through the eye of the camera, directed by my own sense of observation, that the millions of people at home would gain their only first-hand knowledge of what was happening at the front.'[8] Nonetheless, he was not without courage, being frequently under fire and gassed at least once. McDowell was later awarded the MC. The GHQ 'minder' to both McDowell and Malins, the Military Director of Kinematograph Operations, Captain John Faunthorpe, wrote that they 'necessarily have to run great risks to get good pictures, and must break down in time. It is a considerable strain to be constantly under fire armed only with a camera and taking pictures over the parapet of a front trench involves additional exposure.'[9] Each hand-cranked camera, together with its tripod and magazines of highly inflammable cellulose nitrate film, weighed in excess of 100 pounds: McDowell suggested that, after carting it 4 or 5 miles up the front line and through the communication trenches, the camera seemed more like 4 hundredweight.

The intention was not originally to produce a documentary on the Somme offensive when Malins and McDowell were sent to the British Fourth Army front on 25 and 28 June 1916 respectively. Malins went to 29th Division in the north and McDowell to 7th Division in the south, merely to take general scenes. The official war photographer, Ernest 'Baby' Brooks, accompanied Malins. The day for the opening of the Somme offensive was postponed from 29 June to 1 July, enabling them to take additional scenes of preparation. Much of Malins's initial work on 1 July was around 'White City' opposite Beaumont Hamel and from 'Jacob's Ladder', a convenient elevation nearby. It was from White City that Malins filmed the famous sequence of the blowing of a large British mine under the German Hawthorn Redoubt at 0720 hours on 1 July. In his own account, Malins had begun turning the crank at, 0719 hours: 'Then it happened. The ground where I stood gave a mighty convulsion. It rocked and swayed. I gripped hold of my tripod to steady myself. Then, for all the world like a gigantic sponge, the earth rose in the air to the height of hundreds of feet. Higher and higher it rose, and with a horrible, grinding roar the earth fell back upon itself, leaving in its place a mountain of smoke.'[10]

Malins apparently changed the film magazine during the course of his attempts to capture the subsequent advance, from which the sequence of distant figures in No Man's Land was taken. Malins then took scenes of British wounded at the 'Tenderloin' collecting post at 'White City'. On the following day, Malins moved to La Boiselle, and may also have gone to the area between Carnoy and Montauban on 5 July.

McDowell filmed around 'Minden Post' close to the main road between Albert and Peronne at Carnoy on 1 July, first filming the British wounded, and German prisoners. He then moved forward to film the forward German trenches captured between Carnoy and Mametz. No footage by McDowell has been positively identified as filmed after 3 July, but both men seem to have left the front on 10 July. They appear to have each taken about 4,000 feet of film, a cartridge of 400 feet lasting some six minutes. Based on Malins's own estimate, it is usually suggested that 80 per cent of the footage eventually used was his, but the latest careful shot-by-shot analysis has concluded that the balance was rather more even.

The first negative rushes were seen in London on 12 July and it was at this point that William Jury of Imperial Pictures, who was on Wellington House's cinema committee, realised that the film could be made into a documentary rather than used for a series of newsreels. The faked 'over the top' scenes were taken at the Third Army's Mortar School at Ligny-St-Flochel near St Pol sometime between 12 and 19 July, presumably once the initial unedited film had been viewed. Malins was probably the cameraman, going back to France expressly to film the added scenes. The War Office accepted Jury's offer and settled for 40 per cent of the profits for war charities. Jury and Charles Urban worked quickly: Urban liked to edit whilst smoking a cigar, despite the risks of the film catching fire. Malins claimed to have helped edit the film, but this is unlikely. With its five reels lasting seventy-two minutes, *The Battle of the Somme* was given its trade screening on 7 August. There was a swift censorship check by the military authorities in London and at GHQ, with some alterations to captions, and some deletions of scenes of dead and wounded at the request of Lieutenant General Sir Henry Rawlinson of Fourth Army, who had commanded the offensive.

The completed film had a special premiere screening to an invited audience on 10 August at the Scala. The film then opened in thirty-four London cinemas on 21 August 1916. It became available in the provinces a week later in a general release of one hundred prints, Jury dropping the hiring

charges to maximise distribution. He also endorsed the 'musical suggestions' of J. Morton Hutcheson, musical director of the Premier Electric
Cinema chain, to accompany the film. Jury reminded accompanists that
they '*must* realise the seriousness and awfulness of the scenes depicted
most realistically, and even where the scenes are showing the brighter side
of events in this Great Push, the "accompaniment" *must* not be too bright'.[11]
Hutcheson had selected over thirty pieces of suitable music including
Suppé's 'Light Cavalry Overture' for the 'over the top' scene. It would
appear, however, that the music varied from region to region, with full
military bands on occasions. Rather less suitably, the screening at the
Theatre Royal Hippodrome in Dublin was part of a variety programme
including a singing comedienne and a one-legged dancer. The film was
also accompanied by the publication of an illustrated booklet, *Sir Douglas
Haig's Great Push: The Battle of the Somme*, which included stills no longer
in the surviving copy of the film.

Quite what the film's purpose was meant to be is uncertain. Strictly
speaking, it was not a propaganda film, since it had been made at very
short notice and was assembled from film not intended to provide a
continuous narrative. It had not been determined in advance to record the
offensive, but it seems there was some intent to use the example of men at
the front to rally civilian support for the war. This is suggested by a letter
from Lloyd George read to the audience at the premiere at the Scala, in
which he wrote, 'I am convinced that when you have seen this wonderful
picture, every heart will beat in sympathy with its purpose, which is no
other than that everyone of us at home and abroad shall see what our men
at the Front are doing and suffering for us, and how their achievements
have been made possible by the sacrifices made at home.'[12]

The juxtaposition of images from different parts of the battlefield, which
appears confusing and effectively patternless to historians, was probably
not of significance for the contemporary audience. There were five
distinctly labelled 'parts' to the film and it was edited sufficiently well to
convey not only narrative progression but also visual breaks in the narrative to create cinematic 'surprise'. Again, it has been suggested that there
was no particular conception of an enemy, since Germans appeared only
as prisoners or bodies and the film showed only the humanitarian behaviour of British soldiers towards German prisoners. There was just one

moment where a British soldier reacted aggressively to a German, who had jogged his wounded arm. However, the captions referred repeatedly to the Germans. Certainly, the sequences filmed by Malins in the 'sunken road', of the Lancashire Fusiliers waiting to go into action, was a significant contrast from the early scenes of smiling and waving troops. In one sense, these early scenes were as staged for the camera as the faked sequences of going over the top. Exhaustion, however, was very clear in the later scenes, including one sequence of a soldier clearly suffering from shell shock. Some 13 per cent of the footage was also devoted to the wounded and the dead, and though the total of British casualties was never revealed in any way, even the relatively careful selection of footage of the wounded still had much impact. Only one British general appeared, Major General Henry Beauvoir de Lisle being shown in long shot addressing troops before the battle: shots from two different parades were combined.

There was no attempt to hide the physical destruction of a battlefield. In this sense, therefore, as Roger Smither has commented, emphasis on the faked scenes, which lasted for less than twenty seconds, does a disservice to the film-makers 'in obscuring a very real achievement in pioneering the battlefield documentary'.[13] There was some attempt to include as many national representative types of soldier as possible, with eighteen different regiments mentioned in the captions, although battalions were not specified and only three were seen repeatedly: 1st Battalion, the Lancashire Fusiliers and 2nd Battalion, the Seaforth Highlanders, both filmed by Malins; and the 2nd Battalion, the Royal Warwickshire Regiment, filmed by McDowell. The captions provided by the War Office were bald statements of fact and place, though only six towns or villages were mentioned, and there was little subtlety in any message conveyed. A map, suggesting that the German withdrawal to the Hindenburg line in April 1917 was a direct consequence of the Somme offensive, was only added at that time. No follow-up to the film was planned. There was another feature, *The King Visits His Armies in the Great Advance*, shown in October 1916, but it was not until January 1917 that *The Battle of the Ancre and the Advance of the Tanks* appeared, filmed by Malins and McDowell in the autumn of 1916, and introducing audiences to the new weapon, the tank.

The Somme film caused a sensation and, although no overall viewing figures are extant, it was clearly widely seen. It has been suggested that a million people saw the film in the first week and 20 million saw it in the first six weeks. If true, then it would be quite remarkable given that the total British population was approximately 43 million. Nonetheless, the film was enormously popular. It was shown in at least 2,000 cinemas, and made some £30,000. The film was still being booked regularly fifteen months after its premiere. It was shown simultaneously, for example, in twenty cinemas in Birmingham, and 10,000 saw it at Dublin's Theatre Royal alone in a matter of days. Huge queues were reported in towns like Edinburgh, Glasgow and Swansea, with crowd control having to be introduced outside the cinema in West Ealing. Even Jury, Malins and the secretary of the Topical Committee, Joseph Brooke Wilkinson, had difficulties getting into the cinema at Finsbury Park when the film opened there. People were being turned away regularly from full houses. Overseas, it was shown in eighteen different countries, though the film was not well received in the United States, where isolationism still ran strongly and where there was less favourable reaction to scenes of death and destruction.

The response evoked in audiences was generally a mixture of pity and horror. Whatever Lloyd George's intention, the domestic reaction suggests that sacrifice on the Western Front was seen as immeasurably greater than that on the home front. Far more than censored letters home, censored newspaper reports, and perhaps veiled allusions in the comments by those servicemen on leave, film images conveyed a much greater reality than even lengthy lists of casualties in the provincial press or acquaintance with those convalescing from wounds. The images were far from the conventional depictions of high Victorian battle art in which saving the guns or saving the Colours was utterly devoid of any real sense of death. The greatest reaction was to the faked scenes purporting to show men leaving the trenches. The audience and the press universally took these as genuine, the *Manchester Guardian* announcing on 11 August that the film was 'the real thing at last'. The *Daily Mirror* reported one woman calling out, 'Oh, God, they're dead.' The *Spectator* commented on 26 August, 'It is a wonderful example of how reality – remember this is no arranged piece of play acting but a record taken in the agony of battle – transcends fiction.' In the same way, *The Times* suggested that, if historians in the future wanted to know what the war was like, 'they will only have to send for these films'. The *Bioscope*, a leading trade journal, proclaimed it 'the most remarkable film ever made in this country'.[14] Henry Rider Haggard wrote of the faked scenes in his diary on 27 September 1916, 'There is something appalling about the instantaneous change from fierce activity to supine death. Indeed, the whole horrible business is appalling. War has always been dreadful, but never, I suppose, more dreadful than today'.[15] The Dean of Durham, Hensley Henson, expressly condemned the film as presenting war's tragedy as entertainment. A leading zoologist, Professor Ray Lankester, supported him, and a few other dissenting voices were heard. A few reports of screenings, for example, suggest some limited expressions of the need to avoid any future wars.

Serving soldiers had equally mixed reactions. Some clearly felt that it was useful for civilians to know something of the reality, whereas others believed it better not to expose women and children to such images. Lieutenant Colonel Rowland Feilding of 6th Battalion, the Connaught Rangers, wrote on 5 September 1916 after seeing the film in France, 'This battle film is really a wonderful and most realistic production, but must of necessity be wanting in that the battle is fought in silence, and moreover, that the most unpleasant part – the machine gun and rifle fire – is entirely eliminated.' Feilding doubted at first whether it was wise to show the film to soldiers until he overheard two newly arrived recruits discussing it: 'Said one, "As to reality, now you knows what you've got to face. If it was left to the imagination you might think all sorts of silly b-things". I wonder where his imagination would have led him had he not seen the Cinema.'[16]

Those who had lost relatives in the war seemed to feel that the film helped them to understand the sacrifice. As one wrote, 'I came away feeling humiliated and ashamed, for at last I was able to realise what Britain's soldiers were doing for her. If my turn comes, I hope that the memory of that film will stay with me to keep me as brave and smiling as they are.'[17] Inevitably perhaps, some audience members claimed to recognise relatives. At a screening in Droylsden near Manchester, a woman claimed to see her husband being carried wounded from the front, having just been notified that he had died of wounds. Others in the audience also identified him, though the most recent careful analysis of the film has suggested that it is impossible, since the sequence was filmed on 1 July and the unfortunate soldier in question was mortally wounded five days later on an entirely different part of the battlefield. A pet dog lying dead in No Man's Land, filmed by McDowell on 2 or 3 July, is almost certainly that of Lieutenant Colonel Harold Lewis of the 20th Battalion, the Manchester Regiment. It is not certain the body next to the dog is Lewis, as was claimed by his niece when she saw the film. Subsequently, a number of soldiers have been identified with some certainty, but only as a result of substantial research, which has even used lip readers to identify what some men filmed are saying.

Unlike other films of the time, the audiences viewed *The Battle of the Somme* often silently, with considerable intensity of emotion, sighing audibly or weeping. As Lloyd George's secretary, Frances Stevenson, wrote in her diary, it reminded her of the loss of her brother, 'I have often tried to imagine myself what he went through, but now I know, and I shall never forget. It was like going through a tragedy. I felt something of what the Greeks must have felt when they went in their crowds to witness those grand old plays – to be purged in their minds through pity and terror.'[18] As Nicholas Reeves has suggested, the film may have fulfilled its purpose in bridging the chasm between front and home, and in demonstrating that the sacrifice was worthwhile for, as he puts it, the film was 'incorporated within the audience's own existing ideology'.[19]

The depiction of death in the sense of seeing falling soldiers, as opposed to dead bodies, was not repeated in other British wartime films. Moreover, the Topical Committee was reorganised in November 1916, with a new War Office Cinema Committee being established consisting of Max Aitken, Brade and Jury, partly as a result of the Topical Committee's failure to pay the War Office the agreed royalties to war charities. After a third film, *The German Retreat and the Battle of Arras*, was produced in June 1917, Aitken, now Lord Beaverbrook and head of the Ministry of Information, into which Wellington House had been subsumed in February 1918, ordered a change in policy. It was believed that the novelty of battle films had worn off, and that the public was jaded. Attention turned to twice-weekly newsreels such as 'The Pictorial News', to cartoons, and to fictional films. The latter included *The Leopard's Spots*, also known popularly as 'Once a Hun Always a Hun', and *The National Film*, a somewhat tawdry drama filmed in Chester, with British troops drafted in as extras to play brutal and licentious Germans. Interestingly, the German authorities were so impressed by the films' impact that they had their own Somme film, *Bei Unseren Helden an der Somme* (*With Our Soldiers on the Somme*) produced and premiered on 17 January 1917. However, much of it was staged in training areas, and it was widely condemned in Germany for not looking sufficiently authentic.

Still photographs also played their part in establishing the image of the war. Wellington House formed a pictorial section in April 1916, which then published *War Pictorial* as a means of making use of the photographs being taken: over 40,000 official photographs were taken, well over half of the Western Front. On the home front, Horace Nicholls, appointed as 'official photographer of Great Britain' in July 1917, produced a memorable series of scenes in munitions and ordnance factories. Later war photographers of the Spanish Civil War and the Second World War had smaller, more compact cameras, and pushed back much further the parameters of what was acceptable. The photographers of the Great War, however, began the process and helped transform photography into a mass medium. Photographic exhibitions were arranged by Beaverbrook, the Ministry of Information opening a shop to sell official photographs in October 1918. Sales were also licensed through postcards issued by the *Daily Mail* and stereoscopic prints produced by various firms. Photographs, of course, were also a means of commemoration. The Imperial War Museum initiated an appeal for photographs of serving soldiers in July 1917, but was so swamped that the museum called a halt in 1919 after 15,000 images had been deposited.

In reaching mass audiences, film and photographs had a far greater impact in shaping the popular memory of the war than officially sponsored war art, much of which was influenced by pre-war modernist artistic movements such as cubism and futurism. The public much preferred more traditional art forms, as was also apparent in the wide choice of entirely neoclassical monuments to the memory of the war dead. Similarly, little literature or poetry of 'disillusionment' appeared in print much before the late 1920s. It was often rather ambiguous, being aimed against wartime propaganda and those who had manufactured it. Much wartime literature was decidedly patriotic, and post-war fiction about the war continued in the same vein. Children's literature, often written by war veterans, continued to display a positive view of the war as justified sacrifice, pre-war writers for the juvenile market simply reusing old plots and stereotypes without varying the heroic ideal.

Much of post-war film, too, was not intended to be critical of the conduct of the war, or to depict the war as a grisly horror, even when film-makers began to try and convey more of the reality. In Britain, there was a whole series of films made between 1919 and 1927 almost as documentaries – 'reconstructions' as they were billed at the time – by Harry Bruce Woolfe's British Instructional Films, in cooperation with the War Office and the Admiralty. Mostly, these films, which included versions of Mons, the Somme, Jutland, and the Zeebrugge Raid, concentrated on the exploits of winners of the Victoria Cross. A concern to make sacrifice heroic and palatable persisted into the era of sound: the Hollywood film version of *All Quiet on the Western Front* in 1930 was as much an anomaly as the 1928 novel on which it was based.

Yet, the power of image merely compounded the effect already produced by real wartime film such as *The Battle of the Somme*. The meaning of war was now understood in an entirely different way from what had been the norm prior to 1914. The visual reference points that the film established have proven unshakeable by the efforts of historians. In 1964 the script-writers of the landmark BBC television series, *The Great War*, sought to counter what they regarded as the pervasive misrepresentation of the war. Audience research reports showed that, whatever the narration, the visual content had simply reinforced the popular concept of the war's futility for a mass audience estimated at 8 million per episode. The successful television comedy, *Blackadder Goes Forth*, first broadcast in 1989, had characters and situations that needed no explanation, so familiar was the audience with the received version of the war. In 1999 the final moments of the series, where the characters became freeze-framed as they went over the top, counted as first among the ten clips voted, with no apparent irony, 'the nation's all-time favourite' moment from a television comedy. 'Blackadder' also became the only fictional entry in the Top Ten of '100 Greatest Television Moments' voted for in 2000.

Despite Malins's bombast, he and McDowell could have had little true idea of just what an impact their efforts would have. Malins continued to work in France until invalided home in the spring of 1917. He returned to France in January 1918, and was then discharged in June 1918. He made a number of post-war documentaries, before moving to South Africa in 1928, where he died in 1940. McDowell worked in France until the end of the war, receiving the MBE for his services. He worked as a freelance cine-matographer after the war, then for Agfa between 1926 and 1936. He died in 1954. Their flickering silent images transformed the public perception of the war, both at the time and for posterity. Appropriately, in July 2005, as the first feature-length battle documentary, *The Battle of the Somme* was one of the very few films accepted on UNESCO's Memory of the World global register of key cultural artefacts. It is ranked alongside the Bayeux Tapestry and Beethoven's Ninth Symphony.

CHAPTER 6

THE DEATH OF KINGS

The Passing of Emperor Franz Joseph,
21 November 1916

O N 30 NOVEMBER 1916 a ceremony first supposedly enacted in 1657 on the death of the Habsburg Holy Roman Emperor, Ferdinand III, took place at the Kapuzinerkirche (Church of the Capuchins) in Vienna. As the coffin reached the gate of the Kaisergruft crypt, Prince Montenuovo, the Lord Chamberlain, knocked three times with the golden staff of his office. A voice from within enquired, 'Who Knocks?', to which Montenuovo replied, 'His Apostolic Majesty, the Emperor of Austria.' The response was, 'Him I know not.' After another three knocks from Montenuovo, the same question was asked. The reply this time was, 'The King of Hungary', which received the same response from within. Another three knocks, and the same question elicited, 'Franz Joseph, a poor sinner who begs for God's mercy'. This time, the response was, 'Enter then.' Thus was the body of Franz Joseph laid between the tombs of his empress, Elizabeth of Bavaria, assassinated in 1898, and his son, Crown Prince Rudolf, an apparent suicide in 1889. The bodies of 138 Habsburgs lie in the Kaisergruft though, traditionally, their hearts were placed in caskets in the Loreto Chapel of Vienna's Augustinerkirche (Church of the Augustinian Order), and the entrails in the catacombs of the Stephansdom (St Stephen's Cathedral). Franz Joseph was not the last imperial ruler of Austria-Hungary to be buried in the Kapuzinerkirche. His successor and the last emperor, his great-nephew Karl, died in exile on Madeira in 1922, but Karl's empress, Zita of Bourbon-Parma, was buried in the Kapuzinerkirche with the appropriate ceremony after her death in 1989.

In so many ways, the passing of Franz Joseph on 21 November 1916 sounded the death knell of the Austro-Hungarian Empire. Despite the accession of the seemingly dynamic young couple of Karl and Zita, the loss of the father figure of the old emperor undermined any remaining faith in the ability of traditional imperial paternalism to mitigate increasing wartime sacrifice and privation. Had he lived for eleven more days, Franz Joseph would have marked the sixty-eighth anniversary of his accession as emperor. Britain's Queen Empress, Victoria, reigned for sixty-four years from 1837 to 1901 and, though Louis XIV was King of France for seventy-two years from 1643 to 1715, his mother was regent for the first eight years of the reign. Not initially popular, the ageing Franz Joseph had become the very embodiment of his empire, a symbol of permanence and, seemingly, the last true believer in the concept of Austria-Hungary. In 1904 he had remarked to his aide, Albert von Margutti, that the monarchy 'is a place of refuge, an asylum for all those fragmented nations scattered over central Europe who, if left to their own resources would lead a pitiful existence, becoming the plaything of more powerful neighbours'.[1] That vision, however, had long been seriously undermined by rising nationalism. It was fear of the appeal of militaristic Serbian aspirations to the subject Southern Slav population within the empire's boundaries that propelled Austria-Hungary into war in July 1914. It was a fateful decision and one that an aged emperor had accepted with too great a degree of fatalism. As the Foreign Minister from 1916 to 1918, Count Ottokar von Czernin und Chudenitz wrote, 'We were bound to die. We were at liberty to choose the manner of our death, and we chose the most terrible.'[2]

On being told the news of the death of his empress, who had been murdered while visiting Geneva in 1898, Franz Joseph had exclaimed, 'So I am to be spared nothing in this world.'[3] At least he did not experience the final collapse of his empire, but the signs of impending disaster could hardly have failed to escape the old man's notice. Not least there was the failure during the summer of 1916 of the Austro-Hungarian offensive in Italy, and the near total collapse of the Austro-Hungarian position on the Eastern Front during the Russian 'Brusilov' offensive. Reviewing the situation on the Eastern Front, the German staff officer Max Hoffmann remarked that the Austro-Hungarians were like a mouth full of bad teeth, 'every time there's a slight breeze, there's an ache somewhere'.[4] Similarly, the

Chief of the German General Staff from 1914 to 1916, Erich von
Falkenhayn, had dismissed the Austro-Hungarian Empire as a 'cadaver'
and, in imitation of the Greek stoic philosopher of the first century AD,
Epictetus, German officers frequently said that they were shackled to a
corpse.[5] On the home front, the portents were just as ominous. There were
serious food riots in Vienna in both May and September 1916. In October
the Austro-Hungarian minister-president, Count Karl von Stürgkh, was
assassinated while he was dining in a Vienna hotel. At a time of shortages
and the perceived failure of the state to maintain food supplies, reports of
Stürgkh's death dwelt on what he was eating rather than on the murder
itself: he even continued to receive hate mail after his death. In such
circumstances, the death of the old emperor seemed to set the seal on a
collapse of imperial power that a younger, more vigorous Franz Joseph
might have succeeded in averting.

Austria-Hungary was already an unlikely survivor amid the growth of
the ideal of the nation state and the emergence of nationalism as the dominant ideology in nineteenth-century Europe. Austria, as it had emerged
after the Napoleonic Wars, was a multinational empire with eleven major
racial groups and fourteen recognised languages. An emerging Prussia
could see the natural frontiers of a potential united Germany as being
bounded by the North Sea, the Baltic, the Rhine, the Alps, and perhaps
the Vistula. Austria could not aspire to the leadership of such a Germany.
Any Austrian appeal to wider German nationalism would raise the spectre
of self-determination by others. The subsequent emergence of a united
Germany and a united Italy in 1870–71, both effectively at the expense of
Austria, inevitably increased the pressure on Vienna. Indeed, the great
compromise, or *Ausgleich*, of 1867, creating the dual monarchy of Austria-
Hungary, had resulted directly from the political pressures of defeat in the
brief Austro-Prussian War of 1866. The common government controlled
finance, defence and foreign policy but, in effect, there were now three
administrations since Austria and Hungary were separately administered.
Yet, notwithstanding the difficulties arising from diversity of language,
nationality, religion, class and politics, there remained some unifying
factors. First, there was the sense of an institutionalised state in its widest
sense, once characterised as a standing army of soldiers, a sitting army of
officials, a kneeling army of priests and a creeping army of informers.

Second, there was a certain economic integration deriving from the great international trade route represented by the Danube. Third, there was a recognition even by some of the subject nationalities that other great powers such as Russia and Germany would pose a threat to the integrity of small states, and that it was better to press for autonomy within existing state structures than to seek full independence. Adding to this was the effective use of divide and rule generally: neither Austria nor Hungary had a majority of Germans or Magyars respectively. Above all, there was the unifying role of the common monarchy in the person of Franz Joseph, not just as emperor, but also as King of Hungary and King of Bohemia.

The increasing respect in which Franz Joseph was held was certainly the empire's 'strongest centripetal force'.[6] If the emperor was his empire's greatest strength, he was also its greatest weakness. By nature a conservative and centralist, he had never sought popularity and, in many respects, the affection in which he was held grew from his dignified acceptance of personal tragedy, as well as from sheer longevity. Franz Joseph had never cared for liberalism, but had tolerated periods of liberal government when necessary and was prepared to countenance expediency if it served the dynasty. Universal male suffrage was embraced in Austria in 1907 as a means of reconciling democratic elements to the empire, but Franz Joseph stepped back from insisting on a similar suffrage in Hungary for fear of alienating the entrenched Magyar elite. At heart, Franz Joseph's dynastic instincts prevented him from using his powers to impose the kind of changes that might have maintained the empire: the preservation of a personal dynastic identity compromised the construction of an Austro-Hungarian state identity.

Franz Joseph, then eighteen, had succeeded to the Austrian throne on the abdication of his ineffectual, feeble-minded and epileptic uncle, Ferdinand, in the revolutionary year of 1848 when Hungary, Bohemia and Italy were all in revolt, and Vienna itself was affected by rioting. In what amounted to a coup of doubtful legality from above, orchestrated by the army, Franz Joseph bypassed his own father at the insistence of his mother, Archduchess Sophie. She thought her son far more capable of securing the dynasty than her husband. In many ways, Franz Joseph, or Franzi as he was known within the family, was a man of contrasts, and even those who had closest contact with him rarely penetrated the exterior veil. On the one hand, he had expected a military career and was seemingly shy with no gift for small talk, frugal and austere in his habits, with a rigid conception of duty, and a desire for a carefully ordered private life. A strict observer of court ritual, he always stood to receive his ministers, whom he tended to treat as he would military subordinates. Habitually, his everyday wear was the uniform of a junior officer, and it was said that one major relaxation was reading the Army List. He slept on a simple iron bedstead and, lacking a bathroom at the Schönbrunn palace, made do with pitchers and bowls. To the end of his life, he rose daily at 4 a.m., working on his papers from 5 a.m. until breakfasting at 7.30 on coffee, rolls and butter. After a walk, he would eat two or three slices of sausage and bread at 10.00 a.m., then return to his work until lunch in his private study at 12.30 or 1 p.m., consisting always of soup, fish, vegetables, a light dessert, fruit, coffee and a small glass of wine. Meetings and other official duties consumed the afternoon and evening and, following a supper of bread roll, slice of ham and another small glass of wine or beer, he would retire at 9 p.m.[7]

Subjected to a rigid and illiberal educational programme as a boy, Franz Joseph spent long hours at his desk hoping to promote the welfare of his people, for he saw himself as their 'first servant'. However, he always resisted self-government for his subjects, believing firmly in the strength of paternalism. The significance of imperial paternalism was evident in the thousands of petitions and begging letters – as many as 30,000 annually in the 1870s – sent by his people to the emperor every year, ranging from requests for advice to those for financial help. In reality, the police dealt with most such correspondence from ordinary citizens, but imperial propaganda and rhetoric played assiduously on Franz Joseph's role as 'father of his people'.

On the other hand, as a young man Franz Joseph enjoyed hunting and dancing and had a lifelong interest in women. He had fallen in love at first sight with his beautiful sixteen-year-old first cousin, his mother Sophie's niece, Elizabeth of Bavaria, known as Sisi. Notwithstanding sexual indiscretions, he remained infatuated with her until her death. Sophie had actually wanted Sisi's elder sister as her son's bride and thought Sisi inadequate, leading to an increasingly frosty relationship between them. Spirited and wayward, Sisi was resentful of the stiff protocol surrounding the court in Vienna compared to the freer atmosphere in Bavaria. Brittle, wilful and self-absorbed, she steadily grew more distant from Franz Joseph, her frequent illnesses brought on by the rigorous diets she inflicted on herself to keep her figure. Yet, though frequently absent from Vienna, Sisi was a great asset to the empire. Her affection for Hungarian culture, albeit partly embraced in defiance of her mother-in-law, who hated Hungarians, did much to persuade Franz Joseph to accept the division of the monarchy in 1867. He tried often to attract Sisi to stay longer in Austria-Hungary, even creating a Hungarian home she had long wanted at Gondollo. Realising, however, that she could not give him the emotional support he craved, Sisi encouraged Franz Joseph's close friendship with the actress Katherina Schratt, who remained a comfort to the old man for the last thirty years of his life.

The marriage was also overshadowed by frequent personal tragedy. Franz Joseph's younger brother, Archduke Maximilian, was executed in Mexico in June 1867 following the failure of a French-inspired attempt to install him as emperor there. Franz Joseph's second brother, Karl Ludwig, died of typhoid in 1896: he had drunk contaminated water from the Jordan on a pilgrimage to the Holy Land. Franz Joseph and Sisi's son and heir, Rudolf, whom some saw as the great liberal hope for a future of increasing recognition for the minorities, died apparently by his own hand alongside his seventeen-year-old mistress, Marie Vetsera, at Mayerling in the Vienna Woods in January 1889. Much remains unexplained and conspiracy stories abound. Sisi was then assassinated by a deranged Italian anarchist armed with a sharpened file while she was visiting Geneva in September 1898: his actual target had been King Umberto of Italy but, lacking enough money to get to Rome, he had chosen Sisi instead. As it happened, Franz Joseph had narrowly escaped assassination himself by a Hungarian nationalist in 1853. The heir was now the eldest son of Karl Ludwig and the emperor's nephew, Archduke Franz Ferdinand, a humourless and unpopular auto-crat with violently anti-Magyar and anti-Semitic prejudices. At least Franz Ferdinand was energetic, with decided views on restructuring the empire that appealed to radical conservatives. He was also devoted to his wife Sophie Chotek, an impoverished Czech aristocrat he had been forced to marry morganatically as a result of Franz Joseph's disapproval. Their children, therefore, were barred from the succession and she was allowed no royal precedence, bearing the purely courtesy title of Duchess of

Hohenberg. Ironically, it was an unusual honour for her to be allowed to accompany Franz Ferdinand on his visit to Sarajevo on 28 June 1914, the 525th anniversary of the destruction of the old Serbian kingdom by the Turks in 1389. Both fell victim to the young Bosnian Serb student, Gavrilo Princip. On hearing the news, according to an aide, Count Eduard Paar, Franz Joseph's first comment was, 'A higher power has restored that order which I myself was unable to maintain', the new heir presumptive being a young man of whom he thoroughly approved.[8] This was the emperor's great-nephew, the young Archduke Karl, the son of Karl Ludwig's second son (the dissipated Otto, who had died in 1906) and thus the nephew in turn of Franz Ferdinand.

Precisely how Sarajevo propelled Europe into a global conflict remains a matter of debate, but there is little doubt that there were those within Austria-Hungary who saw Franz Ferdinand's demise as an opportunity to neutralise the threat of Serbia. Influence in Central Europe was lost to Germany after the Austro-Prussian War of 1866 and, having lost Venetia and Lombardy to Italy in 1871, Austria-Hungary's only opportunity to preserve the notion of great-power status lay in the Balkans. Here, however, the empire was confronted with the emergence from within the Ottoman Empire of new nation states with irredentist claims on her own imperial possessions. Serbia had doubled the size of its territory and increased its population by 1.5 million between 1912 and 1913 as a result of victories in the Balkan Wars. A more militaristic Serbian dynasty had taken power in Belgrade by a coup in 1903. Its aim was for a greater Serbia embracing Montenegro, parts of Macedonia and, ultimately, the two southern Slav provinces of the empire, Bosnia and Herzegovina. The latter had been occupied by Austria-Hungary in 1878 and formally annexed in 1908. Dalmatia, Croatia and Slovenia also appeared to be in the sights of the Serb leadership. Vienna had mobilised its forces against Serbia both during the annexation of Bosnia and during the Balkan Wars, and influential younger policymakers in Vienna's Foreign Ministry all looked to solve the empire's problems through a preventative war against Serbia. The Chief of the Austro-Hungarian General Staff, Franz Conrad von Hötzendorf, for example, pressed for war against Serbia in 1906, 1908–09, 1912–13, and an astonishing twenty-five times between January 1913 and January 1914. The Foreign Minister, Leopold, Count Berchtold, shared

Conrad's determination and the assassination of Franz Ferdinand on 28 June 1914 therefore seemed a gift. Indeed, the Austro-Hungarian ambassador to Belgrade was instructed as early as 7 July that war must be forced on Serbia.

Ironically, Franz Ferdinand had led those advocating a peaceful solution to the empire's relationship with Serbia. His idea of reconstructing the empire by giving the Slavs the same autonomy enjoyed by the Hungarians since 1867 was precisely what made him a target for the Serbian secret society known as the Black Hand, though its real title was Union or Death. The Black Hand's leader was Serbia's chief of the military secret service, Colonel Dragutin Dimitrijevic (nicknamed 'Apis', or the Bull), but the Serb government was not actually involved in the Sarajevo assassination. Theoretically, the Black Hand was also distanced from the deed, since the assassins were members of the Young Bosnia movement and Austro-Hungarian subjects. Clearly, however, Conrad and Berchtold were determined to exploit the assassination from the beginning. No one mourned Franz Ferdinand, for all that mattered was to act decisively to preserve the empire and Austria-Hungary's status as a great power. The Austro-Hungarian leadership therefore consciously risked a general war, though without contemplating how war would achieve their objective. Only the Hungarian prime minister, Count Tisza, hesitated. Tisza, however, was sympathetic towards Germany. He accepted war once he was assured of German support and of Romanian neutrality, and that Serbia itself would not be annexed after its intended defeat, since he feared the consequences of incorporating more Slavs into the empire. German support, without which Vienna would not act, was secured as early as 5 July, a letter from Franz Joseph to the Kaiser receiving an unequivocal statement of support, known henceforth to history as the 'blank cheque'. For its own reasons of securing the general war that it felt necessary to preserve Germany's status, the German military and political leadership were fully committed to backing Vienna and knew all too well the likely outcome. They were also fully aware of the weaknesses of the Austro-Hungarian army from the detailed reports of the German military attaché in Vienna.

Finalised on 19 July, the Austro-Hungarian ultimatum was presented to the Serb government on 23 July. It was always intended to be unacceptable. It demanded the suppression of the Black Hand and of anti-Austrian propaganda, the dismissal of Serbian officers implicated in anti-Austrian activities, the arrest of named suspects, the tightening of border controls and the participation of Austrian representatives in an official inquiry to be carried out by the Serbs. The Serbs accepted the ultimatum on 25 July with the exception of allowing Austrian officials on Serbian soil, but this was still sufficient for Vienna to go to war. The draft declaration of war was put before Franz Joseph on 27 July, Berchtold having argued that a compromise might be found 'unless a clear situation is created by a declaration of war'. Thus, Vienna was determined to seek a 'final and fundamental reckoning' with Serbia, as Berchtold informed the German ambassador, at all costs.[9] War was declared on Serbia on 28 July, though not on Russia until 6 August, with Britain and France declaring war on Austria-Hungary only on 12 August 1914.

The role of Franz Joseph himself in the crucial decision-making that summer was a peripheral one. The emperor still enjoyed unchallenged authority but, at eighty-four, understandably, there was not the same vigour as of earlier years, though he had continued to attend the annual military manoeuvres on horseback until 1912. Moreover, he was still recovering from a severe attack of bronchitis in April 1914. Back in 1881, Crown Prince Rudolf had written of his father's perceived isolation, 'Only those people now in power have access to him, and they naturally interpret matters in the way that is most satisfying to them.' Rudolf concluded that his father was 'kept from any purely human contact, from any non-partisan, truly thoughtful advice'.[10] Nonetheless, in earlier imperial crises, Franz Joseph had been firmly at the centre. During the run-up to the Franco-Prussian War in 1870, for example, Franz Joseph had presided over five conferences in twelve days, but he had attended none of the thirty-nine Common Ministerial Conferences in the three and a half years leading up to war in 1914. Now he did not return to Vienna for three weeks, remaining on holiday at Bad Ischl, some five hours' travelling distance from Vienna, until 30 July, forcing Berchtold to travel there on five occasions to consult him. With Franz Ferdinand's alternative circle of advisers at the Upper Belvedere Palace effectively dissolved by his death, Berchtold and Conrad had considerable freedom of action, though their decisions still required the emperor's formal written agreement. According to his aide, Albert von Margutti, Franz Joseph was reluctant to go to war and came under pressure from Conrad and Berchtold. Franz Joseph seems to have expected any war to be localised and, though apparently surprised by the harshness of the ultimatum to Serbia, made no effort to alter it. Nor, apparently, did he believe breaking off diplomatic relations would necessarily mean war. Certainly, he was aware of the risks of the ultimatum, remarking to the joint Finance Minister, Leo von Bilinski, 'Yes I know, Russia cannot possibly tolerate such a note.' Nonetheless, there was the honour of the dynasty to consider, Berchtold suggesting that the issue for the emperor was that 'it was clear our role in world history would be over if we feebly allowed fate to do what it willed'. Thus, in remarkably similar terms to Czernin's fatalistic judgement, Franz Joseph told Conrad, 'If the monarchy has to perish, then it shall perish honourably.' In signing the mobilisation order, in 'a muffled, choked voice', the emperor remarked only, 'So, after all'.[11]

Fatalism had always been part of Franz Joseph's make-up. Back in 1866 he had written, 'When the whole world is against you and you have no friends, there is little chance of success, but you must go on doing what you can, fulfilling your duty, and, in the end, going down with honour.' Again, despite early, relatively good news from the front, Franz Joseph remarked to Karl's wife, Zita, on 17 August 1914, 'My wars have always begun with victories only to finish in defeats. And this time it will be even worse and they will say of me, "He is old and cannot cope any longer".'[12] Fatalism appears to have been the predominant mood.

The Austro-Hungarian ultimatum to Serbia had been held off because Conrad, after such frequent demands for preventative action in the past, had to admit that it was not possible immediately to recall men furloughed for the annual harvest. To do so would also alert Europe's diplomats to Austro-Hungarian intentions. Thus mobilisation of between 2.5 and 3 million men would be delayed. Conrad was another complex personality and by no means a conventional soldier. In 1915 he was able to marry his long-term mistress, the married Gina von Reininghaus, bypassing difficult Austrian divorce and remarriage laws through having her convert to Protestantism, and becoming a Hungarian national in being adopted by a compliant friend. Gina was then installed in Conrad's headquarters at Teschen in Silesia for the remainder of his wartime command, which at least meant that he no longer devoted the hours he had previously in writing a long daily letter to her. At one point before the war he had said that his best chance of marrying Gina was to return home a victorious war hero, as her husband would then divorce her, and some have even suggested that this was an additional motivation for his bellicosity in 1914. Conrad dabbled in philosophy and, as a convinced Social Darwinist and fatalist, believed in the inevitability of war. In the past, his search for a likely enemy had often bordered on fantasy: he had contemplated war against both Japan and China. He had been dismissed as chief of staff in December 1911 for his aggressive stance, only to be reinstated in December 1912 during the diplomatic crisis arising from the outbreak of the First Balkan War. The volatile Conrad had also resigned in September 1913 when Franz Ferdinand had insisted he attend Mass on manoeuvres. Espousing scientific materialism rather than the archduke's ardent Catholicism, Conrad testily replied that he was there 'to conduct manoeuvres, not to go to Mass'.[13] The emperor ordered Conrad to retract his resignation. For all his warmongering, however, Conrad feared war on different fronts simultaneously, with Russia, Italy and Serbia all posing threats. But, if he was apprehensive of the outcome, war had to be waged 'since an old monarchy and a glorious army must not perish without glory'.[14] Isolated in his headquarters at Teschen, Conrad visited the front only three times, yet was ultimately the longest-serving director of any belligerent's war effort, only finally being dismissed by Karl in February 1917.

In pre-war talks with the German General Staff, Conrad had formed the erroneous impression that Germany would support Austria-Hungary by an early offensive against the Russians. The Germans had formed the equally erroneous impression that there would be Austro-Hungarian help in defending East Prussia against the Russians through an immediate Austro-Hungarian offensive. Thus, in 1914, Conrad had his conscript army divided into three groups, one opposite the Russians in Galicia, one opposite Serbia, and one as a reserve. Conrad assumed he could safely attack Serbia in the expectation that Russia would not intervene and decided to commit the reserve to this front as well. In order to redirect the reserve to the Russian front, Conrad had to do so no later than five days after mobilisation began, for all Austro-Hungarian military trains moved at the speed of the slowest – about 10 miles per hour. Conrad knew that the Russians had mobilised on 31 July, but did not choose to order the recall of his reserves from Serbia until 6 August. The head of the Russian section of

1 Exhausted Belgian soldiers from a dog-drawn machine gun section pictured at Louvain during the retreat to Antwerp, 20 August 1914.

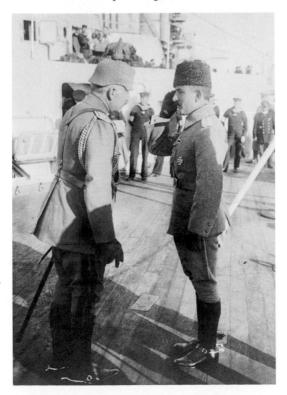

2 Enver Pasha (right) meeting Kaiser Wilhelm II on the former German battle cruiser, *Goeben*, in Constantinople, October 1917.

3 The scene at Anzac Cove, *c.*0800 hours on 25 April 1915, the Australian 4th Battalion coming ashore together with the mules of the 26th Indian Mountain Battery.

4 The Ministry of Munitions' National Shell Filling Factory No. 6 at Chilwell, Nottinghamshire, 1916.

5 Geoffrey Malins films British and French leaders leaving Beauquesne Chateau on 12 August 1916: King George V walks ahead with President Poincaré, while Haig and Joffre come down the steps.

6 The funeral procession of Emperor Franz Joseph in Vienna, 30 November 1916. Emperor Karl and Empress Zita with Crown Prince Otto, and the kings of Saxony, Bavaria and Bulgaria.

7 Torpedoes being loaded onto a German U-boat at Bruges, 1917.

8 An apprehensive crowd outside the Winter Place in St Petersburg, 29 July 1914, the day before the announcement of full Russian mobilisation.

9 London as photographed from a Gotha bomber on 7 July 1917. St Paul's Cathedral is clearly
visible to the lower left.

10 Arthur Balfour leaving No. 10 Downing Street, 1918.

11 President and Mrs Wilson in a carriage outside the Mansion House in London, 28 December 1918.

12 Hindenburg (left) and Ludendorff (right) with the Kaiser at German General Headquarters, 1916.

his Railroad Bureau had assured him that there would be no transportation problem but, in any case, Conrad had determined on destroying Serbia. As a result, the Austro-Hungarian offensive against Serbia failed, despite the shortcomings of a Serbian army badly affected by losses in the Balkan wars. Bizarrely, the Serbian commander-in-chief, Radomir Putnik, was taking the waters in Austria-Hungary when war broke out and had the only set of keys with him to the safe containing Serbia's mobilisation plans: Franz Joseph's old-world courtesy allowed Putnik's return to Belgrade. In the oft-quoted words of Winston Churchill, Conrad's reserve left the Serbian front 'before it could win him a victory. It returned to Conrad in time to participate in his defeat', for the Austro-Hungarian front in Galicia collapsed at Lemberg between 3 and 10 September.[15] The Austro-Hungarian army lost 300,000 men – a third of its combat effective – in the first three weeks of war and 750,000 men in the first six months. Among the dead was Conrad's son, Herbert. Belgrade was taken on 2 December 1914, but a Serbian counter-offensive soon forced its abandonment.

Failure was due to poor leadership, inadequate equipment as a result of a long-restricted defence budget, and a resolute opponent. Like much else in the multinational empire, the army was also hampered by problems of nationality. In 1914, by one calculation, 26.7 per cent of the army was German, 22.3 per cent Hungarian, 13.5 per cent Czech, 8.5 per cent Polish, 8.1 per cent Ruthenian, 6.7 per cent Croat or Serb, 6.4 per cent Romanian, 3.8 per cent Slovak, 2 per cent Slovene and 1.4 per cent Italian. German officers and NCOs stiffened non-German units and, overall, more than 78 per cent of officers were German, resulting in considerable problems when officer casualties proved heavy. Other than Germans, the Croats, Slovenes and Bosnian Muslims were deemed most reliable and, proportionally, the latter were the most conscripted during the war. Not all nationalities were equally committed to the war effort and the list of those regarded as unreliable steadily grew. One Czech regiment unfurled the Bohemian flag upon mobilisation in Prague in August 1914 and another surrendered en masse to the Russians in April 1915. It soon became the practice to station Italian units in the Balkans or on the Eastern Front. Croats, Slovenes and Serbs were generally content to fight the Italians once they came into the war against Austria-Hungary in May 1915. By 1917, nationalities were increasingly being mixed rather than allowed to serve in separate units.

During the war 2.7 million Austro-Hungarian troops became prisoners. After the collapse of Russia in 1917, 500,000 Austro-Hungarian prisoners were repatriated. Though relatively few had volunteered to fight for the Entente, they were all regarded with considerable suspicion and kept under close supervision, causing yet further resentment. About 60,000 Czechs formed a Czech Legion for the Provisional Government after the fall of the Tsar in March 1917, and subsequently the Bolsheviks recruited between 85,000 and 100,000 prisoners, the majority Magyars. Most joined, however, from hatred of their officers rather than out of ideological sympathy with the cause, though the best-known defector, Béla Kun, went on to lead the short-lived communist republic in Hungary in 1919.

The defeats of 1914 had been a heavy blow and it was said that the surrender of the fortress of Przemysl to the Russians in March 1915 reduced Franz Joseph to tears. Austro-Hungarian success thereafter depended largely on German reinforcements and German commanders, Paul von Hindenburg becoming supreme commander in the east in 1916. After Hindenburg became Chief of the German General Staff in August 1916, Kaiser Wilhelm II became supreme commander on all fronts with Hindenburg acting in his name. Thus, the overrunning of Serbia in October 1915 and of Romania, which entered the war against Germany and Austria-Hungary in August 1916, were essentially German victories. By 1918, the Austro-Hungarian army was falling apart. At least 400,000 men deserted between June and September 1918. By October 1918, many appeared to be just waiting for an allied advance to which they could surrender, as a British and Italian offensive on 24 October broke through at Vittorio Veneto. Indeed, some 500,000 Austro-Hungarian soldiers surrendered between 26 October and 3 November 1918, with only some 30,000 men becoming casualties in the same period. The war as a whole cost Austria-Hungary 1.2 million dead.

German military domination raises the question of the relationship within the alliance generally. It has often been said, reflecting a remark by Conrad in early 1915, that Germany was effectively a 'secret enemy' rather than an open ally of Austria-Hungary.[16] Germany continued to pursue expansion when Austria-Hungary had essentially achieved its own war aims by 1916 with the defeat of Serbia, the containment of Italy and the pushing back of the Russians. Austro-Hungarian ambitions with regard to

Poland and Romania clearly rested on German largesse. Vienna was forced to agree to a public commitment to a post-war independent monarchy in Russian Poland in November 1916, rather than achieving its preferred solution of unifying Russian Poland and Austrian Galicia as an autonomous kingdom with a Habsburg sovereign. In May 1917 Germany agreed to offer Romania to Austria-Hungary (though with a substantial German interest in Romania's oil fields) by way of compensation for the loss of Poland, but subsequently demanded part of Austrian Silesia.

Realisation of the dangers threatening the empire fuelled the desire for a separate peace. In July 1916 Franz Joseph remarked to Margutti, 'Things are going badly with us, perhaps worse than we suspect. The starving people can't stand much more. It remains to be seen whether and how we shall get through the winter. I mean to end the war next spring whatever happens. I can't let my Empire go to hopeless ruin.'[17] It might be suggested, given Karl's subsequent failure to free himself of Germany's all-encompassing war aims, that Franz Joseph would not have succeeded either. However, as yet, Britain and France were not ill disposed towards a future for Austria-Hungary in Europe whatever Italian expectations of the potential spoils of participation in the war. Franz Joseph still had significant symbolic influence and the German leadership would have been less able to cower him into submission.

Moreover, there were occasions when the emperor still clearly asserted himself. It was his absolute refusal, for example, to contemplate making concessions to Italy as a means of preventing the Italians coming into the war against Austria-Hungary that precipitated Berchtold's resignation in January 1915, and the subsequent Italian declaration of war in May 1915. War against Italy was one that all the diverse nationalities within the empire could happily support. Nonetheless, it is possible that Franz Joseph may have succeeded in forging peace with Russia, notwithstanding what would have been considerable German opposition. Equally, when the Viennese authorities suggested that Jewish refugees in the city should be moved to camps in Moravia, Franz Joseph quashed the idea by saying that he would instead open up Schönbrunn for them.

It was not just a matter of unrest among subject nationalities, for the empire as a whole failed the wider challenges of war. In Austria, the Reichsrat had been prorogued in March 1914 due to obstructionist tactics by Czech deputies, though the Hungarian Parliament sat throughout the war. Neither government managed to grasp the situation. Although much of the civil jurisdiction was handed to a new Kriegsüberwachungsamt (War Supervisory Office), there was little initial attempt to establish effective control over the economy, with a series of ninety-one ad-hoc agencies, or *Zentralen*, established with general oversight of production. There was only limited industrial capacity in 1914 and Austria-Hungary confronted shortages of raw materials of all kinds. Recourse was had to such expedients as reopening abandoned mines, and melting down church bells, pots and pans. Such measures, and drawing emergency supplies from Germany, could never alleviate the shortages. Lack of manpower planning had denuded the industrial labour force and closed factories. Austria-Hungary was also chronically short of rail transport with which to carry war production or, indeed, anything else. The situation was exacerbated by coal shortages, which further reduced not only production of engines and rolling stock, but also the ability to keep the rail system running.

The empire appeared largely self-sufficient in food and, therefore, no preparations were made in advance of the war. Supply depended, however, upon Hungarian-grown agricultural produce, exchanged in peacetime for Austrian manufactured goods under protective tariffs excluding foreign competitors. Unfortunately, the 1914 and 1915 harvests were poor and, with the best Austrian agricultural areas now in Russian-occupied Galicia, prices rose sharply. Hungary effectively closed its frontiers with Austria, no longer regarding food supplies as common to the empire, so that Austrian imports of flour and cereals were by 1917 only 2.5 per cent of what they had been in peacetime. Bread rationing was introduced in Austria in April 1915, followed by rationing of coffee, fats, milk and sugar. By 1916, even potatoes were in short supply. Food shortages created increasing unrest, food riots occuring in Vienna as early as May 1915, and there were then the serious riots caused by rising prices in both May and September 1916. Women, who had entered industry in large numbers in Austria-Hungary as elsewhere, were less inhibited by the likely application of military discipline than men, and they were prominent in the riots and strikes. Prices rose over 1,000 per cent between 1914 and 1918.

In the face of the growing unrest, the authorities proved ultimately powerless. The Common Council of Ministers met only about forty times during the war and, for all practical purposes, the Austrian and Hungarian administrations operated entirely separately. Parliamentary opposition to Tisza in Hungary coalesced around the issue of the extension of the suffrage, which he opposed. Ultimately, it was the suffrage issue that cost Tisza his office when Karl forced his resignation in May 1917. Tisza retained a parliamentary majority, and his resistance continued to frustrate his successors. Consequently, only a limited franchise reform was passed in July 1918, which increased the size of the electorate to just 13 per cent of adult males.

In Austria, the Reichsrat remained prorogued until 1917. Stürgkh attempted to rule by decree for fear that parliamentary recall would open a can of worms. In part, Stürgkh's assassination in October 1916 reflected wider disaffection with the failure of the state to maintain food supplies, though the murder was primarily intended as a protest against wartime absolutism. Citizen was set against citizen and neighbour against neighbour in terms of the struggle for survival, as evidenced by the so-called 'pillory decree' of January 1917, by which the names of profiteers were published, and also by the routine denunciations received by the police. The state and the emperor as the symbolic head of the national family were becoming thoroughly discredited. Over 54,000 letters and petitions had been sent to the emperor since the outbreak of the war, but the pretence of imperial paternalism could no longer alleviate widespread suffering and discontent.

As Franz Joseph grew weaker, he was more easily exhausted by his insistence on maintaining his heavy daily schedule. His bronchitis returned in October 1916 and developed into a fever. He refused to stop smoking cigars, and continued his usual regime of work. On 17 November, however, Conrad noted that the emperor seemed much weaker and dozed off during his report, though he rose to take leave of the chief of staff. In the early evening of 21 November 1916 Franz Joseph was compelled to take to his bed, instructing his valet to waken him at 4.30 a.m. Instead, he died at 9.05 p.m. that same evening, his reported last words being 'I am behind with my work.' Large crowds turned out for the funeral on 30 November on a wet and foggy day, but their reaction was muted, the liberal Bohemian politician Josef Redlich recording in Vienna only 'a deep tiredness, akin to apathy', for the emperor had been little seen outside Schönbrunn since the outbreak of war.[18]

The amiable Karl, though inexperienced, was highly realistic about the need for reform. He subscribed to aspects of Franz Ferdinand's political programme but lacked the support of his late uncle's political constituency. It was all too late for the dynasty, the death of the old emperor having severed any lingering loyalties that might have overridden the manifest failings of the state to meet the challenges of war. Indeed, Karl's attempt to cultivate the goodwill of the Magyars through dismissing Stürgkh's conservative German successor, Ernest von Körber, was a serious error, for the new minister-president, Heinrich Clam-Martinic, a Bohemian noble, was far less able. Karl attempted an approach to the British and French through his brother-in-law, Prince Sixtus of Bourbon-Parma, a French national serving in the Belgian army, in the hope of ending the war. He was prepared to evacuate Serbia but it would have required concessions to Italy, at which even Karl balked. The revelation of Karl's role by the French prime minister, Georges Clemenceau, in April 1918 resulted in the emperor's abject apology to the Germans and capitulation at Spa on 13 May 1918 to a binding political, military and economic alliance that committed Vienna to do Germany's bidding. It is unlikely that a separate peace would have saved the empire. Czernin, indeed, believed any pursuit of a separate peace apart from Germany would represent 'suicide for fear of death' in triggering an instant German response.[19]

Karl was also constrained from responding adequately to the demands for far more autonomy from the subject nationalities when Poles, Czechs and Slavs were all confronted with a potential dilemma as to whether it would be better to remain loyal to the empire or to hope for an Entente victory. Karl's announcement of a federal system in the Austrian half of the empire on 16 October 1918 came far too late to satisfy national aspirations. Though the British and French came round only belatedly to allowing self-determination to prevail so far as the empire was concerned, the collapse of Russia simplified matters and Britain edged towards recognition of the Polish National Committee on 15 October 1917, and of the Czech National Committee on 2 August 1918. The war ended before the Yugoslav Committee could receive British recognition, by which time British approval was largely academic as the empire was already falling apart.

In October 1918 Karl appealed to the American president, Woodrow Wilson, for peace on the basis of Wilson's Fourteen Points as outlined in his speech of 8 January 1918, but Wilson replied only through Berlin.

In response to Karl's introduction of a federal structure into Austria, the German-speaking deputies constituted a Provisional National Assembly on 21 October and proclaimed an Austrian state. In Hungary, a National Council was established on 25 October under Count Mihály Károlyi, this being recognised as the government on 31 October. That same day, Tisza was murdered by soldiers who blamed him for the war. An independent Czechoslovak Republic was proclaimed in Prague on 21 October, and Austrian Galicia announced it would join a Polish state, though this was not formally proclaimed until 16 November. On 22 October the Zagreb diet proclaimed the cessation of constitutional ties between the South Slav lands and Vienna. On 30 October the port of Fiume declared its independence and its wish to be united with Italy. Much of the Austro-Hungarian army was now affected by mutiny and, on 27 October Austria-Hungary requested an armistice. It was signed at Villa Giusti near Padua on 3 November and did not come into effect until 4 November. Karl abdicated political power on 12 November, though not formally renouncing the throne. Karl had feared that he might not be able to leave Vienna, but unexpectedly the new Socialist chancellor, Dr Karl Renner, arrived at the Schönbrunn to announce allegedly, 'Herr Habsburg, the taxi is waiting.'[20] Karl and his family were driven to Ackartsau Castle and from there took a train to Switzerland. His post-war attempts to regain the Hungarian throne thwarted, Karl died of pneumonia in April 1922 at only thirty-four years of age.

The events in Austria were not a social revolution but one in power and authority. By contrast, subsequent events in Hungary were assuredly a revolution, albeit one soon extinguished. The new Hungarian authorities initially declined to accept that the armistice applied to Hungary, but they signed one officially at Belgrade on 15 November 1918. Hungary was proclaimed a republic on 16 November in a bloodless process controlled largely by a middle-class alliance of social democrats and radicals. Károlyi, however, proved a disappointment to the poorer peasants in not pressing for land redistribution. Still faced with the Entente blockade, the government also found itself incapable of curbing the soldiers' and workers' councils that had emerged at the end of the war. Amid a series of damaging strikes and the demands by the Entente that Hungary surrender territory to Romania, the social democrats were compelled to accept a coalition with the Hungarian Communist Party in March 1919. A so-called

Revolutionary Governing Council of what was now the Hungarian Soviet Republic emerged on 23 March. In April, Czech, Yugoslav and Romanian forces all intervened in Hungary to seize the territory they claimed. The Romanians broke the 'Hungarian Red Army' and occupied Budapest from August until November 1919.

Of the various peace treaties negotiated at Paris, the Treaty of St Germain concluded the war with Austria on 10 September 1919 and, delayed by the Hungarian revolution, the Treaty of Trianon concluded the war with Hungary on 4 June 1920. The break-up of Austria-Hungary was established fact before the Paris conference convened and the situation created thereby was irreversible as Poland, Czechoslovakia and Yugoslavia were all already in practical existence. In many respects, Hungary was the greatest loser from the treaties, being dispossessed of 60 per cent of its former population and two-thirds of its former territory. Indeed, it could be suggested that 6.2 million Austrians and 7.6 million Hungarians bore disproportionate blame for the perceived sins of the 52 million inhabitants of the Austro-Hungarian Empire. Since clauses from the Treaty of Versailles were incorporated wholesale into the Treaty of St Germain, land-locked Austria found itself prohibited from possessing submarines.

Austria-Hungary after 1867 was a fragile construct of a common monarchy, an economic union, and two separate states. In many respects Germans and Hungarians went their own ways, but few within the empire could imagine life without the Habsburgs, and few had actually desired their end. Indeed, it was the perceived external threat from Serbia rather than any real internal threat that propelled Austria-Hungary into a war waged upon such a scale that the Habsburgs seemed increasingly irrelevant to its survival. In more normal times, the death of such a long-reigning monarch as Franz Joseph would have seemed significant enough. In the midst of such a war, however, his passing was a far more symbolic evocation of a rapidly disappearing past. Only a single regiment was available in Vienna to line the funeral route and, rather than the full assembly of the crowned heads of Europe, the last ceremonial rites at the Kapuzinerkirche were attended only by the kings of Bulgaria, Bavaria and Saxony. Like the Habsburgs, their rule, too, had only two more years to run. As A. J. P. Taylor memorably wrote, 'a pebble was removed and an avalanche started'.[21]

CHAPTER 7

THE UNGENTLEMANLY WEAPON

The German Declaration of Unrestricted Submarine Warfare, 1 February 1917

O N 3 OCTOBER 1914 the *Bucks Advertiser and Aylesbury News* reported the 'thrilling experience' of an Aylesbury man, Alfred Brown, from the armoured cruiser, HMS *Aboukir*. On 22 September, in company with HMS *Cressy* and HMS *Hogue*, the *Aboukir* had been cruising the 'Broad Fourteens' off the Dutch coast. At about 0615 hours 'there was an explosion like a terrific clap of thunder, accompanied with a flash like lightning' as the *Aboukir* was hit by a torpedo on the port beam and quickly began to list.[1] Only one of the larger lifeboats could be lowered as the explosion had affected the main steam derrick, while heavy seas a few days previously had smashed the smaller boats. Brown began to swim towards the *Hogue* and was being hauled aboard by rope when this, too, was hit by a torpedo. Almost sucked under, Brown made for the *Cressy*, which was also standing by. No sooner had he reached the *Cressy* than it was torpedoed also. A keen athlete, having 'learned to swim in the canal at Aylesbury', Brown was eventually rescued by a Lowestoft fishing smack.

The loss of all three vessels of the 7th Cruiser Squadron together with 1,459 lives to a single German submarine, Otto Weddigen's *U-9*, within just 47 minutes was a striking demonstration of the weapon's potential. In Germany, the date would be known as 'Weddigen Day' well into the Nazi era. Ironically, the old cruisers had been nicknamed the 'live bait squadron' for their supposed vulnerability to surface attack. Such was the scale of the resulting 'periscopeitis' that Admiral Sir John Jellicoe commanding the

British Grand Fleet moved it from the main fleet base of Scapa Flow in the Orkneys to Lough Swilly off Ireland until the defences of Scapa could be improved. Earlier the same month, *U-21* had become the first submarine to destroy a ship at sea, when sinking HMS *Pathfinder* in the Firth of Forth on 5 September. The only previous successful attack had been by a primitive Confederate craft, the *Hunley*, using a 'spar torpedo' in Charleston harbour in 1864 during the American Civil War.

Neither side had envisaged war at sea in anything other than conventional terms, as a decisive clash of capital fleets, although it was recognised that mines and torpedoes rendered capital ships vulnerable in more confined waters. As First Sea Lord from 1904 to 1910, Admiral Sir John ('Jackie') Fisher certainly envisaged submarines playing a prominent role in a blockade of the German coast, and 'flotilla defence' in the North Sea. Though he was a torpedo officer by background, the architect of the new German Imperial Navy, Admiral Alfred von Tirpitz, had declared submarines a waste of money in 1901, and a luxury to be left to 'wealthier states like France and England'.[2] For Tirpitz, it was simply an article of faith that the Royal Navy must offer battle. In 1914, Germany had only 21 U-boats capable of operating in the North Sea, of which only 9 were diesel-powered craft capable of reaching the Atlantic. The Royal Navy had 73 submarines but, as in the German case, the majority were coastal craft of limited range and the intention was to integrate them into surface operations. Little thought had been given to anti-submarine warfare.

As for using submarines for attacking merchant shipping, Churchill had proclaimed in January 1914 that it would never be done by 'any civilised power', though he certainly saw the potential for submarines in naval warfare in the future. Jellicoe said much the same thing. Fisher's successor, Admiral Sir Arthur Wilson, had likewise suggested submarines were 'underhand, unfair and damned un-English'.[3] Similarly, a fictional story by Sir Arthur Conan Doyle in *Strand Magazine*, 'Danger! Being the Log of Captain John Sirius', in early 1914, suggesting submarines would be used successfully against merchantmen, was met by general incredulity among the naval experts contacted by the magazine for comment.

There were also international legal implications to consider in deploying submarines against merchant ships. With a decisive naval engagement proving elusive, German frustration led to a decision to wage unrestricted submarine warfare – the sinking of merchant vessels without warning by submerged submarines. Its first manifestation in 1915 was abandoned for fears of American reaction. In January 1916 the German chancellor, Theobald von Bethmann-Hollweg, suggested its revival would equate to a second decision for war.[4] The subsequent resumption of unrestricted submarine warfare on 1 February 1917 certainly had global implications, not only for the United States, but also for other neutrals through the tightening of the allied economic blockade on the Central Powers. It also marked the strengthening influence of the Chief of the German General Staff, Paul von Hindenburg, and his First Quartermaster General, Erich Ludendorff, over the reins of power in Germany, the adoption of ever-widening German war aims, and the rejection of a negotiated peace.

The decision to resume unrestricted submarine warfare, which reveals much about military dominance in Imperial Germany, was taken in January 1917 at Pless (now Pszczyna) in Silesia, an elegant castle remodelled for the Hochberg family in the 1870s that served as Imperial Headquarters from May 1915 to February 1917. Chosen for its closeness to the Austro-Hungarian headquarters at Teschen, Pless was owned by a personal friend of the Kaiser, Prince Hans Heinrich, Duke of Hochberg. Ironically, the prince was married to an Englishwoman, Lady Mary 'Daisy' Cornwallis-West.

The Treaty of Paris in 1856 had outlawed privateers – vessels licensed by one belligerent to prey on those of another. The first conference on the laws of war held at The Hague in 1899 had simply applied the Geneva conventions of 1864 intended for land warfare to the sea, prohibiting attacks upon hospital ships. Reaffirming this prohibition, the 1907 Hague conference prohibited the naval bombardment of towns, and placed restrictions on the use of contact mines, as well as outlining the rights of neutrals in maritime conflict. Framed in the expectation of surface action alone, the rules stated that neutral vessels could be stopped and searched. Even if a merchant vessel was identified as a belligerent, all due regard had to be paid to the safety of crew and passengers before it was sunk. The Anglo-American War of 1812–14 had centred on the issue of the rights of neutral shipping. The American Civil War had then resulted in a long-running dispute over the *Alabama* claims, the Americans seeking compensation for the damage done by Confederate commerce raiders constructed in British yards. More recently, a British economic blockade of the Boer republics during the South African War of 1899–1902 had resulted in renewed Anglo-American tension, and a determination on all sides to review maritime law with regard to belligerent and neutral rights.

In February 1909, therefore, the Declaration of London saw a measure of agreement on the definition of those commodities that might be defined as 'contraband' and, hence, liable to seizure or destruction. The British delegation was prepared to give way on the so-called concept of 'continuous voyage', by which even a vessel sailing between neutral ports might be stopped on the assumption that the goods being carried were intended ultimately for conveyance to the enemy. Fears that too much was being conceded, however, persuaded the House of Lords to reject legislation ratifying the declaration in December 1911. There was still an assumption that belligerents would comply with the declaration, which required any detained neutral vessels to be taken to a port for adjudication by a prize court. The conventions were then restated at the meeting of the Institute of International Law in Oxford in August 1913, the resulting 'Oxford Manual of Naval War' establishing what could be regarded as the accepted laws of maritime warfare.

Whatever the precise interpretation placed on various aspects of customary convention, it was clear that merchant vessels of any description could not be sunk without proper identification, or without due warning sufficient to evacuate those on board. Submarines, however, were handicapped in playing by any such rules. Initially, submarines carried few torpedoes with the result that most relied on surface gunfire to sink merchant vessels – no U-boat had deck guns prior to 1915 – or boarding parties despatched with demolition charges. At first, too, different propulsion systems were required for surface and underwater operations, and, in the cramped conditions, submarine crews suffered from constant damp, human odours and fumes, with a build-up of carbon monoxide a distinct danger if they were submerged for too long. As Paul König of even a large 'submarine cruiser', the *U-155*, recorded, when submerged, a 'frightful' smell of oil 'kept whipping and whirling through all the chambers of the boat'.[5] Moreover, a submarine was extremely vulnerable on the surface and a number were lost to Q-ships – heavily armed vessels disguised as harmless merchant ships. As designs improved to extend range, so it made sense to submerge a submarine in order to approach surface vessels and to evade detection. As the British children's writer Arthur Mee put it, 'There is no objection to playing cricket, only one side must not bowl with a bomb for a ball. We must play the game and keep the rules, and the submarine can do neither, because it must make haste to be gone, and cannot wait to make sure of its ship; and it has no means of saving the lives of the crews.'[6]

Although its original purpose had been as a deterrent, the Imperial German Navy had banked all on fighting a single decisive naval battle in the North Sea to annihilate the British Grand Fleet. Tirpitz had not considered any alternative should the Royal Navy resort to a long-distance blockade by closing the Straits of Dover and the waters between Norway and Scotland. In effect, the North Sea became, in the words of Holger Herwig, a 'Dead Sea' in strategic terms.[7] The Royal Navy did not need to risk a decisive engagement in order to win the naval war, as did the German High Seas Fleet (Hochseeflotte). Yet the latter could not risk doing so in the face of British naval superiority. There was some success in commerce raiding on the part of the 10 German naval vessels at sea when the war began, but, with the exception of the *Goeben* and *Breslau*, the others had all been lost by July 1915. Moreover, 69 per cent of the German mercantile marine were interned in neutral ports and 16 per cent detained in allied ports at the outbreak of war.

Initially, the submarine did not appear to be an answer to the German naval problem. With so few U-boats available, it was inevitable that there would be some in, or travelling to or from, port at any given moment. By February 1915, only 10 British merchant ships had been lost to submarine attack, compared to 14 to mines and 51 to surface commerce raiders. Even after the first German declaration of unrestricted submarine warfare, Rear Admiral Alexander Duff of the Royal Navy's 4th Battle Squadron still wrote that, with submarines alone, the Germans 'cannot hope to inflict any serious damage on our merchant shipping'.[8]

Faced with the deadlock on land and sea, Tirpitz changed his mind as to the value of submarines: his advocacy of unrestricted submarine warfare in a press interview in December 1914 had struck a chord with public and politicians alike. Bethmann-Hollweg argued against it on the grounds that it would antagonise neutrals, and possibly bring Italy and other Balkan states into the Entente. His opposition was steadily eroded and the commander of the High Seas Fleet, Admiral Hugo von Pohl, reluctant to risk the fleet in battle, persuaded the Kaiser to agree to the introduction of unrestricted submarine warfare on 4 February 1915. Consequently, Germany declared that the waters around Britain were a war zone, in which enemy shipping would be sunk on sight rather than being stopped and identified first. The Germans warned that, since allied merchantmen might fly neutral flags, neutral shipping should avoid the designated zone altogether. The campaign began on 28 February. There was an immediate impact, with 115 vessels lost to U-boats between February and May, even though there were rarely more than 6 at sea at any one time. In June a total of 114 ships went to the bottom, followed by 86 in July, and 107 in August.

The Germans argued that they had not been the first to violate the accepted conventions at sea since, by the Order in Council of 20 August 1914, and, without formally announcing it as such, Britain had imposed an economic blockade on the Central Powers. This clearly repudiated the restrictions on belligerent rights implicit in the Declaration of London. The British definition of contraband was extended to include foodstuffs, which had previously not been regarded as contraband. The Germans argued this was an illegal 'hunger blockade'. The British similarly extended the definition of 'continuous voyage', compelling ships headed for neutral ports to stop in Britain to obtain details of safe passage. Mining of the North Sea, which Britain declared a military area on 3 November 1914, also impeded neutral shipping. Britain then responded to the German declaration with another Order in Council, on 11 March 1915, making all neutral trade subject to confiscation.

US reaction was crucial. Most Americans recognised that Germany was the aggressor, but British blockade posed the most potent threat to American interests. Publicly the American president Woodrow Wilson endorsed the view held by many Americans that the conflict was one 'with which we have nothing to do, whose causes cannot touch us'.[9] On the other hand, he concluded that long-term American interests would not be served by a German victory. Wilson was ever mindful that, in 1812, the United States had sided effectively with Napoleonic tyranny. Moreover, British actions endangered only American property, not American lives. Wilson therefore declined to confront the British openly and chose instead to make representations through his Anglophile ambassador in London, Walter Hines Page. There was thus de facto acceptance of the blockade. A US protest to the German government was despatched within six days of the declaration of unrestricted submarine warfare, but the response to the British retaliatory action in March 1915 took a month. While the Germans signalled acceptance of an American suggestion that they should stop submarine warfare in return for the British suspending their blockade on foodstuffs, Britain rejected it out of hand. Inevitably, neutral ships were sunk, although Wilson chose to act cautiously over the loss of the British steamship *Falaba* in March, in which a single American life was lost. Wilson had spoken of holding the Germans to 'strict accountability' but inclined at this stage more towards the non-interventionist policy of his Secretary of State, William Jennings Bryan, whose view was that Americans took passage on belligerent ships at their own risk.

Then, on 7 May 1915, the British passenger liner *Lusitania* was sunk by *U-20* off the Irish coast with the loss of 128 Americans among the 1,198 dead, who included 291 women and 94 children. Recorded in many contemporary lists as a merchant cruiser of the Royal Naval Reserve, the liner was carrying cases of rifle ammunition and fuses, but the event was still shocking. This produced an American note to the German government that, while representing neither an ultimatum nor a threat, made it clear that an unrestricted submarine campaign was unacceptable. The wording of the note was still sufficiently strong to force the resignation of Bryan, who was replaced by Robert Lansing.

The equally strong US reaction to the sinking of the liner *Arabic* outside the technical 'war zone' on 19 August, in which two Americans died, then brought a German declaration on 1 September 1915 that passenger ships would not be attacked without warning. U-boats were also withdrawn from the Western Approaches. On 6 October the Germans also offered an indemnity for the sinking of the *Arabic*. Effectively, therefore, unrestricted submarine warfare was suspended, though attacks continued in the Mediterranean. Bethmann-Hollweg's concern to modify the rules of engagement struck a chord with the Chief of the German General Staff, Erich von Falkenhayn, who feared that the Dutch, too, might abandon their neutrality. Not surprisingly, the Germans believed that Wilson should also take a firm line against the British blockade. Wilson did send a harsher note on blockade policy to the British government in October 1915. The British delayed their reply but took particular exception to the naive suggestion by Lansing in February 1916 that they should agree not to arm merchant ships in return for a German promise not to sink unarmed ships without warning.

The Germans resumed 'intensified' submarine warfare on 29 February 1916, albeit under accepted 'cruiser' rules of stop and search. With the sinking of an unarmed French-owned passenger ferry, the *Sussex*, in the Channel, by *U-29* in March 1916, costing four American lives, there was another strong US public reaction against Germany, to which Wilson responded with a further note demanding that all merchantmen be treated according to the accepted rules. In line with their generally inept propaganda machine, the Germans initially claimed that they had not torpedoed the *Sussex*, but another vessel at the same time and place. It was also claimed that the British had sunk it using German torpedoes, an excuse that even the Chief of the Kaiser's Naval Cabinet, Admiral Georg von Müller, found 'very picturesque'.[10] Bethmann-Hollweg managed to stave off any irrevocable decision being taken for the time being and, not for the first time, Tirpitz threatened to resign as navy minister. This time his resignation was accepted, and there was another German pledge of restraint on 4 May 1916. The 'Sussex pledge', however, marked the end of the chancellor's success, for the German military leadership increasingly believed that any American intervention in the war could not be in sufficient strength quickly enough to offset the advantages from an intensification of the submarine war. That view coincided with the waning of the influence not only of the chancellor but also of Falkenhayn.

A lawyer by background and chancellor since 1909, Bethmann-Hollweg was a bureaucrat by instinct, ever ready to compromise rather than come down firmly on one side or the other. Given to depression, he had faced a situation of constant political and social flux. The emerging working-class political organisation of the Social Democratic Party (SPD) vied with a traditional landed elite able to co-opt a lower middle class of white-collar workers, artisans and shopkeepers through a strongly articulated nationalism. Though becoming the largest party in the Reichstag in 1912 under a system of universal male suffrage, the SPD's political leverage was restricted by a federal electoral system that gave real power to Imperial Germany's largely autonomous constituent states. These had narrower franchises and held the real power. Bethmann-Hollweg could hope to restrain the political right only by an appeal to a loose coalition of the Catholic Centre Party, the Progressives and those Social Democrats who supported the war effort. The German military collectively enjoyed a prestige that Bethmann-Hollweg found it difficult to challenge, albeit there was no adequate mechanism for overall strategic decision-making. Even within the army, the Prussian Minister of War and the Kaiser's Military Cabinet could challenge the Chief of the General Staff. No fewer than forty army and eight naval officers had the right of direct access to the Kaiser, whose mood swings only increased his growing political marginalisation. It should not be thought that Bethmann-Hollweg was some kind of pacifist for he fully subscribed to the inevitability of war in 1914, and he accepted the sweeping war aims articulated in the so-called September Programme of 9 September 1914 readily enough. The conduct of the war for him was, therefore, always a matter of means rather than ends, his principal concern being to limit the risk Germany ran by war though it was always risk he believed worth taking.

Clever and hard working but arrogant, sarcastic and aloof, Falkenhayn had been the Kaiser's surprising choice as Minister of War in 1913. He was relatively young at just fifty-two and had spent little time serving on the General Staff due to an extended tour of service in China. Consequently, he was always something of an outsider when he replaced Helmuth von Moltke as chief of staff in September 1914, and he had lost a great deal of political capital through the failure of the Ypres offensive in October and November 1914. Falkenhayn identified Britain as the main opponent to Germany. Thus, he advocated reaching a compromise peace with the Russians, his emphasis on the Western Front not endearing him to Hindenburg and Ludendorff, whose victories on the Eastern Front had won them heroic cult status with the public.

Bethmann-Hollweg agreed with Falkenhayn only to a limited extent, doubting that Tsar Nicholas II would act independently of his allies. Moreover, the chancellor believed it important to inflict a heavy defeat on the Russians before negotiating and, therefore, was persuaded by Hindenburg and Ludendorff of the need to replace Falkenhayn. The Kaiser, however, refused to dismiss Falkenhayn when his chancellor broached the subject in January 1915. The uneasy relationship between Bethmann-Hollweg and Falkenhayn was exacerbated further by Falkenhayn's conversion to the necessity for unrestricted submarine warfare in December 1915 as a means of increasing pressure on Britain, a course that Bethmann-Hollweg still resisted.

Over the winter of 1915–16, Falkenhayn resolved to destroy the French army to compel the French and British to negotiate, but the resulting Verdun offensive failed. Coupled with the success of the Russian Brusilov offensive, and Romanian entry into the war against Germany, this resulted in Falkenhayn's dismissal on 29 August 1916 despite the Kaiser's reluctance to see him go. Hindenburg and Ludendorff, who subscribed to the wilder visions of German expansion, were summoned to take over. One member of the Kaiser's Military Cabinet, Colonel Ulrich, Freiherr von Marschall, noted in August 1916 that Ludendorff 'in his boundless pride and ambition will wage war until the German people are completely exhausted, and will saddle the monarchy with the blame'.[11]

Hindenburg and Ludendorff were convinced that a decisive victory could be won against Russia. It would force the Russians to negotiate a separate peace, which would give Germany access to raw materials and food supplies from the Ukraine, and thus avoid the consequences of the British naval blockade. A stable peace in the east would also allow Germany to transfer troops to the west to launch a major offensive in due course. Another consequence of Hindenburg and Ludendorff's success in effectively gaining control of the German governmental machine was renewed unrestricted submarine warfare. Indeed, given the usual lack of cooperation between army and navy generally, the decision to pursue submarine warfare was the only German strategic decision taken during the war that was 'comprehensively co-ordinated'.[12]

In August 1916 the Chief of the Naval Staff, Admiral Henning von Holtzendorff, circulated a memorandum calling for the implementation of unrestricted submarine warfare. A pre-war head of the navy, Holtzendorff had been recalled from retirement in September 1915 precisely because he was seen as a moderate and a sceptic on submarine warfare. Characterised by an American journalist as a 'small, plump, energetic man, with thick white whiskers and a hearty handshake',[13] Holtzendorff had quickly become converted to the view that an unrestricted campaign was necessary despite his usual caution. A meeting at Pless on 3 September 1916, however, concluded that any decision should be delayed while the military situation appeared unclear. Hindenburg and Ludendorff, indeed, were wary of the reaction of Denmark and the Netherlands in the light of warnings from the German ambassador at The Hague of possible Dutch intervention. Bethmann-Hollweg, the Foreign Secretary, Gottlieb von Jagow, and the Interior Secretary, Karl Helfferich, all stressed the risks of American intervention. Vice Admiral Reinhard Scheer, who had succeeded to the command of the High Seas Fleet in January 1916, had been convinced of the efficacy of the submarine for some time. Despairing of Holtzendorff, Scheer sent Adolf von Trotha, chief of staff of the High Seas Fleet, to see Ludendorff. According to Trotha's later account in an interview in 1939, Ludendorff rang up army headquarters on the Western Front and received a gloomy situation report. He therefore told Trotha that unrestricted submarine warfare 'must be implemented'.[14] Scheer himself then went to see Ludendorff on 21 November to press the need for removing all operational restrictions.

Urged on by Scheer, Holtzendorff submitted a new memorandum to Hindenburg on 22 December 1916, calling for the implementation of unrestricted submarine warfare no later than 1 February 1917. In his accompanying summary Holtzendorff argued, 'A decision must be reached in the war before the autumn of 1917, if it is not to end in the exhaustion of all parties, and consequently disastrously for us. Of our enemies, Italy and France are economically so hard hit they are only upheld by England's energy and activity. If we can break England's back the war will be at once decided in our favour.'[15]

Holtzendorff argued that Britain was particularly vulnerable to interdiction of wheat supplies and had at most 8 million tons of merchant shipping available to carry food. This could be sunk at small cost and small risk at a rate of up to 600,000 tons a month for the first four months, and 500,000 tons for each of the following two months. Neutral vessels would be frightened from the seas, reducing available shipping still further, and the crews of German ships interned in neutral ports would scuttle their vessels rather than allow the British to seize them to make up for the tonnage sunk. British shipping would be reduced by 39 per cent within five months. Since the 1916 harvest in the US and in Latin America had proved poor, Britain could be brought to its knees within six to eight months. It was assumed the British would not introduce rationing, since the British national character could not accept its discipline, for 'the people of England have not been educated to submit to such coercion'.[16] The British economy could easily be knocked off course by rising prices. In addition, the British coal industry was dependent upon Scandinavian timber for pit props, and closing off this trade, in turn, would damage the iron and steel industries, rendering Britain incapable of replacing lost ships. Thus, the war could be concluded successfully before the next harvest in the autumn of 1917. US intervention was a risk but one that should not hinder the decision.

The figures had been worked out for Holtzendorff by a number of economic experts drawn from academe and commerce, including Dr Richard Fuss from a Madgeburg-based banking institute and Professor Hermann Levy of the University of Heidelberg. The apparent ability to achieve significant results had also been proven to the navy's satisfaction by the 'intensified' submarine campaign from October 1916, which accounted for 757 vessels by January 1917, since the Germans now had over 100 operational U-boats available. All the assumptions, however, were questionable.

Buoyed by American credit, the British economy and people were far more adaptable than supposed. Holtzendorff's advisers failed to take into account cereals other than wheat, the British ability to bring more acreage under cultivation, and the temporary nature of a single bad harvest in the US. Diplomatic necessity compelled the Germans to allow the Scandinavian neutrals to continue to trade commodities with Britain, including timber. The Germans also equated tonnage with cargoes, failing to appreciate that prioritisation of cargoes could offset overall shipping losses. There was little consideration given to possible British countermeasures.

Bethmann-Hollweg, who welcomed the elevation of Hindenburg and Ludendorff, failed to understand that Ludendorff was utterly opposed to any question of compromise. Indeed, the chancellor's enquiry of the military and naval High Commands as to potential bargaining positions in preparation for a peace offer to the Entente, which was announced on 12 December 1916, elicited sweeping statements of war aims. Attempting a conciliatory move, Bethmann-Hollweg suggested he would be prepared to consider introduction of unrestricted submarine warfare if it could 'outweigh the handicap of America joining our enemies', but reserved the decision for himself. Hindenburg bluntly replied that he intended 'with the fullest sense of responsibility for the successful conclusion of the war, to support every effort in the military sphere that I consider to be necessary to that end'.[17] Bethmann-Hollweg was further undermined by the Catholic Centre Party's support for an unrestricted campaign, which stripped away his ability to resist the demands of the political right within the Reichstag. Popular support was also assured, the mystique of the U-boats having been fed by a flood of books, verse, propaganda posters and other images since the spring of 1915.

Hindenburg and Ludendorff now fully supported reopening unrestricted submarine warfare, because victory over Romania had freed troops to mask the Netherlands and Denmark should they come into the war. The assumption was that the war could be won before the Americans arrived in sufficient numbers to make any difference. Given the calculation that the United States was already a de facto part of the Entente in economic and even political terms, only an American military presence was considered as an additional consequence, Ludendorff remarking, 'I don't give a damn about America'.[18] Rather similarly, Tirpitz's successor as navy minister, Admiral Eduard von Capelle, proclaimed that American troops would not arrive in Europe as their troopships would be sunk, 'Thus America from a military point of view means nothing, and again nothing, and for a third time nothing.'[19] Hindenburg and Ludendorff were prepared to threaten resignation if unrestricted submarine warfare was not reintroduced.

Arriving at Pless for a conference on 29 December 1916, Bethmann-Hollweg received a less than warm welcome from Hindenburg, while Helfferich, who accompanied him, was barred altogether from participating in the talks. The discussion, however, centred mostly on German General Headquarters (OHL) war aims. One of the naval representatives present, Captain von Bülow, urged Ludendorff to persuade Bethmann-Hollweg to accept unrestricted submarine warfare, but Ludendorff said it was Holtzendorff's task. Holtzendorff meanwhile felt a united naval and military front was needed to force the Kaiser, who had moral scruples with respect to unrestricted submarine warfare, to take the decision against Bethmann-Hollweg. Though not yet aware of Holtzendorff's memorandum, the chancellor had grasped the weakness of his position, his difficulties being compounded by the news on 31 December that the Entente had rejected his peace offer. It was not clear, therefore, how much longer he could hold out.

Holtzendorff finally showed his memorandum to Bethmann-Hollweg on 4 January 1917. Informed that same day by an emissary from Scheer, Captain Magnus von Levetzow, the head of the High Seas Fleet Operations Division, that the navy had lost confidence in his leadership, Holtzendorff then told Hindenburg that he would go direct to the Kaiser to appeal for a decision. Bethmann-Hollweg clung to the rapidly disappearing prospect that he could determine the timetable for the introduction of unrestricted submarine warfare and, summoned by the Kaiser to Pless, asked Holtzendorff to meet him there. Having consulted Hindenburg and Ludendorff, Holtzendorff agreed to delay ordering the commencement of unrestricted operations but, meeting the Kaiser, he outlined his arguments in a manner effective enough to win him over. Holtzendorff, Hindenburg and Ludendorff agreed that the chancellor should be forced to resign if he did not accept unrestricted submarine warfare, and they confronted the Kaiser with their demands on the evening of 8 January. Having been forced previously to umpire the disagreement between his advisers, the Kaiser happily agreed that it was a purely military decision. The wording of his invitation to Bethmann-Hollweg should have sounded the alarm bells: 'Since my order to the Navy regarding the U-boat war has to go out no later than the day after tomorrow, I shall be delighted to see you here tomorrow.'[20] Overnight, Holtzendorff prepared a new memorandum to steel the Kaiser for the coming confrontation.

When Bethmann-Hollweg, suffering from a chill, arrived at Pless on the morning of 9 January, Georg von Müller met him. A serious-minded Saxon, whose nickname of 'Rasputin' was a sarcastic comment on his austere nature, Müller had been a sceptic on submarines. However, he had been persuaded by the better than expected German harvest, and evidence of resentment of the British blockade by neutral powers, that it was worth attempting 'this last shot in our locker'.[21] Müller informed the chancellor that all was already settled and asked him not to reject submarine warfare out of hand. Bethmann-Hollweg met Hindenburg and Ludendorff at 11.15 a.m. The chancellor's later account, as expressed to

Helfferich and the head of the Civil Cabinet, Rudolf von Valentini, differed somewhat from the official record. He had continued to express his reservations, but ineffectively in face of the military and naval arguments put forward and the inescapable fact that there was little prospect of a negotiated peace: having rejected Bethmann-Hollweg's overtures, the Entente was to reject President Wilson's Peace Note of 18 December on the following day. While Bethmann-Hollweg conceded that the chances of success appeared favourable, they were 'not capable of being demonstrated by proof'. Hindenburg stated, 'We need the most energetic, ruthless methods which can be adopted.' Thus, the chancellor agreed to the necessary diplomatic preparations intended to try and keep the Americans from entering the war, remarking that, since the military considered it absolutely necessary, 'then I am not in a position to speak against it'.[22]

Helfferich had spent the night of 8–9 January reading through Holtzendorff's original memorandum and wired a rebuttal to Bethmann-Hollweg, arguing for a further delay. The wire only reached Pless in the early afternoon, by which time the chancellor's opposition had entirely collapsed. The Crown Council met at 1800 hours, comprising the Kaiser, Bethmann-Hollweg, Hindenburg, Ludendorff, Holtzendorff, Müller, Valentini and the head of the Military Cabinet, Colonel-General Moriz, Freiherr von Lyncker. It was a foregone conclusion.

According to Valentini, 'Everyone stood around a large table, on which the Kaiser, pale and excited, leaned his hand.' Holtzendorff spoke of his confidence in victory 'in at most six months' before 'a single American had set foot on the continent'. Hindenburg observed that he was now ready if the Danes and Dutch entered the war. He also dismissed Bethmann-Hollweg's odd assertion that the Swiss might also come into the war. With 'a visible inner excitement', the chancellor again stressed the danger of American intervention, but closed by saying that he would no longer oppose the measure. Müller, who described Bethmann-Hollweg as speaking in a 'rambling tone', suggested it was not so much approval but 'an acceptance of the facts'. The Kaiser, who quoted a newspaper article by a German industrialist supporting submarine warfare, supposedly listened to his chancellor with sympathy, though it seems the Kaiser's actual mood was one of impatience, snorting 'By God, this man still has scruples', and declaring that 'unrestricted U-Boat warfare was therefore decided'.

Bethmann-Hollweg retired to his room nursing his cold, telling Müller that Germany would ultimately have to 'sign an exceedingly modest peace'.[23]

Helfferich felt Bethmann-Hollweg should have resigned immediately. The chancellor concluded that he should stay to mitigate further military demands, and because he might yet manage to keep the Americans out of the war. His resignation in the face of the overwhelming military, naval and public support for unrestricted submarine warfare would also have required greater moral certainty than the chancellor possessed. Speaking before the Reichstag Finance Committee on 31 January, Bethmann-Hollweg rationalised his capitulation by suggesting that, although it had been indefensible to commence unrestricted submarine warfare, the situation had now changed in Germany's favour and it would be indefensible not to do so. Even Helfferich, appearing before the same committee, now dismissed American intervention, claiming that by the autumn Britain 'will sprawl like a fish in the reeds and beg for peace'.[24]

The Kaiser signed the decree authorising the campaign on 19 January 1917, and on 1 February the Germans announced the revival of unrestricted submarine warfare around the British Isles and in the Mediterranean. One American steamer per week would be permitted through the war zone if clearly identified and carrying no contraband. Compared to 1915, there were now 121 U-boats available – of which 41 would always be at sea – with enhanced underwater capabilities and more torpedoes. The leading German technical expert on submarines, Ulrich-Eberhard Blum, had calculated before the war that 222 U-boats would be needed to wage an effective campaign. Nevertheless, a dramatic increase in Entente shipping losses resulted, rising from 464,599 tons in February 1917 to 507,001 tons in March and 834,549 tons in April. The tonnage lost in the first six months of the campaign averaged 643,000 tons a month, close to Holtzendorff's estimates. Other ships were damaged and the sailing of yet others delayed, but the British economy proved resilient.

The impact was sufficient for Jellicoe, now First Sea Lord, to give his support in June 1917 for what became the Passchendaele campaign, as a means of breaking through to the German submarine bases at Ostend and Zeebrugge. In fact, the menace of the submarine was already being blunted for all that pre-war preparations for anti-submarine and anti-mine warfare had been deficient. Technical advances already meant it was possible for naval vessels to survive torpedo attack. Minefields and nets were also used, as in the Dover Barrage, the Northern Barrage between Norway and the Orkneys and the Otranto Barrage in the Adriatic. Dirigibles and aircraft, too, were used for anti-submarine patrols.

The real solution to unrestricted submarine warfare was a revival of the method well known to the age of sail, the convoy. Convoys had been used from the beginning of the war to protect troopships and, in February 1917, were successfully introduced for the coal trade between Britain and France and, in April 1917, for the Scandinavian trade. The Admiralty resisted their general introduction in the belief that the desirable ratio of escorts to merchantmen would be as high as 2:1. Merchant captains also protested that they could not keep station in convoys, which would be reduced to the speed of the slowest ship, and that they would therefore present a wealth of targets. Ships in convoy, it was further argued, would not be able to zigzag as did single ships.

Convoys, however, would prove as hard to locate in the expanse of the sea as single ships, while the concentration of vessels made escort duties easier and increased the opportunities for the escort vessels to engage submarines effectively, and convoys could also be routed away from danger areas. As a result of strong support from the prime minister, David Lloyd George, an experimental convoy was run from Gibraltar to Plymouth on 10 May 1917 without loss. American entry to the war in itself also removed fears of a lack of available escort vessels. By October 1917, a total of 99 homeward-bound convoys had reached harbour safely, and only 10 vessels had been lost. In all, British shipping losses in the last quarter of 1917, of 702,779 tons (235 ships), were only just over half the peak figure of 1,315,496 tons (413 ships) lost in the second quarter of the year. Only three troopships carrying American troops were torpedoed, with only 68 American soldiers killed.

By November 1917 the convoy system was fully operational and U-boats were forced to attack underwater and largely in coastal waters. Escorts were now more successful, using prototype hydrophones and seabed systems to detect U-boats and equally newly developed depth charges, which had accounted for 30 U-boats by 1918. Early sonar had also been developed by this stage. The U-boats also failed to modify their tactics by operating in more than single numbers. Indeed, the submarine campaign might have been more effective had Holtzendorff not repeatedly rejected proposals for creating what in the Second World War would become known as wolf packs, in the vain belief that covering all sea approaches to Britain with individual submarines would force the British to disperse their escort vessels. Construction had barely kept pace with losses, German yards having to compete for manpower and raw materials against other industrial priorities. Of 335 U-boats deployed by the Germans during the war, 178 were lost with 4,474 crew killed.

U-boats still sank 6,394 ships, amounting to 11.9 million tons, between 1914 and 1918, but the decision had been a disastrous one, for the political fall-out in terms of the American entry into the war decisively tipped the balance against Germany. There were other irritants in US–German relations such as German involvement in Mexico, partly contributing to an American occupation of Vera Cruz between April and November 1914, and to American involvement in Mexico's incipient civil war. There was also some attempted German subversion in the US itself, the most serious of 88 suspicious incidents or accidents being an explosion at Black Tom Island, New Jersey, in July 1916, which destroyed $20-million worth of ammunition destined for the Entente and killed three people. The temperature of Anglo-American relations had been similarly raised by the British suppression of the Easter Rising in April 1916, though other events had also contributed. There was continuing British bending of international maritime law. There was also the continuing rejection of Wilson's mediation efforts as epitomised by Lloyd George's interview with Roy Howard of the American United Press, published in *The Times* on 29 November 1916, in which the new prime minister indicated his intention of delivering a 'knock-out blow' to Germany, and fighting 'to the finish'. Wilson was convinced that he could only keep America out of the war by ending it, hence his increased efforts at mediation in the winter of 1916–17.

The German declaration of renewed unrestricted submarine warfare immediately prompted the breaking off of diplomatic relations by the US. More American lives were lost when the British *Laconia* was torpedoed on 26 February 1917.

Four more American vessels were sunk in March and the Entente cause also received a fillip through the abdication of the Tsar on 15 March 1917, since the new Russian provisional government could be regarded as sufficiently democratic to remove any moral objections to American participation in the Entente. In all, 197 Americans had been killed since 1914 by U-boats. Wilson finally requested a declaration of war from Congress on 2 April, the resolution passing the Senate by 82 votes to 6 on 4 April and the House of Representatives, by 373 to 50, two days later. In declaring war on 6 April, Wilson proclaimed 'submarine warfare against commerce is a warfare against mankind'.[25] Panama and Cuba declared war on Germany on 7 April 1917, as did Brazil on 26 October. Nine other Latin American states also broke off diplomatic relations with Germany between April and October, Peru citing the German sinking of a Peruvian vessel, the *Lorton*, by way of justification. The 'last shot' had failed but, like other manifestations of new technologies, submarines would prove more potent in the future.

Alfred Brown survived the Great War, going on to serve in the Dover Patrol. A butcher after the war, his stories proved sufficiently alluring for his son, Frederick, to join the Merchant Navy as a wireless operator. A few months past his twentieth birthday, Fred was lost, together with the rest of the crew, when SS *Empire Jaguar*, en route from Cardiff to Philadelphia, was torpedoed by *U-103* some 296 miles west of Slyne Head on 8 December 1940. Alfred Brown had not escaped the shadow of the U-boat.[26]

CHAPTER 8

THE PATH TO REVOLUTION

The Abdication of Tsar Nicholas II, 15 March 1917

ONE POPULAR perception of the Great War remains the image of enthusiastic crowds welcoming the outbreak of war in Europe's belligerent capitals. To be sure there were such crowds, but it is now apparent that the European public had relatively little time to react to events. Enthusiasm for war was more an urban than a rural phenomenon. The crowds that did gather were more likely to be of younger and more middle-class composition. Often the national mood was subdued. One clear illustration is a photograph taken on Dvortsovaya Square behind the Winter Palace (now the Hermitage Museum) in St Petersburg, which was to be renamed Petrograd in August 1914 as more suitably Slavic. The date is 29 July 1914, following the announcement of partial Russian mobilisation.[1] Rather than enthusiastic, this crowd is undoubtedly apprehensive.

As events were to prove, they were right to be apprehensive. While there were significant consequences from the collapse of all four empires destroyed by participation in the war – Austria-Hungary, Germany, Ottoman Turkey and Russia – that deriving from the collapse of Tsarist Russia had particular importance. It led to the emergence of the Bolsheviks, shaping and determining European and global development until the collapse of communism in Europe between 1989 and 1991. It is difficult to conceive communism triumphing but for the impact of the First World War on the Russian state. Though the causes were many, the train of events in March 1917 began simply enough as a riot among women workers queuing for bread in a Petrograd suburb. How the autocratic Tsar and his advisers reacted was symptomatic of the malaise within the Russian government. J. A. S. Grenville memorably suggested that, by 1917, Italy, Austria-Hungary and Russia were 'racing each other to collapse'.[2] It was Russia that was always likely to 'win' the race through the enormous additional pressure placed on the Tsarist system by the challenge of war.

Russia had experienced considerable social, economic and political tensions as a result of defeat in the Russo-Japanese War of 1904–05. In the aftermath, a nominally constitutional monarchy had emerged, with a Council of Ministers headed by a chairman and an elected assembly, or Duma, marking a distinct change in a state without democratic tradition. Reform was also begun in agriculture with the abolition of communes. In 1908 plans were announced for the progressive extension of universal primary education by 1922. Stimulated by a rearmament programme for both army and navy, industry grew, especially in metallurgy, engineering and shipbuilding, though the economy was still backward in terms of international competitiveness: productivity also remained relatively low, and there was a dependence upon imported raw materials.

Modernisation was not without its costs. In the countryside the impact of reform was limited and it did not diminish the desire for land redistribution. Rapid industrialisation came at the cost of concentrating the industrial workforce in a few key areas such as Moscow, Riga and St Petersburg. Industrialisation and accompanying urbanisation put considerable strains on housing, and there was already growing industrial militancy before the war. The 90 per cent of the population who were either workers or peasants possessed but 24 per cent of the country's wealth.

As yet, the revolutionary movement was too fractured to fully exploit any militancy, the Marxists of the Social Democratic Workers Party having split into Bolsheviks and Mensheviks in 1903. The Socialist Revolutionaries, founded in 1901, were also divided over revolutionary tactics. The small middle class – generally liberals – was thwarted by a change in the franchise in 1907, which resulted in the return of a more conservative Duma and an end to expectations of further reform. As a result, there was increasingly less support for the Tsar. Neither the Orthodox Church, nor an army badly affected by mutiny in 1905, was quite the bulwark of autocracy it had proved to be in the past. Nonetheless, any revolutionary threat appeared slight.

As elsewhere in Europe in 1914, the fateful decision on war was taken by a relatively small group of individuals. There was some concept of a 'public opinion' as represented by the press and by the Duma. While this was a limited circle, it reinforced the view of the Council of Ministers that Russia could no longer yield to Austro-Hungarian or German demands in the way it had done so in previous diplomatic crises. Revolutionaries had assassinated one opponent of an aggressive foreign policy, Pyotr Stolypin, in 1911. Another, Stolypin's successor as chairman of the Council of Ministers, Vladimir Kokovtsov, had been dismissed in February 1914. Concerned at the possible loss of Russia's status as a great power, Foreign Minister Sergei Sazonov placed too much confidence in the optimism of the Minister of War, Vladimir Sukhomlinov. The influential Minister of Agriculture, A. V. Krivoshein, also favoured a robust response. On 24 July 1914, therefore, the Council took the decision to advise the Serbs to make concessions, but also to mobilise partially in those frontier districts contiguous with Austria-Hungary as a diplomatic lever. The decision was then confirmed by the Tsar at a Crown Council on the following day. Partial mobilisation commenced on 29 July. Since the military warned that this left Russia hopelessly vulnerable in view of the inherent difficulties of only partial mobilisation, the Tsar then ordered full mobilisation. It went into effect on 31 July. On 1 August, Germany declared war on Russia.

The personality of the Tsar was to be a crucial factor in subsequent events. Meeting the Tsar for the first time in October 1914, Sir John Hanbury-Williams, the head of the British Military Mission, expected an austere autocrat. He discovered instead a man with 'a bright, keen, happy face, plenty of humour and a "fresh-air man"'.[3] Similarly, the British ambassador, Sir George Buchanan, found Nicholas to possess attractive attributes, with 'quick intelligence, a cultivated mind, method and industry in his work, and natural charm'.[4] Unfortunately, Buchanan also found the Tsar lacking in moral courage in his desire to avoid confrontation with those around him, and dominated by his wife.

Nicholas was just twenty-six when he succeeded his father, Alexander III, in 1894 and was due to marry the twenty-two-year-old German Princess, Alix of Hesse-Darmstadt, a first cousin of Kaiser Wilhelm II. The marriage duly took place just a week after the late Tsar's funeral, Alix becoming the Tsarina Alexandra. The couple always corresponded and spoke to one another in English – he was 'Nicky' and she was 'Sunny'. As is well known, Alexandra, a granddaughter of Queen Victoria, passed on haemophilia to the couple's youngest child and only son, Aleksei, born in 1904. Aleksei's condition was largely concealed. The resulting influence over Alexandra of the manipulative Siberian peasant mystic, Grigory Rasputin, led to increasing rumours of an improper relationship. Rasputin's influence rested simply on he alone appearing able to ease the boy's symptoms, possibly by some form of hypnosis. That Alexandra was both German-born – though from her Hessian background, she was actually violently anti-Prussian – and also considerably stronger willed than her shy husband added to the impression of the Tsar's weakness once war broke out. Coupled with her own shyness, the constant stress over her son's health made Alexandra appear an ever more distant figure to ordinary Russians. The couple remained passionately in love throughout their marriage, and devoted to their children, their four daughters – Olga, Tatiana, Maria and Anastasia – completing the family. On occasions Nicholas did give way to Alexandra's wishes. 'Our Friend' Rasputin, who was desperate to maintain his own position at the heart of government, often shaped those wishes. Kokovtsov was one of his victims. Another case in point was the continued support of Rasputin and Alexandra for the hopelessly inefficient Minister of the Interior appointed in September 1916, Alexandr Protopopov. Meriel Buchanan, the daughter of the British ambassador, memorably characterised Protopopov as 'a small grey-haired man, with restless, nervous movements and bright, wild eyes that shifted all the time'.[5] His inability to tackle the food shortages in Petrograd played a not inconsiderable part in the riots that triggered revolution.

Nicholas always remained an autocrat at heart, believing in a mythic bond between himself and his loyal people, often attributing discontent to those who were 'alien' elements in the population, or otherwise not truly Russian. He had an almost preternaturally orderly mind, his daily routine unvarying, and his desk always tidy. Arising from his own elevated concept of duty, Nicholas perceived more and more virtue in traditional Russian structures in the face of the forces of change. He had responded to one early expression of liberal expectation on his accession by proclaiming that he would maintain 'the principle of autocracy just as firmly and unflinchingly' as his father.[6] His acceptance of the 1905 constitution was a reluctant one. In any case, the Tsar could dismiss the Duma and appoint or dismiss his ministers as he chose. Ministers were usually confined to departmental responsibilities so that the Council operated more as a bureaucracy than an executive. To give one example, whatever Rasputin's influence, the Tsar himself had believed that Kokovtsov was exceeding his authority. Indeed, where the Tsar was quite prepared to act decisively was in maintaining his own powers, which coincided with what he perceived to be in Russia's best interests.

If anything, Alexandra was even more convinced of the need to maintain the Tsar's supreme authority. In December 1916 she urged Nicholas to 'be the Master' for 'we have been placed by God on a throne & we must keep it firm & give it over to our son untouched – if you keep that in mind you will remember to be the Sovereign – and how much easier for an autocratic sovereign than one who has sworn the constitution!'[7] Just as orderly in her habits as her husband, the deeply religious Alexandra developed a belief not only in the virtue of suffering, but also in the basic loyalty of the Russian people to the Tsar.

The simple fact was that the government did not cope well with the war's demands. There was a spirit of 'patriotic union' in the Duma in August 1914. Only 21 out of 448 deputies in the Duma voted against the war: five Bolsheviks, six Mensheviks and ten Trudoviks (Labour Party). The political truce ended, however, with military failures in 1915, and the continued resistance of the Tsar to reform. Prorogued in January 1915, the Duma was recalled in July, with a new political alliance emerging within it in August 1915. This alliance was the so-called Progressive Bloc, orchestrated by Pavel Miliukov of the Kadets (Constitutional Democrats), a radical party representative of small businesses. Apart from the Kadets, it also embraced the Octobrists (Conservative-Liberals), led by Alexandr Guchkov, a wool manufacturer, which mostly represented the larger industrial concerns; and the Progressists, founded in 1912 by Moscow-based textile manufacturers to seek a wider political role for industry as a whole.

Within a few weeks, however, the Duma was prorogued ostensibly for six months as the Tsar left for the front in September 1915 to assume personal command of his armies. He took up quarters with Russian General Headquarters (Stavka) in Mogilev (the word literally means 'grave'), a small and undistinguished town to the southwest of Moscow. In some respects, the Tsar's decision was logical. It removed the tension that had arisen in civil–military relations from the mutual animosity between the conservative Sukhomlinov, who had expected to have command, and the Tsar's actual commander-in-chief, his cousin, the urbane and liberally minded Grand Duke Nicholas. The Tsar had frequented Stavka since the beginning of the war and was at his most relaxed there, especially when Aleksei joined him. Unfortunately, the decision had been influenced by Alexandra's insidious dislike of the Grand Duke, who had threatened to hang Rasputin if he ever came near Stavka. It also consigned government in Petrograd to Alexandra and Rasputin. A letter from ten of his thirteen ministers objecting to the Grand Duke's removal from his command, which 'shocked & horrified' Nicholas, stemmed largely from their recognition of how the Tsar's absence would enhance Alexandra's influence.[8] Ministers, indeed, were now to be chosen depending upon their acceptance of Rasputin, until he was murdered in December 1916 amid rumours of a wider palace coup aimed at replacing the Tsar.

In all, there were four chairmen of the Council, three war ministers, three foreign ministers, and six ministers of the interior between the Tsar's departure for the front and March 1917. The Bloc maintained a presence as a kind of rump parliament after the suspension of the Duma, but the Tsar declined to offer even the moderate concessions sought by Miliukov. Nicholas was bolstered in his opposition to reform by Alexandra. As she wrote in July 1915 of its recall, 'I assure you only harm will arise – they speak too much. Russia, thank God, is not a constitutional country.'[9] When Sir George Buchanan urged the Tsar to create a more representative government in January 1917, saying it would enable him to regain his people's confidence, Nicholas replied, 'Do you mean I am to regain the confidence of my people or that they are to regain *my* confidence?'[10] On 6 March 1917 Nicholas suggested that he was prepared finally to appoint a 'responsible government' but then changed his mind the following day and left for Mogilev.

Much actual day-to-day administration increasingly fell into the hands of so-called 'voluntary' organisations such as the All Russian Union of Zemstvos (rural councils), headed by a liberal monarchist, Prince Georgy L'vov, and the Union of Municipalities. Both emerged in August 1914, initially to organise relief of the sick and wounded. In June 1915 the two organisations, both of which were largely controlled from Moscow, created Zemgor as an agency to intervene in war supply. The emergence of Zemgor was followed by the creation in June 1915, in a further extension of the self-mobilisation process of business and industry, of the Central War Industries Committee (TsVPK), under Guchkov, and other similar local War Industries Committees (VPKs). The significance of these public organisations and of the Progressive Bloc, which was closely linked to them, was the assertion by the educated middle classes of their role in the state. Consequently, the government was intensely suspicious of the VPKs, of Guchkov's attack on state bureaucracy, and of the Moscow-based challenge to the monopoly of the metal industries centred on Petrograd.

Unfortunately, the duplication of effort between state and public organisations undermined the ability of both to maximise war production. Under the direction of Guchkov and his deputy, A. I. Konovalov, leader of the Progressists, the VPKs became increasingly politicised. By contrast, Miliukov lapsed into passivity in the expectation that only the recall of the Duma could solve Russia's problems. Guchkov addressed criticisms of the government to the army chief of staff, Mikhail Alekseev, in August 1916 and attempted to draw other officers into some kind of action to force the Tsar to abdicate. Alekseev, who had been appointed by Nicholas in September 1915, was a modest man of relatively humble origins, his father having been only a junior officer. Despite the Tsar's presence, Stavka became far less aristocratic and far more effective under Alekseev for all that he appeared unable to delegate. He was honest and notably apolitical but even he called for a single minister to oversee the war economy in June 1916. The most politically damaging aspect of the VPKs, however, was their championing of labour representation within industry. It proved so because the resulting workers' groups failed to achieve any worthwhile gains for labour. This so radicalised the central workers' group in Petrograd that, under Menshevik influence in November 1916, it demanded the immediate establishment of a provisional revolutionary government. Both the Petrograd and Moscow central groups then called for a strike in January 1917 in commemoration of the 'Bloody Sunday' of the 1905 revolution. Most of the leadership was arrested in February 1917, but there was escalating strike action and general unrest in Petrograd through February and March 1917.

Strike action reflected the way in which industry had responded to the war. It has been sometimes assumed that Russian industry simply collapsed under the strain of wartime production. Initially, it was certainly affected by mobilisation and by the loss of Poland in 1915, 15 per cent of the terri- tory, 23 per cent of the population, a fifth of coal and a tenth of iron-ore resources being lost to Germans. As elsewhere, Russia also suffered a shell shortage in 1915. This continued into 1916, the estimated monthly require- ment being 1.5 million shells at a time when only 140,000 were being produced. The government itself declined to believe that its industry could cope, with the result that it ordered large amounts of munitions from Britain and the United States. In any case, the government took the view that resources would be better spent on purchasing shells overseas than in developing new factories, which would be idle in peacetime.

In the event, overseas manufacturers, already struggling to fill orders from their own governments, failed to match Russian expectations. By November 1916 foreign suppliers had delivered only 7.1 million of the 40.5 million shells ordered. Even if they did arrive, there was still the problem of transporting them. The northern ports were closed by ice for much of the year and the Trans-Siberian Railway was capable of handling only 280 railway wagons a day. Little was done to sort out the chaos that developed at Archangel in northern Russia and, while a railway connecting it to Petrograd was completed in 1917, the development of Murmansk as an ice-free port was not finished until 1923. By March 1917 American boot manufacturers had resorted to sending their products by parcel post.[11]

Russia's own industrialists led the demand to be allowed to reorganise the war economy. In the wake of the retreat from Galicia and the shell shortage, the Special Council of Defence was established by industry and the Duma in May 1915 on the model of the British Ministry of Munitions. It was intended to encourage amalgamation and consolidation of industrial units, and to channel government finance to key areas such as munitions and railways. In all, the Special Councils, of which four were created, spent some 15 million roubles between 1914 and 1917, representing about a third of all government expenditure.

The prices charged by private enterprise, however, rose significantly and there was inefficiency and corruption, as well as a failure of coordination.

In the process, the labour force in heavy industry quadrupled between 1914 and 1916. The number of miners doubled, the numbers in the building trade went up by a third, and those employed in the oil industry increased to half a million. The number of women employed in manufacturing also rose by between 30 and 40 per cent by 1916. In all, the total urban population expanded from 22 million in 1914 to 28 million by 1916. Overall, Russia's economy grew by 21.6 per cent between 1913 and 1916, and there was more modernisation and standardisation of manufacturing processes. Though productivity declined rapidly after 1916, therefore, it could be argued that the mounting economic crisis was born of over-rapid growth.

The problem was that industrial expansion was based on a few areas like Petrograd and Moscow, which were precisely those most affected by food and housing shortages. Between 1914 and 1917, the Petrograd labour force increased from 242,000 to 391,000 and in Moscow from 153,000 to 205,000. With municipal authorities forced to compete for food supplies on the open market, prices rose. Inflation was also encouraged by the amount of money the government had to raise in loans since it was reluctant to incur unpopularity by raising taxes. By 1917, the budgetary deficit of 1.9 billion roubles in 1914 had increased to 31.1 billion. There was little check on inflation so that a price index for Petrograd set at 100 in December 1914 would have reached 192 by December 1916. A similar index of 100 set in Moscow in December 1913 would have reached 361 by January 1917. Prices rose even more rapidly between March and November 1917. Effectively, while wages had gone up by between 50 per cent and 200 per cent depending upon the industry, all prices had increased by at least 100 per cent and, in some cases, by 500 per cent. Not unexpectedly, strikes were ever more prevalent, from 1,946 in 1915 to 2,306 in 1916, with 751 in the first two months of 1917.

Exacerbating all the other problems was the sheer number of refugees who moved into central Russia from Galicia, Poland and the Caucasus to escape military operations. There were already 3.5 million refugees by 1915, and conceivably as many as 7.4 million by July 1917. The numbers were fuelled by the Russians themselves forcibly deporting Jews and other minorities such as ethnic Germans from western Russia as they retreated in 1915. As elsewhere, there was much hostility to perceived aliens, over

3,000 premises of supposedly foreign ownership being looted in Moscow in May 1915. Minority groups that would have remained loyal to the state in other circumstances were alienated from it.[12]

All this put much more strain on food supplies. The food crisis afflicting Russia by 1917 was once attributed to declining production, as a result of conscription of the agricultural labour force and the greater mobility of the remaining rural labour force seeking new opportunities in industry. In fact, with women, prisoners of war and refugees making up some of the labour shortfall, agricultural production actually grew with good harvests. The real difficulty was one of transportation. It was not the case, as is sometimes imagined, of grain chasing trains but, as Norman Stone has argued, of trains chasing grain.[13] Food was not a transport priority and track maintenance had declined, but the whole pre-war system had been geared to taking bulk supplies from larger producers. Wartime increase in production took place among smaller producers, thus requiring longer rail journeys and more trains. Such were the difficulties of marketing that many peasants either resorted to feeding surplus to livestock or reverted to subsistence agriculture.

As a result, by 1917, despite some 2.5 billion roubles being spent on the rail network, Petrograd was receiving not much more than half its daily requirement of grain and Moscow only a third. Bread and flour rationing were introduced in Moscow on 11 March 1917, having been resisted previously for fear of raising expectations that could not be fulfilled. Significantly, the revolution erupted in Petrograd on the back of food disturbances compounded by fuel shortages and severe winter weather, which exacerbated the transport crisis. Ironically, crowds on the streets were swelled once the disturbances began by a sudden improvement in the weather, which encouraged people to go outside after several months' confinement.

At this point, another key factor was the disintegration of the army. While shortage of material has been advanced as the primary reason for Russian military disasters in the Great War, these have been exaggerated in the sense that the German and Austro-Hungarian forces on the Eastern Front were also frequently short of supplies. The Russian army also performed better than is sometime suggested, capturing more German and Austro-Hungarian prisoners of war than the British and French combined, and also accounting for a higher percentage of German combat deaths than the Western allies. Indeed, it won significant victories against the Austro-Hungarian army in Galicia in 1915 and at least initially during the Brusilov offensive in June 1916.

The 'old army', however, was effectively destroyed in 1915. Only harsh discipline kept the army together. Increasing fraternisation with German and Austro-Hungarian troops was perceived as growing evidence of war-weariness. Most Russian soldiers were peasants, and they were affected by separation from home and land, and unsettled by events on the home front. They also appear to have had little interest in Russia's wider war aims although they would have fought willingly in defence of Russia itself. In fact, the replication of peasant society in the army's ranks and the bonding of military service helped preserve the army as a military instrument at least until early 1917, when the abdication of the Tsar removed the vital tradi-tional cement underpinning discipline.

The Russians did have a major manpower problem, with almost 6 million casualties by January 1917. Losses badly affected the officer corps. Many new officers, recruited from the middle classes and from students, were, to quote Allan Wildman, 'negatively disposed' towards the government through their previous involvement in politics or their awareness of progressive ideals.[14] At the same time, the gulf between officers and men steadily widened as soldiers increasingly questioned poor treatment of the wounded, censorship of mail, and dwindling rations, a factor made more significant by the relatively generous provision of rations in 1914. Trained NCOs were also a decreasing asset.

By the autumn of 1916, therefore, there was a number of mutinies. Battle fatigue and war-weariness were factors, but politicisation of the army was mainly a feature of rear garrisons and transport centres. As with the indus-trial working force, most recruits tended to be trained in large centres such as Moscow, Petrograd and Kiev, where they suffered the same privations as the civilian population with few officers to control them.

Sailors of the Baltic Fleet were to prove still more radical than the army. The majority of the Russian seamen were of non-peasant background and literate. More significantly, due to a combination of ice-bound ports and German naval domination of the Baltic, they spent long periods in bases such as Helsingfors (Helsinki) in Finland, Reval (Tallinn) in Estonia and Kronstadt close to Petrograd, where they were frequently in contact with shipyard and other industrial workers. Moreover, many naval officers were of Baltic-German or Finnish origin, and were thus distanced from their men by both class and nationality.

Discipline amid the enforced idleness of naval life was often harsh. In the case of the cruiser *Aurora*, for example, which was sent to undergo repairs in Petrograd in September 1916, a new commanding officer attempted to tighten discipline at a time when the crew were working alongside workers in a Socialist Revolutionary stronghold. When the disturbances broke out in Petrograd in March 1917, the crew were confined to the ship and some workers were detained in the ship's brig. The crew mutinied on 13 March, murdering the captain and his executive officer. There is little evidence that the majority of sailors belonged to any political organisation and revolt was almost certainly spontaneous. It spread to Kronstadt on the same day, to Reval on 15 March, and to Helsingfors on 16 March. At least 76 naval officers were killed and over 300 arrested in the course of a few days.

In Petrograd the chain of events leading to revolution was set off on Thursday, 8 March 1917 by a riot of women textile workers from the Vyborg district who were queuing for flour. Ironically, it was International Working Women's Day, an event first suggested by the German Social Democrat, Clara Zetkin, in 1910: it had then been held in a number of European states in 1911, and had been observed in Russia for the first time in 1913. As suggested earlier, the number of women in industry had increased, women comprising some 43.2 per cent of the Russian industrial labour force by 1917. As elsewhere, they experienced at first hand the problems of keeping their families fed. One calculation is that, by 1917, the average working woman in Petrograd spent forty hours a week in queues for food or other requirements. Police agents had been reporting mounting distress for months. The women were quickly joined by militant metalworkers.

There were at least 180,000 troops available in the capital. Most, however, were under training or recovering from wounds, with only perhaps 12,000 regarded as reliable. Protopopov had worked on a plan to maintain order with the war minister, General Mikhail Beliaev; the City Prefect, General A. P. Balk; and Lieutenant General Sergei Khabalov, whom he had recommended to Alexandra as military governor of the Petrograd region. It did not amount to much, however, and the strikes took all by surprise. Spreading out from Vyborg, large crowds of women gathered on the Sampsonesvsky Prospect on 8 March and headed for the Aleksandrovsky bridge over the Neva, which would have given them access to the city's main thoroughfare of Nevsky Prospect. Police blocked the bridges, but large numbers of people got across the frozen river. On 9 March, with workers joining the women, the police were unable to hold the bridges and there were some violent clashes and widespread looting. More troops were apparent on 10 March but they were not called upon to open fire, and generally mingled with crowds in what now amounted to a general strike. In any case, the troops would have been reluctant to fire on women representing wives and mothers of servicemen. Therefore, when on Sunday, 11 March, Khabalov in the Tsar's name ordered the army to suppress the disturbances and to open fire, as well as threatening to conscript strikers, troops began to mutiny. Opening fire on the crowd by a training company of the regiment located at the Pavlovsky Barracks led to mutiny by the rest of the regiment. The Volynsky Regiment of the Imperial Guard also went over to the crowds. With further reinforcements unable to move on the frozen rail lines, the Tsar's younger brother, Grand Duke Michael – the ineffectual 'Misha' – took the decision to abandon the Winter Palace on the night of 11/12 March at a time when crowds had actually dispersed.

The atmosphere that Sunday was curious. Stella Arbenina, an actress from an English family long resident in Russia and the wife of Baron Paul Meyendorff, went to the theatre. Driving through virtually empty streets, she found not much more than fifty people present for a performance of what had been a wildly popular play. By contrast, when returning to his residence, the French ambassador Maurice Paléologue witnessed the lights burning brightly and a party in full swing at the town house of Prince Léon Radziwill. Returning to Petrograd from Reval in the early hours of Monday, 12 March, Meriel Buchanan found the city strangely deserted: 'In the bleak, grey light of that early morning the town looked inexpressibly desolate and deserted . . . the streets seemed completely empty, nearly all the shops were boarded up, not a face showed at the windows of any of the houses.'[15]

The change later that morning was dramatic. Hearing sudden firing and 'a strange and prolonged din' from the direction of the Aleksandrovsky bridge while he was at breakfast, Paléologue went to the window. He recorded 'a disorderly mob carrying red flags appeared at the end which is on the right bank of the Neva, and a regiment came towards it from the opposite side. It looked as if there would be a violent collision, but on the contrary the two bodies coalesced. The army was fraternising with revolt.'[16] Similarly, looking from his window at soldiers thronging the street outside, the British military attaché, Alfred Knox, thought himself like a spectator 'in a gigantic cinema.'[17] In the normally quiet Sergvievsskaia district, Stella Arbenina was equally startled by the sudden sight of two lorries full of soldiers, workers and 'horrible disreputable women, whom they were embracing in the street', with others running alongside. It soon dawned on her that the soldiers were Imperial Guardsmen. It was a 'hideous, nauseating spectacle that remains graven in my memory. I could not believe my eyes.'[18]

By the evening of 12 March the Council of Ministers had dissolved itself and surrendered authority to an ad hoc executive committee of the Duma hastily convened in the Tauride Palace, and dominated by Alexandr Kerensky, a lawyer and Trudovik deputy. A Provisional Government then emerged on 14 March under Prince L'vov with Miliukov as Foreign Minister, Guchkov as Minister of War, and Kerensky as Minister of Justice. Kerensky authorised the arrest of a number of Tsarist ministers and officials. The authority of the new government, however, was already being challenged ominously by the self-appointed and Menshevik-dominated Petrograd Soviet of Workers' and Soldiers' Deputies, led by Irakli Tsereteli, which had emerged on 10 March.

At the time of the initial disturbances, Nicholas and Alexandra were preoccupied with the measles that had struck Aleksei and his eldest sister, Olga. Alexandra merely reported to Nicholas on 9 March that 'the poor people stormed the bread shops', before passing rapidly on to the condition of the children. The following day, by which time Tatiana had also succumbed to measles, Alexandra was attributing 'a hooligan movement' of 'young boys & girls running and screaming', and 'work men preventing others fr. work', to the long spell of cold weather. She felt it would soon quieten down. She was at least aware that lack of bread was a problem and proposed sending an officer to speak to Khabalov about using military ovens to bake bread for the population. On 11 March Alexandra suggested that 200,000 people were now involved in the disorders but that 'all adore you & *only* want bread'. She accepted the assurances from some Duma members that all would be calm by the following day. She feared above all that, without her presence by his side, Nicholas might be forced to sign 'some paper of theirs, constitution or some such horror'. Indeed she did not learn of her husband's abdication until the day after it had occurred.[19]

Nicholas, meanwhile, who had only returned to Stavka on 7 March, was aware of the transport difficulties resulting from the bad weather, with locomotive boilers frozen and tracks blocked by snow. However, he confined his replies to Alexandra almost entirely to his children's health. He expressed the hope that Potopopov would direct Khabalov to act firmly against the 'street rows'. A telegram on 11 March from Mikhail Rodzianko, the Octobrist chairman of the Duma, specifically warned Nicholas that the situation was out of hand and that concessions had to be made immediately. Nicholas ignored it, telling the Swedish-born minister of the imperial court and household, Count Vladimir Fredericks, 'That fat guy Rodzianko has again written me all sorts of nonsense, to which I will not even give a reply.'[20] Nicholas, who believed recuperating soldiers were primarily responsible for the disorders, told Alexandra that Alekseev, who had only just returned from sick leave, was one of the few at Stavka who remained calm. But Alekseev, too, urged the appointment of new ministers to take action. According to Lieutenant General Alexandr Lukomsky, Nicholas refused to discuss the matter with Alekseev who, still feeling ill, took to his room with a temperature of 102°. Having considered the issue, Nicholas subsequently sent for Alekseev, but Lukomsky reported he was in bed. The Tsar handed Lukomsky a telegram for the Council of Ministers, telling him to relay to Alekseev, 'that this is my last word, that I will not change my mind, and that consequently it will be useless to report anything more on the subject'.[21] Other warnings were also equally casually dismissed, including those of Aleksei Brusilov, commanding the Southwestern Front, Nikolai Ruzsky, commanding the Northern Front, and the Tsar's brother, Michael. Telegrams from Beliaev, Protopopov and Khabalov had all tended to suggest that the disorder had been contained. It was only on 12 March that Khabalov requested units to be sent to Petrograd urgently from the front, though Beliaev was still insisting that 'I am firmly convinced that calm will soon arrive.'[22]

Having prorogued the Duma, and ordered the Guard Cavalry and other troops under General Nikolai Ivanov to Petrograd to restore order, Nicholas set out to return the 500 miles to his capital from Stavka early on 13 March.

The Tsar's train was halted in the early hours on 14 March by the news of mutinous troops blocking the line. The train diverted to Ruzsky's headquarters at Pskov. Alekseev now took the initiative with his fellow generals in cooperation with the Duma, the liberal opposition having been assiduously cultivating the army's leadership ever since 1915. Having effectively suspended any military coercion by informing Ivanov that the Tsar would almost certainly appoint a new government, and this would 'change your manner of action', Alekseev drafted a new manifesto for the Tsar to sign.[23] Ruzsky, who was the most committed of the increasing number of military dissidents, had supposedly been wearing rubber galoshes as a token of disrespect when he arrived late to greet the Tsar at Pskov station. He also urged concessions on the Tsar. Finally yielding, Nicholas sent a telegram to Rodzianko indicating he was now prepared to make the concession of a government responsible to the Duma. Rodzianko tersely replied, 'It is too late.'[24]

Rodzianko, who was in close touch with Ruzsky, now communicated the belief of the Provisional Government that the Tsar must abdicate. On 14 March, too, the imperial family itself had begun to break ranks. The Tsar's brother Michael, his uncle Grand Duke Paul, and his cousin Grand Duke Cyril all signed a declaration recognising the Provisional Government. As the Tsar slept, Alekseev contacted leading commanders, including Grand Duke Nicholas now commanding in the Caucasus, all of whom supported the decision. These replies came in during the morning of 15 March and were presented to Nicholas. He now realised that, without the military's support, he had little alternative. At 1500 hours on 15 March, therefore, and without visible emotion, Nicholas signed a document pre-prepared by Lukomsky. Initially, Nicholas abdicated in favour of his son but, having taken advice from one of his doctors that Aleksei was incurable and likely to die young, nominated his brother Michael, instead. Unaware of events at Pskov, Guchkov and Vasily Shulgin of the Progressists, representing the Provisional Government, arrived in the evening to try and persuade the Tsar to abdicate. Consequently, they oversaw a redraft of the abdication document favouring Michael, which the Tsar signed at 2340 hours, though it was agreed that it would bear the time of 1500 hours. Nicholas again displayed no reaction though he confided to his diary, 'All around are treason, cowardice and deception.' A telegram to Alexandra did not even mention the abdication.[25]

Whether Nicholas had any legal authority to nominate Michael, who had married a divorced commoner and had been forced as a result to renounce any claim to the throne in 1913, was a moot point. In the discussions with Nicholas, indeed, Guchkov remarked that the Provisional Government had counted on Aleksei's accession 'having a softening effect on the transfer of power'.[26] It was soon clear from the demonstrations outside the Tauride Palace that Michael would be unacceptable in Petrograd. Kerensky pointedly told Michael that the government could not guarantee his safety. Deciding that he could only accept the throne if invited to do so by a proposed constituent assembly, Michael then also renounced the throne at 1800 hours on 16 March. On 21 March Nicholas was arrested at Mogilev, to which he had returned from Pskov. He was moved to Tsarkoe Selo to be reunited with Alexandra next day. The imperial family was transferred to Tobol'sk in August 1917.

In March it still seemed that Russia would survive as a belligerent. The basic aspirations of workers and peasants alike, as expressed in resolutions of various workers and villagers' committees, or soviets, which began to spring up in March 1917, were largely economic rather than political. Nationalist aspirations appeared a more serious threat to the state, particularly those emanating from the Baltic States and the Ukraine. In response, the Provisional Government recognised the principle of Polish independence and granted autonomy to Finland. Other reforms were also implemented, including freedom of the press and of association, the disestablishment of the Orthodox Church, the independence of the judiciary, and the replacement of the police with a militia. The new government erred, however, in not pushing land redistribution. Similarly, influenced by the opposition of industrialists to price controls and increased taxes, it mismanaged the economy. A division of authority soon emerged between the government on the one hand, which was backed by the generals, the bureaucrats, industrialists and the Duma, and the soviets on the other. Above all, the Provisional Government committed itself to a new military offensive in order to establish its military and diplomatic credibility with the Entente. It soon ground to a halt, with further disintegration in the army, and paralysing chaos within government.

The Bolsheviks were the only group advocating peace at any cost, one reason why the German General Staff facilitated Lenin's return to Russia from Switzerland in April 1917. Most of the Bolshevik leadership had been in exile and the overthrow of the Tsar clearly took the party by surprise. The continuation of the war, however, enabled it to begin to gain ground, leading ultimately to its successful coup in Petrograd on 6–7 November 1917. The resulting civil war continued until 1921. Estimates of the deaths in Russia between 1917 and 1921 as a result of the civil war, and concomitant disease and starvation, range between 2.8 million and 6 million.

In the short term, the democratic credentials of the Provisional Government benefited the Entente. Not least, this played well in the United States, which joined the war against Germany in April 1917. Initially, too, Russian pledges to its allies suggested continued effort on the Eastern Front: Russia had been rather more responsive to its partners' military demands and needs since 1914 than Britain and France had been in return. In the medium term, the Provisional Government's collapse, and the peace treaty signed between Lenin and the Germans at Brest-Litovsk in March 1918, freed German resources for a new offensive in the west. That provided a severe challenge to the Entente before substantial US forces could arrive in Europe. In the longer term, however, the overthrow of Tsarist Russia had its most dramatic impact with the emergence of communism.

Communism claimed many victims. Several of those intimately connected with the events of March 1917 ultimately escaped Russia but Protopopov, Ruzsky and Beliaev were executed by the Bolsheviks in 1918. Alekseev died of disease while fighting against them that same year. The imperial family was not spared. Grand Duke Paul was executed in January 1919. Michael was killed at Perm on 10 July 1918, supposedly while trying to escape from detention in what was almost certainly an attempt staged by the Bolsheviks themselves. Nicholas and his family were seized by local Bolsheviks at Tobol'sk in April 1918. Moved to Ekaterinburg in May, Nicholas and Alexandra, their five children, the family doctor, the cook, a footman, a maid and the pet dog were all slaughtered on 16/17 July 1918. The remains of all but Aleksei and Maria were discovered in 1979: remains of the two missing bodies were found subsequently in 2007. The remains of Nicholas and his family were reinterred in the St Peter and Paul Cathedral in St Petersburg in July 1998, just across the Neva from Dvortsovaya Square where that revealing photograph was taken eighty-four years previously.

CHAPTER 9

THE SHADOW OF THE BOMBER

The First Gotha Air Raid on London, 13 June 1917

THERE IS a number of ceramic plaques commemorating the heroism of ordinary Londoners in 'Postman's Park' off Aldersgate Street in the City, named for the nearby headquarters of the old General Post Office. Originally conceived by the artist and sculptor G. F. Watts in 1900, the 'memorial to heroic self-sacrifice' has 120 spaces for plaques. A total of forty-eight spaces had been filled by 1908. One more was added in June 1919, three in 1930, one in 1931, and the fifty-fourth only in 2009. That added in 1919 remembers Police Constable Alfred Smith 'who was killed in an air raid while saving the lives of women and girls'. It bears the date of Wednesday, 13 June 1917. Smith was on duty in Central Street in Finsbury when he pushed women and girls from the Debenhams warehouse back inside a building. He closed the door on them just as a bomb exploded outside, killing him instantly. It was one of 72 bombs that fell across central London that day.

The subsequent coroner's inquiry heard from the widow of thirty-seven-year old Smith that he had gone on duty at 0830 hours. He was feeling unwell but 'he said that he "wanted to do his duty"'. One of the 'large number' of young women testified that they had tried to flee the building when the cry of 'Bombs' went up, because it seemed 'natural' to do so. It was also alleged that they had run into the street 'from excitement and curiosity'. Smith's body was found in the porch some 41 feet from where the bomb fell, a doctor suggesting that he would have been able to take

shelter 'if he had not been keeping the young women in'. Having observed
to one female witness that 'I should have thought the best thing to do was
to keep under shelter,' the coroner concluded of Smith that 'in helping to
save lives he sacrificed his own'.[1]

London had experienced raids since May 1915 but this was different
in being in broad daylight, and by aircraft. Previous raids had been by
Zeppelin airships, the threat of which had been largely neutralised by
improving air defences and by the technical deficiencies of the Zeppelins
themselves. Only nine Zeppelin raids had actually reached central London,
the largest on the night of 13/14 October 1915 involving just three airships.
A total of 47 Londoners had been killed on that occasion and, in all, only
181 lives had been lost to date, with a further 504 injured. But the raid on
13 June 1917 by 14 of the new Gotha GIV heavy bombers killed 162 people
in London, Essex and Kent, and injured a further 432: two of the dead and
eighteen of the injured were from falling shrapnel from anti-aircraft guns.
Among the dead were eighteen children from the Upper North Street
School in Poplar, sixteen of them from the infant class aged between four
and six. All the German aircraft returned safely to their bases despite
ninety-two separate sorties by home defence fighter aircraft. Only five of
the eleven pilots who got close enough to the Gothas to exchange fire
claimed to have caused any damage, and one British air gunner was killed.
On 7 July a further 21 Gothas appeared over London, killing another fifty-
four people. It was a shocking demonstration of the potential of aerial
bombing that shaped public attitudes to the coming of war in Britain and
Europe in the 1930s.

The psychological impact of new weapons may be far greater than their
actual physical effect if the sheer novelty induces fear among the public.
Fear may then lead to predictions about the future of warfare based on
only limited operational experience: precisely this resulted from the Gotha
raids. Zeppelins had seemed terrifying enough but the introduction of the
Gotha caused near panic, not least around the War Cabinet table. A few
months later, the Chief of the Imperial General Staff, Sir William Robertson,
took the British liaison officer at French General Headquarters, Sidney
Clive, to a War Cabinet meeting. Clive expressed surprise at the unedifying
wrangling. Robertson laconically observed, 'They were very good today.
You should see them after an air raid.'[2] The raids led to riotous attacks on

supposed German-owned property in the East End. They also persuaded King George V to change his dynastic name from Saxe-Coburg-Gotha to Windsor on 27 July 1917. A whole myth that 'the bomber always gets through' developed, partly due to the conclusions of a committee chaired by the South African statesman Jan Smuts in response to the raids. Yet, only 1,413 deaths and 3,408 injuries from air attack occurred in Britain throughout the entire war.

Technically, aerial attack on non-military targets was prohibited by the Hague Conventions of 1899 and 1907. Since Germany had not signed either, any prohibition was not operative, for it only applied to conflicts between signatories and only Britain, the United States, Belgium and Portugal had signed up to this particular prohibition. In any case, since the wording of the conventions was obscure with regard to aerial warfare, most states assumed bombing military targets would be legitimate once greater accuracy could be achieved. The 1899 Convention had applied to balloons, since Count Ferdinand von Zeppelin's first rigid airship flew for the first time only in July 1900, and the Wright brothers only made the first heavier than air flight in December 1903. A further attempt to codify the rules for aerial warfare in Paris in June 1911 was first adjourned until November, and then put off indefinitely.

There had been some expectation of air attack since the 1890s, dramatic aerial bombardment being as much a part of pre-war popular literature as invasion or spy stories. Lord Northcliffe, proprietor of the *Daily Mail*, warned of Britain's vulnerability to air attack from 1906 onwards, while H. G. Wells also predicted aerial warfare in his influential *The War in the Air* in 1908. In July 1909 Louis Blériot flew across the English Channel, increasing anxieties. R. P. Hearne's *Aerial Warfare* of the same year then helped precipitate a so-called Zeppelin scare, as did Charles Urban's feature film, *The Airship Destroyer*. Anxiety increased steadily, climaxing in the appearance of the German passenger airship, *Hansa*, over Britain in February 1913. Once war broke out, however, the press tended to emphasise initially the difficulties the Zeppelins would encounter from wind and cloud over Britain. By 1914 the Germans had built 11 airships, 10 of them aluminium Zeppelins and one similar wooden Schütte Lanz model. The Deputy Chief of the German Naval Staff, Paul Behncke, urged their immediate use against London, but ten of the airships were army operated and, of these, seven were allocated to support land operations. There were not sufficient airships available, therefore, to undertake bombing raids on Britain until early 1915.

On 22 September 1914 the Royal Naval Air Service (RNAS), which had a wider view of the potential of offensive airpower than the army's Royal Flying Corps (RFC), carried out the first genuine strategic bombing mission against a military target. This was aimed at the Zeppelin sheds at Düsseldorf and Cologne. One aircraft scored a direct hit on a hanger at Düsseldorf but the bomb did not explode. In turn, Zeppelins undertook the first attack on ships at sea on 25 December 1914, ironically intercepting the British naval force launching the first seaborne air attack – by seaplanes – on the Zeppelin sheds at Cuxhaven. The first air raids on civilian targets were those by Zeppelins on French and Belgian Channel ports on 21 August 1914, followed by a raid on Paris on 30 August. Great Yarmouth became the first British town attacked by airship on the night of 19/20 January 1915. The German army-operated Zeppelin *LZ 38* then attacked London for the first time on the night of 31 May/1 June 1915, 28 bombs and 91 incendiaries being dropped over East London in accordance with restrictions placed on the operation.

Behncke certainly believed that aerial attack would have a significant psychological impact on civilian morale in Britain, in much the same way it was also assumed later that unrestricted submarine warfare would have a longer-term impact through the effects of starvation. It suggests perhaps more a calculation as to the general impact of such strategies on civilians than any specific belief about the nature of British society in particular. The Kaiser had resisted authorising an air attack on London, but agreed that the docks might be a legitimate target in February 1915. Similarly, he agreed to the bombing of areas to the east of the Tower of London on 5 May 1915. *LZ 38*, therefore, was governed by the limitation, 16 Alkham Road in Stoke Newington having the dubious privilege of being the first house in the capital to be hit: the inhabitants fortunately escaped injury though there were seven fatalities as a result of the raid as a whole. German Chancellor Bethmann-Hollweg finally agreed to attacks on central London on 9 July 1915. He stipulated, however, that they should take place between Saturday afternoon and Monday morning so as to minimise casualties, and that no historic buildings should be bombed.

The former restriction took little account of the vagaries of the weather. The Kaiser removed most restrictions on 20 July except that forbidding the targeting of historic buildings, somewhat impracticably given the primitive nature of bombing. Trying deliberately to hit the Admiralty and War Office buildings on 14 October 1915, for example, the German navy's *L15* dropped its bombs and incendiaries instead on the theatre district north of the Strand, the Inns of Court and the City. Its commander, Joachim Breithaup, later wrote that the scene was 'indescribably beautiful – shrapnel bursting all around (though rather uncomfortably near us), our own bombs bursting and the flashes from the anti-aircraft batteries below. On either hand, the other airships, which, like us, were caught in the rays of the searchlights, were visible. And over us the starlit sky! Still, at such a moment one is inclined to be a little insensitive to the beauties of nature and to the feelings of the people below. It is only afterwards that all comes to one's consciousness.'[3]

In one sense, the British public had already become aware of the likelihood of coming under attack. The first, brief, use of German unrestricted submarine warfare in 1915 was certainly an indirect means of attacking civilians by trying to starve Britain out. Direct attack, however, had also featured prior to the arrival of the Zeppelins. On 16 December 1914 the German High Seas Fleet bombarded West Hartlepool, Scarborough and Whitby in an attempt to lure the British Grand Fleet into a naval engagement. Over 1,500 shells were fired, causing 127 deaths – the majority in Hartlepool – and forcing thousands to flee temporarily. The youngest victim was six months old and the oldest eighty-six. The event was so unprecedented that it was said over 10,000 visitors went to Scarborough to see the damage. Visiting the town herself over Christmas, Sylvia Pankhurst reported, 'The big amusement "palaces" on the front were scarred and battered by shell-fire, iron columns twisted and broken, brickwork crumbling, windows gone. Yawning breaches disclosed the pictures and furnishings, riddled and rent by the firing, dimmed and discoloured by blustering winds and spray.' There was a sense of panic: 'People could not sleep now; many would not even go to bed. Everyone had a bundle made up in readiness for flight; but how little one could carry in a bundle! One could not afford to move's one's home; and one's living was here in Scarborough.'[4] In fact, the Germans had actually opened fire on Great Yarmouth and Lowestoft on 3 November 1914 but at such a distance that few were aware of what had taken place. Naval bombardment of civilian targets was not repeated on a large scale, some twelve incidents taking place over the war as a whole.[5] In an emotive phrase that was later to become commonplace in reference to bombing, Churchill sent a message to the town's mayor on 20 December referring to the 'baby killers' of Scarborough.[6]

Rather like the naval bombardment of the east coast, Zeppelin raids attracted a mixture of emotions: fear and anger, but also curiosity. The first Zeppelin raid on Great Yarmouth resulted in two dead, a fifty-three-year-old shoemaker, Samuel Smith, and a seventy-two-year-old, Miss Martha Taylor. A woman playing the piano at the Fish Wharf Refreshment Rooms was blown off her stool but survived, while the door had been blown off the vestry of St Peter's Church. The landlord of the First and Last on Fish Quay picked up still-warm bomb fragments and handed them to the police. Two unexploded bombs were displayed in the Drill Hall. According to The Times the town had received only a 'slight headache'.[7] As in the case of Scarborough, the East End of London also attracted crowds in 1915 once bombing began. According to Sylvia Pankhurst, 'Impatient passengers on the tops of buses were asking before they had yet passed Bishopsgate: "Is this the East End?". Sightseers paused at Shoreditch Church because rumour declared it had been injured, though not a sign of damage was to be seen. Crowds stood with chins uncomfortably upstretched arguing whether the thin shadow cast by the lightning conductor might really be a crack.'[8]

Rumours were rife of German night surveys of potential targets, and the authorities attempted to play down the risks of so-called 'visits', primarily to prevent the Germans from gaining accurate intelligence. Consequently, the press resorted to printing German communiqués on the location of raids. On 31 April 1915 an explosion was heard in Greenwich and at the Royal Arsenal, Woolwich. Word spread of a 'terrible air attack on North London', to the extent that the lack of warning received caused arsenal workers temporarily to refuse to resume labour after the 'all clear' was announced. Those responsible for air-raid precautions at Woolwich enquired whether there had been a raid: 'Not an official one was the laconic reply.'[9] Bombs had actually fallen on Dalston, Leyton and Stoke Newington. The sensation of being under attack was itself an unusual experience. One worker at Woolwich leaning out of a window saw a

Zeppelin 'hovering about overhead' and heard a 'strange buzzing sound' followed by a crash and a 'cold blast of air' as a bomb hit a storeroom with a corrugated roof nearby, which 'rose into the air several feet and smashed down on the cobblestones'. A woman in London heard 'an odd chunkety, chunkety noise. It sounded as if a train with rusty wheels were travelling through the sky. I ran out on to the balcony and saw something which looked like a large silver cigar away to my left, and I realised that it was a Zeppelin.'[10]

The random (and seasonal) nature of Zeppelin attacks meant that there was no sustained pressure on domestic morale. Restaurants began to offer sausage and mash as 'Zepp and a portion of clouds'.[11] London theatres, however, reported audiences trailing off in 'Zeppelin weather' of dark, fine nights as the moon waned. The longest interruption of work at the Royal Arsenal in Woolwich was just six hours on 31 March 1916. But, at the same time, the unexpected occurrence of raids could bring criticism of the lack of defences. When Hull was bombed on 5 March 1916 – the Zeppelins had been struggling against high winds to reach the Firth of Forth – an RFC vehicle was stoned by indignant civilians. Soldiers were also attacked in Beverley. Backed by the *Daily Mail*, the colourful Noel Pemberton-Billing resigned from the RNAS and stood at a by-election at Mile End in January 1916 as an Independent, campaigning for more air-raid defences. A former soldier in the South African War, Pemberton-Billing had tried his hand at being a chauffeur, a bricklayer, an actor and a playwright before he became 'air-minded'. Establishing the first aerodrome in England at Fambridge in Essex in 1908, he also founded the Supermarine aviation company at Southampton in 1912. He was unsuccessful at Mile End but then won another by-election for East Hertfordshire in February 1916, demanding an 'Imperial Air Fleet', an air ministry and mass bombing of German towns. Known as the 'Member for Air', Pemberton-Billing's influence declined after the Smuts report was published. Subsequently, he featured in an extraordinary libel case in May 1918. Having alleged that the Germans had a list of 47,000 British men and women open to blackmail for sexual depravity, Pemberton-Billing stood accused of libelling the dancer and actress, Maud Allen, as a lesbian. He was acquitted amid the general hysteria concerning declining wartime sexual mores: he eventually retired from politics through ill health in 1923.

The Germans had originally intended to use conventional aircraft to bomb Britain in November 1914, establishing the euphemistically named 'Ostend Carrier Pigeon Detachment' in Belgium with the intention of basing it at Calais once the port fell into their hands. The failure of the 1914 offensive saw it transferred to the Eastern Front. The Aviatik B1 aircraft originally allocated would not have been effective as bombers. Re-equipped with heavier aircraft, the renamed Bombing Wing No. 1 was deployed to Bulgaria in 1915. The crews were sent back to Belgium in 1916 as Bombing Wing No. 3, or the English Squadron, under the command of Ernst Brandenburg. They received the new Gothas in March 1917. Now thirty-three, Brandenburg had transferred to the German air force as an observer in 1915 after a wound had rendered him unfit for further ground combat duties. Too capable to be restricted to such a relatively minor role, he was soon selected to organise and train the squadron for missions against Britain, the squadron being divided between four airfields around Ghent. Crewed by a pilot, a navigator and a rear gunner, the Gotha had no radio and no instruments for blind flying, necessitating good visibility for navigation. It was an unwieldy aircraft, quickly exhausting pilots, who grappled with the controls. Indeed, in the raid of 7 July 1917, three of the Gothas crashed over Belgium on the way back from London as a result of high winds. The Gotha could carry up to 880 pounds of bombs, however, typically comprising a mix of 22- or 110-pounds bombs, and incendiaries.

A lone German LVG aircraft had dropped six bombs over London on 28 November 1916, injuring ten people in the area of Harrods and Victoria Station, but the Gotha promised an impact of far greater magnitude. The first appearance of the Gotha was on 25 May 1917, 23 aircraft dropping 159 bombs on Folkestone. They killed 71 people, a number of whom had been queuing outside a shop for food. The scrambling of 74 defending aircraft succeeded in downing only one of the Gothas. There was an 'indignation' meeting in the town, and a deputation waited on Field Marshal Lord French, commanding Home Forces, on 30 May to enquire why there had been no warning. This first Gotha raid had been meant to reach London but had turned back amid dense cloud cover over Essex. Folkestone had become accustomed to attack, Thanet suffering the most air attacks during the war. One raid on 3 September 1917 resulted in 131 deaths in the naval barracks at Chatham. Dover was especially targeted in the autumn of

1917, the authorities opening up cliff shelters capable of holding over 25,000 people. Indeed, Dover was the first British town bombed by an aircraft, a lone German FF 29 floatplane having dropped two bombs in the sea close to Admiralty Pier on 21 December 1914, and another then dropping a bomb in a garden close to the castle on Christmas Eve. Dover had twenty-nine warnings in three months from September to November 1917: one every three days. At one point, there were thirteen consecutive nights when the sirens sounded. It was said that those 'who were free to change their residence at pleasure left for safer quarters'.[12]

The raid on London on 13 June 1917 should have involved 20 German aircraft but two turned back with engine trouble and a third did so after dropping its bombs on Margate at 1045 hours, killing four people. Three more broke away once over the English coast, one dropping bombs on Shoeburyness at 1120 hours, injuring two people, and another on Southweald, while the third flew a presumed reconnaissance flight over Greenwich without dropping any bombs. The remaining 14, flying in a rough diamond formation, appeared at about 15,000 feet over London at about 1130 hours in bright sunshine that made all the major sites quite visible to the Gotha crews. Many people on the ground assumed they were British aircraft and took no cover. Brandenburg fired a flare at 1135 hours, his aircraft dispersing at the signal to bomb individual targets. The attack was centred on Liverpool Street Station. Sixteen people were killed in the station, another nineteen in an office building at 65 Fenchurch Street, and thirteen including Constable Smith in Central Street, Finsbury. Those aircraft with bombs remaining released them over East London. Southwark and Dalston received hits; five bombs fell in East Ham; and fifteen across Blackwall, Poplar and Limehouse, including that on the Upper North Street school. Preliminary police reports submitted at 1900 hours recorded serious damage to an iron foundry in Beech Court, Barbican, and eight other premises in the City, mostly shops or warehouses, with Liverpool Street Station and a further sixty-four City buildings slightly damaged.[13] It was later calculated that £130,000 worth of damage had been done to property.

A Special Constable walking down Yeomans Row off the Brompton Road was mesmerised by the appearance of so many aircraft: 'the sight was so magnificent that I stood in the yard spellbound. The noise of the air being churned up by this fleet of aeroplanes was very loud.' His wife was on a bus in Knightsbridge when the raiders appeared and took cover in Hyde Park House, used as offices by the Admiralty: 'The basement was packed with women clerks, some of whom were crying hysterically. One caught hold of me. "Oh, I'm going to be killed! I'm going to be killed!" she moaned, pinching my arm so violently that what with pain and excitement I flared up and replied quite venomously, "I hope you *will*," which so surprised her that she stood still staring at me with her mouth open, the picture of idiocy. A girl near who also had been crying, but quietly, remarked, "You aren't very sympathetic." "I'm sorry," said I, beginning to recover my temper, "but my sympathies are with the men who have to bear this kind of thing day after day and night after night." I wasn't in the least brave, but I *was* excited.'[14] An American journalist on a bus noted that 'men and women strangely stood still, gazing up into the air. The conductor mounted the stairs to suggest that outside passengers should seek safety inside. Some of them did so. "I'm not a religious man," remarked the conductor, "but what I say is, we are all in God's hands and if we are going to die we may as well die quiet." But some inside passengers were determined that if they had to die quiet they might as well see something first and they climbed on top and with wonderstruck eyes watched the amazing drama of the skies.'[15] Generally remarking on the apparent excitement caused by the raid, *The Times* commented on the 'tendency of people to rush into the streets and stare skywards' rather than taking cover.[16]

There was widespread criticism at the lack of warning, most Londoners only becoming aware of the raid when bombs started dropping. As might be expected, there was particular outrage at the deaths of the Poplar infants, the bomb having penetrated two upper floors, killing two children on its way, before detonating in the infant class on the ground floor. London County Council denounced 'innocent victims of German barbarity'. A public funeral for the victims conducted by the Bishop of London took place on 20 June, the bodies being interred in a common grave in East London Cemetery. The mayor of Poplar, Will Crooks, announced that the victims had 'died as truly for their country and for everything worth dying for as any of our men at the front or on the high seas'.[17] Four teachers subsequently received the OBE and the public raised £1,455 19s. 11d for a memorial, which still stands in Poplar Recreation Ground in the East India Dock Road. A resolution was passed demanding reprisals at a meeting at the Opera House attended by the Lord Mayor on 17 June, and he headed a deputation to the Home Secretary four days later demanding better air-raid warnings.

The second raid, on 7 July, by 22 Gothas – two more had turned back, with one bombing Margate yet again – was centred on the City and the East End, with many falling close to Fenchurch Street. Anti-aircraft fire and a total of 101 RFC and RNAS fighters sent up to engage the Gothas made little impression. Only one Gotha was shot down on its return across the North Sea, and one forced down at Ostend through damage. Three more, as recounted earlier, were lost to high winds encountered on landing. Moreover, anti-aircraft fire had caused at least ten of the deaths in London from falling shrapnel.

Since the government had assured everyone that everything would be done to protect against air raids after the earlier raid, there was even greater indignation at 'the irritating and humiliating impunity' of the Gothas.[18] Riots occurred after the second raid in Bethnal Green, Dalston, Hackney and Holloway, with disturbances continuing for three days. In Dalston, for example, the local police station was attacked in an attempt to free those arrested. On 13 July a delegation of MPs waited on Lloyd George to call for improved air defence for London. The prime minister was naturally anxious to dispel false rumours, suggesting that bringing down four enemy machines was not only a reasonable effort but also urging a sense of proportion as to deaths from the raids and the losses incurred daily by the army on the Western Front.

Despite some examination of the problem of air defence by a subcommittee of the Committee of Imperial Defence in 1909, little thought had been given to coordinating it, and inter-service rivalry had continued to bedevil its evolution. There were only 33 anti-aircraft guns in the whole of England in August 1914, of which just 12 were allocated to London. Nearly all available RFC aircraft were also sent to France on the outbreak of war, though the RNAS had a number available for home defence. The RNAS was made primarily responsible for home defence against air raids, but the Zeppelin raids on London forced the RFC to divert additional aircraft from the Western Front in September 1915. The retired Admiralty gunnery expert, Admiral Sir Percy Scott, was also given the task of increasing the number of anti-aircraft guns available to defend the capital. By 1917 there were 11 fighter squadrons attached to the Home Defence Wing of the RFC, of which four were allocated to London. With the apparent decline of the Zeppelin threat, however, a number of pilots trained in night flying were sent to the Western Front in February 1917. On 6 March 1917, to facilitate manpower reductions in home defence when men were needed in France and Flanders, it was also decided to restrict anti-aircraft batteries from firing on even identifiably hostile aircraft outside of coastal areas: this was rescinded on 7 June 1917 following the initial Gotha raid on Folkestone.

From the beginning, it was left to local authorities to determine what precautions should be implemented. A blackout or rather 'dim out' was introduced for defended harbours in August 1914 and was extended to other designated areas including London on 1 October 1914. In April 1915 a blackout was extended to Middlesborough, Hartlepool and the Tees under permissive clause of the Defence of the Realm Act, it being arranged to dowse all lights and the glare of the local blast furnaces within twelve minutes of a warning. Zeppelin attacks on inland targets such as Burton-on-Trent and Walsall in January 1916 forced a more general extension. Lighting restrictions caused more difficulties than the raids themselves, leading to increased traffic accidents. Bizarrely, the chiming of public clocks was also stopped due to the fear that it might provide a navigational aid to Zeppelins. There were suggestions in London that lowering gas pressure or ringing telephones could be an additional means of warning of raids but not all people had gas, and even fewer had telephones. At the Royal Arsenal at Woolwich, where noise from factory machines made verbal warnings impossible, notices were held up, though these were eventually replaced by klaxons.

At least Zeppelins could be caught through their slow rate of climb. Flight Sub-Lieutenant Rex Warneford successfully dropped bombs on a LZ 37 on 6 June 1915 over Ghent, and Lieutenant W. Leefe Robinson shot down a similar Schütte Lanz SL 11 airship with new incendiary bullets over Cuffley in Hertfordshire on 2/3 September 1915. Not surprisingly, in view of the effect on morale, both Warneford and Leefe Robinson were awarded the Victoria Cross. Warneford was killed in a flying accident only a few days after downing the Zeppelin; Leefe Robinson died of influenza in the pandemic of 1918. Poor wireless security on the part of Zeppelin crews also greatly assisted British signals intelligence once the Naval Intelligence Division and Military Intelligence Division began to cooperate fully. The British often had a better idea of the location of Zeppelins than the latter's own crews. Losses mounted steadily, the doyen of Zeppelin commanders, Heinrich Mathy, jumping to his death from the burning and stricken *L31* on the night of 1/2 October 1916 over Potters Bar. In all, Germany lost 17 airships in combat, with 21 lost in accidents.

The Gotha raids were a different matter. Earlier warnings had not been given in the belief that false alarms would disrupt production and prove counter-productive. The Gothas compelled the introduction of an official air-raid warning system in July 1917, though there were doubts as to how effective it would prove in a major city. Generally, it was believed that people should have the opportunity to take cover should they wish, since it was not felt that the raids could seriously affect normality. Policemen on bicycles issued the warnings, though maroons were also fired. Boy Scouts sounded the 'all clear', and Automobile Association vehicles carried 'all clear' notices. Public shelters had to be improvised such as the caves at Chiselhurst, the London Underground, and the tunnels under the Thames at Rotherhithe, Blackwall, Greenwich and Woolwich. Surprisingly, it was not until July 1918 that the Metropolitan Police carried out a detailed survey of larger public shelters available in London, although they had surveyed the capacity of tube stations in early 1917. The public had taken to the tunnels before the War Office, the LCC and the Metropolitan Police could agree that they should be officially opened at night in August 1917. It was reported as early as September that up to 30,000 people were taking shelter in the Rotherhithe tunnel, between 10,000 and 12,000 in the Blackwall vehicle tunnel, and up to 3,000 in the small Greenwich and Woolwich pedestrian tunnels.[19] In the case of the underground, police were put on duty at 1700 hours each evening to control the crowds following the realisation that there was considerable overcrowding. It has been suggested, indeed, that as many as 300,000 people were sheltering in the London Underground in September 1917, there being six raids over eight nights. It was reported that the stations echoed to 'rollicking choruses' of popular songs, while the 'more youthful' danced.[20] Conceivably, therefore, more used the underground for air-raid shelters in proportion to the capital's population than in the Second World War.

On 28 January 1918 a raid caused panic at both Mile End underground station and the Bishopsgate Railway Goods Depot, where people were trying to get to shelter: a total of fourteen died at Bishopsgate when anti-aircraft fire was mistaken for falling bombs. In the same raid a bomb also hit Odhams Printing Works in Long Acre, killing thirty-eight, the floor giving way and sending the printing machines tumbling into the basement where people were sheltering. Others had taken to camping overnight in parks such as Richmond, and it was reported to the War Cabinet in October 1917 that Brighton was full of Jews from the East End, reflecting wider anti-Semitism. It was suggested by the coroner that the deaths in Bishopsgate were due to 'panic almost entirely on the part of persons who might be called foreigners', one newspaper carrying the headline, 'Cowardly Aliens in the Great Stampede'.[21] But it was not just aliens who were tempted to leave the capital. Following the raids in June and July 1917, *The Times* carried a full page of advertisements from potential havens. The Royal Beach Hotel at Southsea pronounced its 'perfect immunity from air raids', while it was similarly proclaimed, 'For safety and rest Bath is the best'.[22]

In 1915 the Metropolitan Police had simply advised remaining under cover in basements and keeping away from windows. Later, those unable to get to shelters were advised to avoid top-floor rooms, place mattresses on upper floors to cushion impact, turn off electricity and gas supplies, and to make sure of escape routes if the building was hit. More important buildings were draped with steel nets and national treasures were moved out of London. Two large paintings at the Royal Naval Hospital, Greenwich, of the *Battle of the Glorious First of June* by Philippe-Jacques de Loutherbourg and of the *Battle of Trafalgar* by J. M. W. Turner, were sent to the Welsh National Library at Aberystwyth: the crates were so large, a hole had to be cut in the wall. The 'Nelson relics' from Greenwich were distributed between the vaults of the Bank of England and the GPO Parcels Tube Station in King Edward Building. Public records were despatched to Bodmin Gaol. Following the Poplar tragedy, the LCC introduced specific measures for schools, directing that upper floors be evacuated, and gates locked to prevent parents, or the public, from gaining access. Air-raid drills were to be implemented, and teachers would tell stories and encourage children to sing.

Eventually, London was ringed with 353 searchlights and 266 anti-aircraft guns, with 159 day fighters and 123 night fighters for additional protection. The whole was coordinated by the London Air Defence Area (LADA) headquarters, the latter a key recommendation of the first Smuts report. Following the raid on 13 June 1917, the War Cabinet requested Field Marshal Haig to withdraw two fighter squadrons from the front, one to be sent to London and the other to Calais. Haig argued that he needed both for the forthcoming Passchendaele offensive and was allowed to keep one, but 24 aircraft intended for France were held back. The squadron sent to London was returned to France on 5 July, just two days before the Gothas struck again. Thereafter defences steadily improved, with better communications systems installed between anti-aircraft guns, home-defence squadrons and observation posts. The latter had originally been established on an ad hoc basis in 1915 to report sightings of Zeppelins, but were now incorporated into the LADA system. The Special Constables who had initially manned such posts were supplemented by army personnel. Reports were now telephoned to ancillary operations rooms and then on to a central control room established in Westminster's Spring Gardens that was the model for the even more elaborate system developed during the Second World War. There were even experiments with concrete sound mirrors to try and detect incoming aircraft. Anti-aircraft balloons were also introduced in January 1918, such experimentation being encouraged by Smuts. On raid nights, therefore, the capital was a cacophony of sound and light, the cumulative effect of bombs, guns, flares and searchlights.

The Germans switched to night raids in September 1917 as a result of the increased defences. But, even given more forewarning, air-defence fighters remained technologically limited and were groping for contact with the Gothas and the heavier Riesen (Giant) Staaken RVI bombers. The latter were introduced by the Germans in September 1917, as the Gothas were diverted to tactical operations on the Western Front. The Giants were armed with single bombs of far greater tonnage: the heaviest was a 2,200-pound bomb dropped in February 1918. Only six Giants, however, were available to supplement the Gothas, as they were expensive to build and each required a ground crew of 51 men. The last appearance of any bomber over London was on 19/20 May 1918, when 8 out of the 41 bombers used were destroyed by fighters or ground fire, and others in accidents. Yet, despite the greater losses inflicted on the Germans, air defence had not really proved effective, and the biggest impact of the raids was to tie up

British aircraft that might have been used more profitably on the Western Front. In 397 sorties, the Germans lost only 24 Gothas over England – while tying up over 300 British aircraft – although another 37 Gothas were lost in accidents. Moreover, it was calculated that the anti-aircraft guns had needed to fire 14,540 rounds to bring down one aircraft.[23] It was concluded, therefore, that there was no effective defence against the bomber.

That expectation was fuelled by the establishment of the Smuts committee in response to the raids of 13 June and 7 July 1917. Now forty-seven years old, the Cambridge-educated Smuts had been the Transvaal State Attorney at the start of the South African War in 1899. A leading Boer commando in the guerrilla phase of the war, Smuts subsequently worked with Louis Botha to negotiate the restoration of self-government. With Botha becoming prime minister of the Union of South Africa in 1910, Smuts occupied a number of key ministries. He established the Union Defence Force, and was appointed the allied commander-in-chief in East Africa in 1916. Arriving in Britain in March 1917 as head of the South African delegation to the Imperial War Conference, Smuts was then offered a place in the War Cabinet by Lloyd George in June though, constitutionally, he could only be in attendance. Smuts knew nothing of airpower other than having witnessed the raid on 13 June from the Savoy Hotel, but had already made his mark on the public with a series of morale-raising speeches. The War Cabinet itself had devoted little time to consideration of air matters since the waning of the Zeppelin threat. Its members were actually sitting during the raid on 13 June. Lord Derby merely reported that a raid was taking place and that Poplar and Woolwich had been bombed: there was no discussion of the news at all. The public outrage stirred a brief flurry of concern before the War Cabinet returned to what appeared the more pressing business of discussing the damaging report of the Mesopotamia Commission into the failures of that campaign. Then came the second raid. Assuaging public opinion was unavoidable. In fact, Lloyd George had already considered the establishment of a new air ministry before the raid of 13 June as a means of bringing Churchill back into government. Smuts had seen Churchill on 5 June to discuss this very possibility, which Lloyd George had first raised six months previously. Appointing Smuts to an inquiry into air defence and air organisation on 11 July, therefore, satisfied public opinion while also fulfilling Lloyd George's intended political agenda.

Lloyd George was supposed to be co-chairing the committee with Smuts in order to deal with political issues, but advanced various excuses for not attending. Smuts's suggestions of adding Churchill, Lord Hugh Cecil or Leo Amery to the committee were also not heeded. Instead, the assistant secretary to the Committee of Imperial Defence, Major Lancelot Storr, who had some knowledge of aviation, undertook much of the work. Smuts also received conflicting memoranda and advice from a number of quarters. A brief first report on 19 July recommended a reorganisation of home air defence with more and better aircraft. Smuts suggested that three home-defence squadrons be formed, as well as LADA under a single commander. In a second report on 9 August 1917, Smuts recommended a single unified air service independent of army and naval rivalries, and the establishment of an air staff and an air ministry. Drafted by Storr, the report had a stark warning, suggesting, 'the day may not be far off when aerial operations with their devastation of enemy lands and destruction of industrial and populous centres on a vast scale may become the principal operations of war, to which the older forms of military and naval operations may become secondary and subordinate'.[24]

Despite opposition from the Unionists in the coalition, Churchill had already been offered the new air ministry on 16 July. This was only five days after Smuts had been initially appointed to his committee, and three weeks before he actually formally recommended such a ministry, again suggesting Lloyd George's previous intent. Churchill chose instead to return to government as Minister of Munitions, and there remained some opposition to an air ministry. The War Cabinet only formally adopted the second Smuts report on 24 August. Smuts was then tasked with leading a new Air Organisation Committee to work out the arrangements for unifying the RFC and RNAS. It has been suggested that only Lloyd George's need for another political gesture following the failure of the Passchendaele offensive gave further stimulus to the establishment of an air ministry and air staff in January 1918, with the Independent Force, Royal Air Force (RAF), coming into independent existence on 1 April 1918. On 6 June 1918 the RAF was tasked with retaliatory attacks on the German homeland.

The RNAS had carried out thirteen bombing raids on some German towns from Lexeuil near Belfort between October 1916 and March 1917. The Admiralty's enthusiasm for extending the campaign had been opposed by Haig, who believed the resources better devoted to support of ground operations. Frederick Sykes, the new Chief of the Air Staff, calculated that 80 per cent of Germany's chemical industry lay in range of British bombers using French bases. Sykes made a virtue of the difficulty of obtaining command of the air to argue that aircraft could deliberately avoid opposing aircraft and thus overcome the deadlock on land. Hugh Trenchard, Sykes's predecessor, preferred to target railways and airfields. Having briefly occupied Sykes's post before resigning in a clash with the new air minister, Lord Rothermere, Trenchard now commanded the RAF. In any case, he believed that the most effective defence of London from the air would be to force the Germans on the defensive in the skies over France and Flanders. Some 242 raids were carried out on Germany and 543 tons of bombs dropped, at the cost of 109 aircraft lost and 243 wrecked. The tonnage was too small to do much damage and, as early as June 1918, it was concluded that only 23.5 per cent of bombs were falling within the designated target area. Nevertheless, the Germans were forced to divert resources to air defence, and some war production was disrupted. All wartime raids by British, French and Italian aircraft resulted in 797 German dead, 380 wounded and an estimated 15 million marks' worth of damage. The new Handley Page V-1500 bomber, with a 126-foot wingspan and a bomb load of 3,500 kilograms, was poised to make the first raid on Berlin on the day the armistice was signed.

The Italians and Austro-Hungarians also carried out strategic bombing attacks during the war, the Italians being in the forefront of the use of airpower for strategic purposes. Gianni Caproni had developed the first true strategic bomber in 1913 and, by 1916, Italy had 40 of his massive three-engined triplanes with a 98-foot wingspan, a bomb load of 1,500 kilograms, and fuel capacity for a seven-hour flight. Giulio Douhet had also begun to develop his theories of strategic air power, although he was only director of the Italian army's aviation section from 1913 to 1914, and returned to it only briefly in 1918: he may never have learned to fly. While Austro-Hungarian aircraft raided Verona, Venice, Padua and Milan, the Italians struck at Adriatic ports, but the Italian air offensive did not really become of any significance until 1918. Paris was also subjected to aerial bombardment, 267 people being killed in Zeppelin or Gotha raids during the war compared to the 256 killed by the long-range artillery bombardment during the German spring offensive in 1918.

In all, there had been 51 Zeppelin raids and 57 bomber raids on Britain during the war, accounting for 1,913 and 2,907 casualties respectively. Of the dead, Zeppelins accounted for 557, and aircraft for 856. It was pointed out in the 1920s that this was not many more than the then 700 annual fatalities on Britain's roads. The estimated cost of all direct German bombardment or bombing of Britain was a relatively modest £3,087,098.[25] In reality, neither the Gotha raids nor those of the RAF proved or disproved the evolving theories of strategic airpower in which both sides were to invest so much subsequent expectation. Instead, crude multiplication of the results of the Zeppelin and Gotha raids combined with public anxiety to establish the idea that there was no defence against bombing.

As suggested by Constable Smith's plaque, there are a number of reminders of the first sustained aerial attack on a modern city, including the remains of a bomb dropped on the church of St Edmund the King and Martyr in Lombard Street on 7 July 1917 and incorporated into the altar. There is a plaque, too, on the wall of the Royal Hospital, Chelsea, that has particular resonance. On the night of 16 February 1918 a Giant dropped a single 2,200-pound bomb on what its commander took to be the City. It fell instead upon the northeast wing of Sir Christopher Wren's building, killing five. Not only does the plaque commemorate that raid, but also further destruction wrought on the Royal Hospital by a V2 rocket on 3 January 1945. In strategic bombing, as in so many other ways, the Great War cast its shadow.

CHAPTER 10

THE PROMISED LAND

The Balfour Declaration, 2 November 1917

Pᴇᴏᴘʟᴇ ᴀᴛ war need to know that the sacrifices they are making are worthwhile, and that there will be a suitable payoff in the future for the country, and for themselves. Making promises that may not be fulfilled is a danger for politicians in the midst of conflict. Vagueness in making 'war aims' public is sensible, but it may become counter-productive because the failure to achieve them may appear akin to defeat. Agreements made with different allies, and promises made to potential allies in order to draw them into the war, may be equally problematic. As the Chief of the Imperial General Staff, Sir Henry Wilson, nicely expressed it in June 1919, war against Ottoman Turkey led Britain into making 'so many promises to everybody in a contradictory sense that I cannot for the life of me see how we can get out of our present mess without breaking our word to somebody'.[1]

It was not just a question of the agreements forged with France, Russia, Italy and Greece, but also of the promises made to subject peoples within the Ottoman Empire, including Arabs, Armenians and Kurds. In addition, however, British Foreign Secretary Arthur Balfour's almost casual recognition, in a letter to Lord Rothschild on 2 November 1917, of the need for a Jewish homeland in Palestine stored up enormous problems for the future. Balfour's engagement with Zionism was the outcome of his extraordinary intellectual bond with the Russian-born but naturalised British scientist, Chaim Weizmann. It endured for almost a quarter of a century from a crucial meeting in the Queen's Hotel in Manchester's Piccadilly in January

1906, to their last in March 1930, as Balfour lay dying at Fisher's Hill near Woking in Surrey. The consequences of that friendship and of the post-war partition of the Ottoman Empire remain evident to this day. The Balfour Declaration was intended to help win the war. Ironically, it did not have the intended impact on the war's outcome.

The British declaration of war on Ottoman Turkey on 5 November 1914 raised the issue of the present and future security of the British Empire. Fighting alongside the French and Russians did not extinguish older imperial rivalries, and winning the war for Britain meant increasing security against both current allies as well as current enemies. Though Egypt remained nominally part of the Ottoman Empire, Britain's Consul General had controlled it ever since British military intervention ended an Egyptian nationalist threat to European control of the Suez Canal in 1882. Under the Constantinople Convention of 1888, signed between Turkey and the European powers, the Suez Canal – so vital for British maritime trade and connections to India – was declared a neutral zone but under British protection. On 18 December 1914 Britain formally declared Egypt a protectorate, deposing the troublesome and ambitious Abbas Hilmi II as Khedive – technically, the Sultan's Viceroy over Egypt – and installing his uncle, Hussein Kamel, as Sultan of Egypt. Abbas Hilmi was in Turkey when he was deposed.

A Turkish attempt to attack the Suez Canal was easily repulsed in February 1915, ending any real threat. But, apart from the Canal, Middle Eastern oil resources were also vital for a Royal Navy now fuelled by oil rather than coal. The need, therefore, to secure Persian oil, and to keep the Russian military effort concentrated on the Eastern Front rather than the Caucasus, persuaded the British to allow the Russians the post-war control of the Dardanelles in the Straits Agreement on 12 November 1914. The Foreign Office had comparatively little interest in the future of the Ottoman Empire compared to the India Office. It was the latter that determined on mounting a limited demonstration by the Indian army in November 1914 to occupy Basra in the Persian Gulf, to reassure the Gulf rulers of British protection against the Turks. It was generally believed that, in the possible break-up of the Ottoman Empire signalled by the Straits Agreement, Britain could not afford to allow the French to meet their own aspirations to acquire Syria without adequate compensatory protection for British interests in Egypt and Mesopotamia.

It was not until April 1915, however, that an interdepartmental committee was tasked with determining what British war aims – quaintly characterised as 'desiderata' – should be in the event of victory over the Turks. With representatives from the Admiralty, War Office, Foreign Office and India Office, the committee was under the chairmanship of a diplomat with North African experience, Sir Maurice de Bunsen. The decision had only been forced on London by wide Russian territorial demands in March. It might be noted, however, that such Russian demands did not negate their general willingness to accommodate British and French military plans.

Reporting in June 1915, the De Bunsen committee recommended establishing post-war zones of influence over five autonomous provinces to be carved from the Ottoman Empire. As already decided, Russia would get the Straits and zones of influence over Anatolia and Armenia, while French interest in Syria would be recognised. Britain would exercise its influence over Mesopotamia, but also control Haifa on the Mediterranean coast of Palestine as a terminal for the Baghdad Railway that the Germans had been constructing and which the British would now also control.

There was another consideration, however, beyond the Suez Canal and oil, for the Sultan in Constantinople also claimed the Caliphate, aspiring to supreme global authority over Sunni Islam, whose adherents formed the largest proportion of Muslims. About 80 per cent of the population of the Ottoman Empire were Muslim, but by far the greatest number of the world's Muslims – over 100 million – lived under British control, followed by the next largest concentration of about 19 million Muslims within the Tsarist Empire. When the 'Young Turks' of the CUP forced constitutional change on Sultan Abdülhamid II in 1908, the Hashemite Sherif (Sharif) of Mecca, Ali Abdullah Pasha, claimed the Caliphate on the grounds that he was in direct descent from Mohammed's own tribe, whereas the Ottomans were effectively usurpers to the title. The office of Sherif had evolved over time into that of governor of the western part of the Arabian Peninsula known as the Hejaz, and custodian of Islam's holiest shrines at Mecca and Medina. Ali Abdullah died that same year, being succeeded as Sherif and Emir of Mecca by his son, Hussein (Husayn), then aged about sixty.

Real Ottoman control of the Hejaz was limited but Hussein's authority was contested, in turn, by the independent Emir of Nejd in central Arabia,

Abdul Aziz Ibn Sa'ud, an adherent of the fundamentalist Wahhabi variant of Sunni Islam. Secularist as they were, the Young Turks were quite prepared to manipulate Islam and, as Caliph, Sultan Mehmed V duly proclaimed selective jihad against Britain, France and Russia on 11 November 1914: the precise date is disputed. Both the CUP and the Germans intended thereby to undermine their enemies' empires, France also controlling Muslim populations in North and West Africa. Potentially, therefore, this posed a serious threat and there was Muslim unrest in India, Central Asia and Africa. Even before the war, Britain's Agent and Consul General in Egypt, none other than Kitchener, had conceived of Britain nominating and controlling its own Caliph. To Kitchener the obvious candidate was Hussein. By contrast, the government of India, wary of inflaming Muslim opinion in India by supplanting the Sultan as Caliph, saw Ibn Sa'ud as a better potential leader of revolt against the Turks. As a Wahhabi, he had no interest in claiming a Caliphate he believed had been long extinct.

Kitchener and his advisers had met Hussein's second and favourite son, the cultivated but politically ambitious Abdullah, in Cairo in February 1914. Abdullah was anxious to ascertain whether the British would support his father should the Turks move to depose him. Whether any specific promises were made is unclear. Following prompting from Gilbert Clayton, who officially represented the Governor General of the Sudan, Sir Reginald Wingate, in Cairo, Kitchener, now Secretary of State for War, directed Ronald Storrs, the Oriental Secretary of the Agency in Cairo, to contact Abdullah on 24 September 1914. He was to enquire whether Hussein would support the British. When Abdullah's response seemed encouraging, Kitchener indicated to Storrs that Britain would support the Arabs if they took up arms against the Turks, would restore the Caliphate to Arabia, and would 'guarantee that no internal intervention takes place in Arabia'.[2] Encouraged by Clayton, Storrs and the Acting Agent and Consul General, Sir Milne Cheetham, embroidered this in translation into support for the 'independence, rights and privileges of the Sherifate against all external foreign aggression'.[3] It would appear that what Clayton, Storrs and Cheetham meant by independence was only from the Turks, and only for what could be characterised as the Hejaz.

That Kitchener's former officials could run a policy separate from that of the Foreign Office owed much to the cloak of Kitchener's massive authority within the Cabinet. Storrs, who had studied oriental languages and literature at Cambridge, had joined Kitchener's staff in 1909 after serving in the Egyptian civil service. His knowledge of Arabic, however, was imprecise. Storrs struck most contemporaries as a cosmopolitan figure with a broad interest in music, literature and the fine arts, but also as vain and arrogant. A former soldier under Kitchener, the more tactful Clayton had been Wingate's private secretary before acting simultaneously as Wingate's representative in Cairo and the Anglo-Egyptian army's director of intelligence. In October 1914 he was appointed to head all the intelligence agencies in Cairo. While Clayton was undoubtedly shrewd, he tended to make judgements largely on intuition. Storrs also invariably believed what he wished to believe. Thus, Abdullah misled them into believing that there was general support in Arabia for Hussein. But they also saw the Caliphate in purely spiritual terms and did not grasp that Hussein would see the offer of the Caliphate as an offer of an extensive kingdom over Arabia, for the Caliph was both a temporal and spiritual ruler in Islam. An Arab kingdom was precisely what Hussein then demanded through the auspices of Abdullah in July 1915.

The Germans were also courting Hussein. Hussein's third son, Faisal (Faysal), had met the German agent, Max Oppenheimer, in April 1915, as well as Enver Pasha. Recognising the preponderance of Shia Muslims in Persia and southern Mesopotamia, the Germans had also approached Shia clerics. Hussein stood to gain most by playing both sides off against each other, but he feared that the Turks were ready to depose him. Moreover, the Entente's blockade of exports such as Lebanese silk and Palestinian citrus fruit, coupled with bad harvests, led to considerable privation throughout Arabia. Income at Islam's holy places was also cut by the effect of the blockade on the Haj pilgrimages. Hussein was increasingly dependent upon the British readiness to supply grain to compensate for Turkish seizures of crops, and shipping to revive the Haj. Hussein also disliked the CUP's secularism that had led to the attempt to grant women equal rights, and to impose secular schools on Mecca and Medina.

In October 1915 the British Foreign Secretary, Sir Edward Grey, authorised the new Agent and Consul General, the plodding Sir Henry McMahon, to open formal negotiations with Hussein. McMahon had experience only of India and spoke no Arabic. He was dependent, therefore, on Storrs's less than perfect Arabic, and that of Storrs's Consular Oriental Assistant, Ruhi, a Persian, whom Storrs himself later described as 'a better agent than scholar' and T. E. Lawrence as 'more like a mandrake than a man'.[4] In the course of the correspondence that passed between Cairo and Mecca, on 24 October 1915 McMahon committed Britain to an independent Arab kingdom after the war, albeit hedged with nuanced language as to its extent and the degree of British supervision. It would be subject to the exclusion of the Syrian coast, and territories of those already in a treaty relationship with Britain (such as Ibn Sa'ud), and also to the acknowledgement of British interests in Mesopotamia, and any French regional interests. Much has been made of what McMahon supposedly offered, with varied inter-pretations laid upon what he meant by excluding from the Arab kingdom the 'districts' west of Damascus, Hama, Homs and Aleppo. 'District' was translated by Storrs or Ruhi as *wiläyät*, which they interpreted as akin to a Turkish administrative province, or *vilayet* but which Arabs could regard as meaning 'environs'. Palestine, which was not specifically mentioned in the correspondence, lay south rather than west of a line drawn between the four towns, but to the British it lay west of the Turkish province of Damascus. How far Hussein accepted the British interpretation remains a matter of debate, but it is clear that the Arabs made a distinction between accepting Jewish settlement in Palestine and accepting a Jewish state. Faisal certainly accepted Jewish settlement in January 1919.

Whatever the later arguments, McMahon was not guaranteeing anything at all. Jewish settlement in Palestine was not on his mind in 1915, though French claims to the coast were. He later suggested that there had been nowhere of importance south of Damascus worth mentioning and he was clear that Palestine was excluded from any potential Arab state. Clayton, Sykes, Grey and Lloyd George all concurred. No maps were attached to the correspondence, and McMahon chose not to clarify anything in subse-quent correspondence with Hussein, who was prepared to wait for the post-war settlement. The exchanges with Hussein were prompted by the belief in Cairo that an Arab revolt against the Turks was imminent. There had been anti-Ottoman conspiracies by Arab secret societies before the war. Two of these societies, al-Fatat (The Society of the Young Arab Nation) and al-'Ahd (The Covenant), had begun to cooperate in early 1915, following the first wave of executions of Arab activists by Cemal, who now commanded the Turkish Fourth Army based at Damascus. Unrest did not necessarily mean revolt. A complete hoaxer, Muhammed Sharif-al-Faruqi, a junior Arab officer who deserted from the Ottoman army in early 1915, took in Clayton. Al-Faruqi claimed to speak on behalf of the Arab societies, and suggested that they were prepared to back Hussein. Clayton was well aware of the executions in Damascus but chose to ignore them. It was also believed that al-Faruqi spoke for Hussein, though he had never met him. Hussein was now also ready to commit because he knew the Turks did intend to depose him.

The French had agreed only reluctantly in April 1915 to conceding the Straits and Constantinople to Russia, and there was considerable public support in France for securing Syria. Grey was prepared to assuage French suspicions by authorising Sir Mark Sykes to negotiate with them over the frontiers of Syria, since fulfilling promises to Hussein required concessions to the French. Sykes has become best known in recent years for the exhumation of his body by virologists from its lead-lined coffin in 2008 in the hope of obtaining more information on the 1918–19 'Spanish' influenza pandemic, from which Sykes died in February 1919. Tissue was extracted, but the coffin had split and there was more decomposition than anticipated. In 1915 Sykes, the energetic and extremely wealthy thirty-six-year-old baronet and Unionist MP for Kingston on Hull, was regarded as the leading expert on the Middle East. He had travelled extensively throughout the Ottoman Empire after failing to complete his degree at Cambridge. An ebullient figure with a creative mind, Sykes was a gifted mimic and cartoonist. His Catholicism was an additional recommendation to Grey in suggesting an ability to relate to the French. But Sykes, whom many Foreign Office officials saw as a pure amateur, was not without an agenda. He had joined Kitchener's staff at the War Office in early 1915 and had then personally represented Kitchener on the De Bunsen committee, and greatly influenced its conclusions. Sent on an extensive visit to the Middle East and India, Sykes had fallen in with the ideas of Clayton and Storrs for excluding the French from Syria. Sykes had also been struck by the lack of a centrally agreed policy and, as a result, recommended the establishment of what became known as the Arab Bureau in Cairo. The Bureau had less power than Sykes had envisaged, being merely a branch of Clayton's intelligence department, but it had the ear of Kitchener and of Sykes himself.

The talks opened on 23 November 1915, the French delegation being headed by François Georges Picot. The former French Consul General in Beirut, Picot was dedicated to securing all of Syria (including Palestine) for France, albeit with direct control over only the coast. Hashemite rulers directly supervised by French advisers would rule the interior. The French, however, were in a relatively weak position in that Britain was taking on the main burden of the war against the Turks. Sykes was determined to separate Palestine from Syria. He was prepared to see the French control Lebanon and coastal Syria directly, with the French exercising indirect influence over inland Syria as a barrier between British territory and Russian control of Armenia and eastern Anatolia. Since the Italians had joined the Entente in May 1915, they would receive some influence over parts of Anatolia, as would the Greeks, whom the British hoped to bring into the war. With both Sykes and Picot wanting to acquire Palestine, the compromise was that it would be an international zone. Haifa and Acre would be under direct British control, together with a strip of territory from these ports along the railway line to Baghdad. Some within the Cabinet were hostile to any concessions to the French, but the draft was agreed on 31 January 1916 and signed by Britain, France and Russia on 15 May 1916.

Sykes thought he had reconciled the claims of the French and Hussein, not realising that no one in London or Cairo took the idea of an Arab state seriously. Grey told the Secretary of State for India, Austen Chamberlain, that 'the whole thing was a castle in the air which would never materialise'.[5] At the time, however, the war's end seemed a long way off and attracting Arab support seemed sensible. The British war effort in the Middle East had faltered. Gallipoli was to be evacuated in January 1916. There had also been a serious setback in Mesopotamia, for the desire to ensure British prestige in Muslim eyes encouraged extension of the campaign from the occupation of Basra to an advance up the Tigris to Kut el-Amara in June 1915 without an adequate force. The advance to Kut became an advance on Baghdad in November 1915 but, within two days, the overextended expedition was forced to retreat back to Kut. Surrounded, it was compelled to surrender in April 1916.

Any promises made to Hussein were dependent on the Arab Revolt taking place. Hussein duly declared his revolt on 5 June 1916. Far more charismatic than either his father, Hussein, or his elder brother, Abdullah, Faisal became the undisputed leader of the revolt in November 1916 following the withdrawal of 'Aziz 'Ali al-Misra of al-'Ahd. At peak, there were some 40,000 under arms, mostly tribesmen from the Hejaz, but it was by no means the case that all Arabs supported the revolt. Faisal had negoti- ated the so-called Damascus Protocol with representatives of the secret societies in April 1915, envisaging post-war independence for all of Arabia and Mesopotamia. This had then informed Hussein's demand for an Arab kingdom in his approach to the British in July 1915. Al-Misra, however, had purposely not taken Medina at the start of the revolt because he favoured a dual Turko-Arab federation modelled on Austria-Hungary. Nor did advocates of a greater Syria, Lebanese separatists, or Ibn Sa'ud share Hussein's concept of a unified Arab state. Such divisions did not assist the Arab cause in dealings with the Entente, especially as it appeared that the revolt was not yielding any positive results: little was achieved until the capture of Aqaba in July 1917. In such circumstances, supporting the Zionist cause looked more promising. Jews had already formed the Zion Mule Corps at Gallipoli, and would later raise three battalions of the Royal Fusiliers.

The Germans had toyed with Zionism for some years, though this sat uneasily with the equal German support of Islam. The Zionist Executive and its Central Office were based in Berlin in August 1914, though it then moved its headquarters to Copenhagen. Most Jews had little liking for a Tsarist government responsible for innumerable pogroms in the past, and there was a general assumption in London that most Jews were pro- German. Certainly, German officials saw Zionism as just as useful an instrument as Islam for undermining the Entente. In June 1915 Arthur Zimmermann, the Under Secretary of State in the German Foreign Ministry, informed a leading rabbi in Magdeburg that the German government was urging the Turks to lift barriers to Jewish immigration into Palestine. Many German Jews believed that Germany was more likely to deliver on its promises as Turkey's ally. Under German pressure, however, Cemal was prepared at most to ease the oppression of Jews in Palestine. Initially, Zionists in Palestine had offered to raise forces for the Turks, but their leaders were deported, and gradually they recognised that Britain could offer more than the Turks. Some Zionists, however, feared the impact of support for Britain on Jewish communities in Germany and Austria-Hungary.

Despite assumptions about Jewish support for Germany, there was some sympathy for Zionist aspirations in Britain. As long ago as the 1840s, Lord Palmerston had given some consideration to a Jewish presence in Palestine. As prime minister, Balfour and his Colonial Secretary, Joseph Chamberlain, had seriously contemplated offering a Jewish colony in the British East Africa Protectorate (Uganda) in 1903, and Lloyd George had tried to interest the Cabinet in establishing one in Sinai in 1906. In January 1915 the first practising Jew to sit in the Cabinet, Sir Herbert Samuel, President of the Local Government Board, suggested to Prime Minister Asquith making Palestine a British protectorate, and encouraging Jewish emigration there. Grey was interested but only Lloyd George was disposed to support it, and it was rejected.

What triggered a more definite British move to recognise Zionist aspirations was the belief that Germany might pre-empt any public declaration of support. At the same time, a British declaration of support for Zionism promised to curry favour both in the United States and in Russia once the Tsar had been overthrown. Weizmann certainly played on the idea that the Jews were a monolithic force throughout the world that could be so influenced. The Foreign Office had particular expectations of influencing Jewish Bolsheviks like Trotsky, but they were not Zionists. Indeed, the Bolsheviks promptly published the 'secret treaties' between the allies, including the Sykes-Picot agreement, in December 1917. Arguably, winning the support of American Jews was even more significant since Britain was now heavily dependent upon US financial support. Influencing American Jewish opinion might yield leverage to offset President Wilson's evident intention of winning the peace on his own terms. Another potential advantage of declaring support for Zionism was that French and Italian suspicions of British aims in Palestine could be allayed. To all Britain's allies, therefore, the coming operations in Palestine 'could be presented as a campaign of liberation, and Britain's post-war presence could be cloaked as a necessary step towards self-determination.'[6]

Above all, the growing support for the Zionist cause was stimulated by the contact between Balfour and Weizmann. Born at Motol near Pinsk in Belorussia in 1874, Weizmann was predisposed by his progressive timber merchant father, who insisted Weizmann learn Russian as a means of advancement. Showing a flair for science, Weizmann studied chemistry at Charlottenberg in Germany and Fribourg in Switzerland, gaining a post at the University of Geneva. In 1904 he became a lecturer in biochemistry at the University of Manchester, advancing to a readership in 1913. Naturalised as a British subject in 1910, Weizmann combined his love for science with dedication to Zionism, with which he had first come into contact in 1890. By 1911 he was the vice president of the English Zionist Federation and a persuasive advocate of the Zionist cause. Solidly built, Weizmann had a commanding presence but his personality was at best mercurial. He found it difficult to conceal his impatience with those with whom he disagreed, or who fell short of his expectations.

As a result of commercial work for a dye works, its owner, Charles Dreyfus, a leading Manchester Unionist, invited Weizmann to meet Balfour when he was visiting his Manchester East constituency in January 1905. They met again, this time at the Queen's Hotel when Balfour was election-eering in the city on 9 January 1906. The intended subject of discussion was the abortive Uganda scheme for Jewish settlement. What was meant to be a fifteen-minute appointment extended to an hour, Weizmann recalling that 'I dwelt on the spiritual side of Zionism', and on Palestine's 'magic and romantic appeal for Jews'.[7]

Balfour, prime minister since July 1902, was fighting a losing election not only nationally but also locally, being ousted from the Manchester seat he had held since 1885. Originally more interested in philosophy than politics, Balfour had become an MP in 1874. He rose effortlessly through the political ranks, not least through the influence of his uncle, the 3rd Marquess of Salisbury, whom he succeeded as prime minister. It is some-times suggested that the phrase, 'Bob's Your Uncle', originated with Salisbury's appointment of Balfour as Chief Secretary for Ireland in 1887, but it appears unknown prior to the 1930s. Balfour's premiership had not been a success, and he was to prove equally ineffective as Leader of the Opposition, yielding the post to Andrew Bonar Law in 1911. Sufficiently tall to be known as 'Daddy Long Legs', Balfour cultivated an air of languid indolence through his aloof, almost serene, detachment. The Duke of Devonshire once remarked that Balfour's sense of duty was sufficient to overcome both his indolence and also his 'strong contempt for popularity'.[8] The unemotional exterior, however, also concealed a quick mind.

The meeting had a profound impact. According to Weizmann, when they met again in December 1914, Balfour recalled every aspect of the conversation. Later Balfour said that it was from the conversation that 'I saw that the Jewish form of patriotism was unique'.[9] Weizmann had aroused Balfour's intellectual curiosity. Balfour was deeply religious and from his familiarity with the Old Testament – shared with Lloyd George – believed the Jews a gifted race. He remarked to Lady Rayleigh in July 1918, 'The Jews were too great a race not to count and they ought to have a place where those who had strong racial idealism could develop on their lines as a nation and govern themselves.' Similarly, in a speech in the House of Lords in 1922, he said that 'we desire to the best of our ability to give them that opportunity of developing, in peace and quietness under British rule, those great gifts which hitherto they have been compelled to bring to fruition in countries that know not their language and belong not to their race'.[10] Balfour certainly believed that Jewish energy would materially improve Palestine and later told his niece that his declaration was 'the thing he looked upon as the most worth his doing'.[11]

It simply did not occur to him that there would be any Arab reaction. In any case, as he was later to outline to the War Cabinet, the declaration 'did not necessarily involve the early establishment of an independent Jewish state, which was a matter for gradual development in accordance with the ordinary laws of political evolution'.[12] In 1914 there had been about 85,000 Jews in Palestine, mostly from Eastern Europe, living among about 700,000 Palestinians. Yet Balfour considered that Arab claims on Palestine were 'infinitely weaker' than those of Jews. He also observed later that 'planting a minority of outsiders upon a majority population, without consulting it, was not calculated to horrify men who worked with Cecil Rhodes or promoted European settlement in Kenya'.[13]

Furnished with a letter of introduction by C. P. Scott, the editor of the *Manchester Guardian* and a supporter of the Zionist cause, Weizmann was due to meet Lloyd George in November 1914. Lloyd George was also to become an important figure in the acceptance of the Zionist cause, not least through his penchant for pursuing an 'eastern' strategic policy in preference to the costly commitment to the Western Front. On this occasion,

Lloyd George was unable to meet Weizmann but suggested that he saw Herbert Samuel. Samuel duly met Weizmann in December and arranged a meeting with Lloyd George in early January 1915. On 12 December 1914 Weizmann had also renewed his acquaintance with Balfour, who had joined Asquith's War Council the previous month. Balfour was apparently unaware of the depth of anti-Russian feeling among the Zionists until Weizmann recounted the history of the pogroms. According to Weizmann, Balfour was 'most deeply moved to the point of tears'.[14] They met on a number of subsequent occasions. Balfour replaced Churchill at the Admiralty in May 1915 in the Asquith coalition and then became Foreign Secretary under Lloyd George in December 1916. By this time, too, Weizmann had cachet because he was making a contribution to the British war effort through his work for the Admiralty and the Ministry of Munitions, having discovered a means of extracting acetone – a vital component of high-explosive cordite – from maize. There was dispute over patents and Weizmann had his critics within the Ministry, but Lloyd George supported him. Lloyd George later claimed quite erroneously that the Balfour Declaration was a direct reward for Weizmann's contribution to the war effort. At the same time as broadening his contacts in government, Weizmann was becoming better known to the more elitist Jewish circles in the country, principally the Rothschilds.

Sensing an increasing opportunity, the Zionists approached Sir Edward Grey in October 1916 for a firm indication of British support. Grey had been considering some kind of gesture towards Zionism for the past few months. The change of government in December caused a hiatus, but the imminence of the British military campaign in Palestine opened new possibilities. Weizmann, newly elected President of the English Zionist Federation, met Sykes in February 1917, and went on to see both Balfour and Lloyd George. Sykes had displayed anti-Semitic attitudes in the past and saw Palestine as simply part of his wider Middle Eastern scheme. But he was impressed when he met Weizmann and felt that supporting Zionism would help keep Russia in the war because its Jews would then support the allies. Alarmed by rumours fed to him by C. P. Scott of the Sykes-Picot agreement, Weizmann was keen to secure a solely British protectorate. The French also indicated some willingness to recognise Zionist aspirations in April 1917, largely through the efforts of Sykes, and Nahum Sokolow, a Polish member of the Zionist Executive who had fled Berlin in 1914 and become one of Weizmann's closest collaborators. Sokolow even secured the blessing of Pope Benedict XV.

Balfour was absent in the United States for a month but, while there, met a leading Jewish jurist from Boston, Louis Brandeis, who reinforced the Zionist arguments. Brandeis's secretary, Felix Frankfurter, later suggested that Balfour had remarked, 'I am a Zionist.'[15] On his return, therefore, Balfour met Weizmann and Walter, Lord Rothschild, on 13 June 1917, at which point he asked them for their suggestions as to a suitable declaration. A former Liberal Unionist MP who had succeeded his father in the peerage in 1915, Rothschild had no significant office but was acknowledged as one of the leading figures in Anglo-Jewry.

Rothschild forwarded the draft on 18 July, after it had been amended several times. Since Weizmann was absent visiting Gibraltar, Sokolow had presided over a meeting of the newly formed London Zionist Political Committee to prepare the text earlier in July. Another member who had a significant input in the drafting was Harry Sacher, a journalist on the *Manchester Guardian*. Weizmann's mission was itself a further twist in affairs. With the blessing of the Foreign Office, he was to persuade the former American ambassador to Turkey, Henry Morgenthau, to desist in his attempt to negotiate a peace treaty with the Turks. Tentative British efforts to reach an accommodation with the Turks had got nowhere, and there seemed little point in allowing Morgenthau to muddy the waters further. Lord Milner had taken a look at the wording together with Sykes and a young diplomat, Harold Nicholson. Milner, who had joined Lloyd George's War Cabinet, had long been well disposed towards Jews. He had become interested in at least some kind of autonomous Jewish presence in Palestine through contacts with Herbert Samuel. After hearing their suggestions, the final version, drafted by Sacher, was submitted. It read, 'His Majesty's Government accepts the principle that Palestine should be reconstituted as the national home of the Jewish people. His Majesty's Government will use its best endeavours to secure the achievement of this object and will discuss the necessary methods and means with the Zionist Organisation.'[16]

Milner tinkered with the wording again, primarily substituting 'a national home for' for 'the national home of', and it was sent by the Foreign

Office to the Cabinet Office, where it languished. These were anxious days for Weizmann, the strain contributing to a deteriorating atmosphere within the London Zionist Political Committee and to Weizmann offering, though then retracting, his resignation as President of the English Zionist Organisation in September. The War Cabinet considered the Sacher draft, together with alternatives suggested by Milner and Balfour himself, on 3 September 1917. Lloyd George and Balfour were absent, the former resting and the latter on a Scottish holiday. There was little discussion but, presiding in Lloyd George's absence, Andrew Bonar Law approved a request by Lord Robert Cecil, Balfour's cousin deputising for him on behalf of the Foreign Office, that they seek the views of US President Woodrow Wilson.

The only real objection came from the newly appointed Secretary of State for India, Edwin Montagu. Since his cousin, Herbert Samuel, had left office in December 1916, Montagu was now the only Jew of ministerial rank. An Asquithian Liberal, he had broken with his former leader after six months in the political wilderness to join Lloyd George's administration. To Asquith's chagrin, Montagu had also married Venetia Stanley, the young woman with whom the former prime minister had been obsessed, and to whom he had penned indiscreet letters even during Cabinet meetings. Montagu was not a member of the War Cabinet but was in attendance by invitation. Unlike Samuel, he opposed the Zionists. Weizmann characterised Montagu as 'a great Hindu nationalist who thought it his duty to combat Jewish nationalism' and symbolic of those whose 'only claim to Judaism is that they are working for its disappearance'.[17] Montagu feared that the promotion of a Jewish national home in Palestine might lead to fresh questions about the loyalty of Jews in Britain and to anti-Semitism. According to Lloyd George, Montagu said later that 'I have been striving all my life to escape from the Ghetto.'[18] Montagu did not see the Jews as sufficiently homogeneous to claim any homeland. There were others within Anglo-Jewry who shared Montagu's fears, including the President of the Anglo-Jewish Association, Claude Montefiore, and the journalist Lucien Wolf, who was director of the so-called Conjoint Foreign Committee of British Jews, a joint endeavour of the Board of Deputies of British Jews and Montefiore's association. The committee was intended as a means of bringing Jewish views to the attention of the British government. Of the

300,000 or so Jews in Britain, only about 8,000 were members of Zionist organisations. Nonetheless, Anglo-Jewry was deeply split, and Wolf's committee collapsed in May 1917 over the whole issue of Zionism.

Montagu's long-term opposition to Zionism had been reiterated in an August 1917 memorandum for the War Cabinet entitled, with intended irony, 'The Anti-Semitism of the Present Government'. There was a veiled threat to resign, but no one appears to have attached much significance to his arguments. Sir Ronald Graham of the Foreign Office described Montagu as representing 'rich Jews' who feared 'that he and his like will be expelled from England and asked to cultivate farms in Palestine'. Rather similarly, in May 1939, Harold Nicholson made the point that, while the declaration was often represented as an improvisation and expedient intended to placate 'strong Jews', it was intended for the millions of 'weak' Jews 'who lived, not in Kensington Palace Gardens or on Riverside Drive, but at Cracow and Galatz'.[19]

President Wilson wired on 11 September that he considered the time was not yet right for any declaration, the Americans still being interested in reaching a peace agreement with the Turks. Weizmann contacted Brandeis and, through contact with Wilson's adviser, Colonel Edward House, it seemed Wilson might change his mind. Weizmann met Lloyd George on 28 September to apprise him of this, and the item went back on to the War Cabinet agenda for 4 October. At that meeting, Balfour outlined the reasons for proceeding, arguing that there was nothing inconsistent 'between the establishment of a Jewish national focus in Palestine and the complete assimilation and absorption of Jews into the nationality of other countries'.[20] The whole issue was only eighteenth on an agenda of twenty items for consideration: in all, Palestine was only discussed at four of the 261 meetings of the War Cabinet between December 1916 and November 1917, nearly always towards the bottom of the agenda. There was virtually no discussion.

Montagu repeated his fears and Lord Curzon, in the War Cabinet as Lord President of the Council and Leader of the House of Lords, raised the issue of Palestinian reaction, also indicating that Palestine was so economically backward as to hold out little prospect for Jewish settlement. Milner suggested adding some guarantee of equal rights for Palestinians to the declaration, having already asked Leo Amery to draft something suitable.

It was agreed to consult Wilson again, as well as leading Zionists and Jewish anti-Zionists. Soundings were duly taken in the Anglo-Jewish community with six representatives, including Weizmann, Sokolow and Rothschild, for a declaration and four, including Montefiore, against. In the light of the fears that the Germans might pre-empt the declaration, President Wilson signalled his approval on 13 October. A cautious Bonar Law was now procrastinating and Curzon continued to raise the economic arguments. He recognised the diplomatic advantages though, after the war, as Foreign Secretary, he was to declare that the British had a better claim to France than the Jews to a Palestine they had left 1,200 years previously. On 31 October, with Montagu having departed for India thirteen days previously, the War Cabinet approved the final declaration. Weizmann was waiting close to the Cabinet Office when Sykes came out of the meeting to proclaim, 'Dr Weizmann, it's a boy.'[21] Balfour wrote to Rothschild on 2 November 1917 to convey a 'declaration of sympathy with Jewish Zionist aspirations'. It was made public on 9 November. As finally agreed, Balfour wrote, 'His Majesty's Government view with favour the establishment in Palestine of a national home for the Jewish people and will use their best endeavours to facilitate the achievement of this object, it being clearly understood that nothing shall be done which may prejudice the civil and religious rights of existing non-Jewish communities in Palestine or the rights and political status enjoyed by Jews in any other country.'[22]

The Germans felt the declaration an empty gesture, and it was clear that the War Cabinet saw it primarily in terms of its short-term political advantages. As Weizmann appreciated, using the government's 'best endeavours' did not actually imply that a Jewish entity would emerge. Nor did 'home' imply statehood. Weizmann was unaware that the prospect of a negotiated settlement with the Turks had again surfaced at the very moment the War Cabinet had agreed to the declaration. Despite the moral objections of Sykes and Curzon in the light of the promises to the Zionists, the War Cabinet was minded to abandon claims to Mesopotamia, Syria and Palestine in order to secure peace with the Turks. In the event, the prospects of a deal had dwindled by January 1918.

There was a great deal of favourable reaction to the declaration among Jewish communities with, for example, a mass pro-British demonstration in Odessa in late November 1917. In the longer term, however, the

Bolsheviks proved unreceptive to any appeal to Zionism. Moreover, British military success in Palestine owed nothing to the declaration, Jerusalem falling into British hands on 9 December 1917. Physical possession of Palestine negated any advantage deriving from the declaration as a diplomatic lever to offset French claims on a greater Syria. In any case, Georges Clemenceau, who became French prime minister in December 1917, had no interest in the Middle East, and was prepared to give Britain a free hand. As a sop to both the French and the Arabs, aware of the Sykes-Picot agreement through Bolshevik disclosure, a reaffirmation of Anglo-French intentions on 7 November 1918 carefully promised the Arabs emancipation from the Turks rather than independence. Clemenceau then verbally assured Lloyd George on 1 December 1918 that the French did not want Palestine. Nonetheless, nothing could be guaranteed and tortuous negotiations were to continue through the Paris peace conference, at which the views of both Arab and Zionist delegations were heard politely, and ignored.

The Middle East peace process reached its climax at San Remo in April 1920 with Britain receiving the mandates to govern Palestine, Transjordan and Iraq, and France those of Syria and Lebanon, on behalf of the new League of Nations. All were Category A mandates, implying the territories were sufficiently advanced to require only temporary 'guidance' before proceeding to independence. Faisal was proclaimed King of Syria in March 1920, but was then ousted by French military action in July. The British made Faisal King of Iraq instead in August 1921. Abdullah was made King of Transjordan, carved from Palestine, in 1922. Hussein had been proclaimed King of the Hejaz in October 1916, but was defeated by his old rival, Ibn Sa'ud in 1924. Hussein abdicated in favour of his eldest son, Ali, but Ibn Sa'ud ousted Ali too in 1925. Ibn Sa'ud proclaimed himself King of the Hejaz in 1926, and King of Saudi Arabia in 1932.

As for Palestine, the Balfour Declaration was incorporated into the Treaty of Sèvres ending the war with Ottoman Turkey on 10 August 1920. It continued to be regarded as binding, though there were fewer prepared to defend it amid the seemingly intractable problem of reconciling Jews and Palestinians. The prospects of a Jewish national home were dealt a blow by the Labour government's White Paper in 1930 aimed at restricting Jewish immigration. Weizmann, who had founded the Jewish Agency in Palestine and striven to establish viable Jewish communities there, was able to overturn it. In 1937 the Conservative government accepted a partition plan for Palestine, a programme Weizmann supported. In May 1939, however, the declaration was finally abandoned as the British opted for an independent state within ten years but with an Arab majority, a limit on Jewish immigration becoming a prohibition after five years. The Jewish Agency regarded this as a betrayal of the declaration.

In March 1930 Weizmann went to see the dying Balfour. Balfour had left government with the fall of Lloyd George's administration in 1922 but returned as Lord President of the Council from 1925 to 1929. By this stage, he was deaf, in poor health and impoverished by a failed financial venture. According to Balfour's niece and biographer, it was 'a brief and silent farewell' but 'I who saw the look with which Balfour moved his hand and touched the bowed head of the other, have no doubt at all that he realised the nature of the emotion which for the first, and only, time showed itself in his sick-room.'[23] Balfour died a few days later. Weizmann's hopes had been undermined by the inter-communal violence in Palestine, and he steadily lost influence. The declaration remained his abiding achievement, for it had been his single-minded determination to harness Britain to the Zionist cause. In 1948 Weizmann's enduring contribution was recognised by his election as the first president of the state of Israel. He died in 1952.

CHAPTER 11

THE MORAL IMPERATIVE

Woodrow Wilson's Fourteen Points, 8 January 1918

T HE EVENTUAL peace settlement imposed upon Germany and her allies was to be an uneasy compromise between British pragmatism, French concerns for security and US President Woodrow Wilson's 'progressive internationalism'. The United States was not technically an ally of Britain and France after April 1917, but an 'associated power'. Thus, Wilson's unilateral announcement of his peace principles on 8 January 1918 posed a significant challenge to his allies when he spoke of freedom of the seas, restriction on armaments, economic cooperation and self-determination. Subsequently, the Germans were to request an armistice on the basis of an 'American peace' that was not to be realised. The problem was that Wilson, the idealistic former professor, was faced with two unscrupulous realists in British Prime Minister Lloyd George and French Prime Minister Georges Clemenceau. The legacy of the fourteen points, therefore, was a bitter one.

Passionately committed to international arbitration as a means of settling international disputes, Wilson had agonised over entering the war, especially when it might jeopardise his modest domestic social-reform programme. Publicly, he had embraced the view of many Americans that no US interests were directly threatened by war in Europe. He also understood well enough the polyglot nature of American immigrant society. Those of German, Irish, Jewish and Polish descent were not well disposed towards the Entente whatever the American cultural affinities with Britain, or the sentimental attachment to France for its role in American independence.

At least 4 million Americans claimed Irish descent, and 8 million German descent. Wilson suggested on one occasion that the British made the mistake of assuming that Americans were a British people. US interests were most threatened by the Royal Navy's intention to impose an economic blockade on Germany and its allies, but Wilson knew that longer-term American interests would not be served by a German victory. As he expressed it on one occasion in June 1915, 'England's violation of neutral rights is different from Germany's violation of the rights of humanity'.[1] Wilson did not believe that neutral rights on the high seas were sufficiently important to justify an open breach with the Entente. Remonstrations at British policy were largely directed privately through the Anglophile US ambassador in London, Walter Hines Page. It was a de facto acceptance that made the United States at least complicit in the economic blockade. Wilson's first Secretary of State, William Jennings Bryan, a genuine neutralist, resigned in June 1915 over the strong wording of Wilson's note to the German government after the sinking of the liner, *Lusitania*.

The Entente was increasingly dependent upon American raw materials and manufactured goods and, above all, upon American financial credit. By June 1917 Britain owed the J. P. Morgan Bank in New York alone some $400 billion. In theory, this gave Wilson considerable economic leverage in his efforts to compel the Entente to take seriously his mediation efforts. American investment in the Entente was such, however, that the publication of his Peace Note to the belligerents on 18 December 1916 led to the worst fall on the New York stock market for fourteen years. Nonetheless, Wilson expected to be able to use financial pressure in any post-war settlement, remarking of the allies in July 1917 that 'when the war is over we can force them to our way of thinking, because by that time they will, among other things, be financially in our hands'.[2]

The German return to unrestricted submarine warfare in February 1917 compelled Wilson to break off diplomatic relations with Germany. The ineptitude of German diplomacy was further exposed by the publication of the Zimmermann telegram that same month. The German Foreign Secretary, Arthur Zimmermann, had instructed the German ambassador in Mexico to propose an alliance. The Mexicans were promised that, in the event of a German victory, all those territories they had lost to the United States as a result of the Mexican War of 1846–48 would be restored. The

British had intercepted the telegram and handed it to the Americans. Naively Zimmermann confirmed its authenticity. The fall of the Tsarist government in March then conveniently removed any moral obstacles to the United States being seen to ally itself with Russia. The US declaration of war on Germany was passed by 82 votes to six in the Senate on 4 April 1917 and by 378 to 50 in the House of Representatives two days later.

Wilson was prepared to accept the strategic assumptions of his new allies, but there were limitations to American attachment to the Entente. Significantly, the United States did not sign up to the 1914 Declaration of London precluding a separate peace. Thus, the American Expeditionary Force (AEF) was committed to the Western Front because this was identified as the decisive theatre, in which an independent American army would make a recognisable contribution to victory. Since the British army was nearing exhaustion, the political price the Americans could extract was considerable. Once it was clear, in August 1918, that the German offensives were over, the British reduced the shipping available to convey American troops to Europe: there was little advantage either in increasing American leverage or in sacrificing British export trade to do so. Wilson had exactly the same aim as Kitchener in 1914, namely to dictate the peace.

The nature of an American peace had already become apparent in Wilson's Peace Note of December 1916. He had called for a peace without territorial annexations and one founded on equality, self-determination, freedom of the seas, limitation of armaments and a permanent international organisation. Wilson maintained that a war fought for democracy precluded territorial gains on the part of the Entente. The Peace Note had been prompted by the German announcement on 12 December 1916 of willingness to discuss peace terms. The British rightly judged the German approach an attempt to split the Entente. They could not afford outright rejection, which might strengthen German support in the United States. In response, therefore, the British and French were forced into an indication of their own war aims. They called for the restoration of Belgium and Serbia, the evacuation of all territories occupied by Germany, indemnities for war damages, and self-determination for subject nationalities within the Austro-Hungarian and Ottoman Empires. They also accepted Wilson's proposal for a post-war international organisation.

Additional pressure was exerted by the collapse of the Tsarist government in Russia in March 1917, and the call by the new Provisional Government in May for a peace without annexations or indemnities. The Reichstag Peace Resolution on 19 July 1917 similarly called for a settlement based upon no annexations or indemnities. Though the German leadership ignored the resolution, the British responded by a demand for democratisation of Germany in advance of any negotiations. Although rejecting a separate Austro-Hungarian overture for peace, the British War Cabinet did resolve in August 1917 that it would negotiate if the Germans evacuated Belgium. There was a negative reaction, however, to the intervention of Pope Benedict XV in August 1917. Wilson was embarrassed by the attitude of his allies since, in speaking of freedom of the seas, restrictions on armaments, economic cooperation and a degree of self-determination, the Papal note reflected many of his own ideas. But even he could not accept the restoration of the status quo ante also implied by the Papal note.

Growing war weariness and the revolution in Russia necessitated a remobilisation of the national will among all the belligerents during 1917, as suggested by the creation of the National War Aims Committee in Britain, the Union of Associations against Enemy Propaganda in France, and the Fatherland Party in Germany. The public enunciation of war aims was an integral part of the process, as was the denigration of perceived internal enemies such as pacifists and socialists. War aims were best left vague lest the failure to achieve them appeared as defeat, but vagueness also might suggest to domestic opinion that the gain was not worth the sacrifice.

A number of events coincided to make it imperative that the Entente declare its hand publicly. The Bolshevik seizure of power in Russia on 7–8 November 1917 was followed by their publication of all the 'secret treaties' between Russia and its erstwhile allies on 22 November. Negotiations for a ceasefire then opened with Germany and Austria-Hungary at Brest Litovsk on 15 December. The Bolsheviks presented a six-point programme for peace without annexations or indemnities. The Bolsheviks included the idea that any territory in Europe or overseas that had shown nationalist discontent since the late nineteenth century should be able to settle its future by free referendum. The Bolsheviks were no more genuine than their opponents in paying such lip service to self-determination. On Christmas

Day the Austro-Hungarian and German foreign ministers, Ottakar von
Czernin and Richard von Kühlmann, indicated they would accept a peace
without annexations if the Entente were to do the same. They knew that the
Entente would not do so. The armistice talks were suspended for three days
to enable the Bolsheviks to invite the Entente to send representatives to
Brest Litovsk.

In Britain, additional pressure had been placed on Lloyd George by the
publication of a letter on 29 November 1917 by the former Unionist Foreign
Secretary, Lord Lansdowne, calling for a moderate peace, and the declaration of non-expansionist war aims by the Labour Party on 28 December.
In a speech to the Trades Union Congress at Caxton Hall on 5 January
1918, therefore, Lloyd George showed willingness to compromise. Italy's
claims on Austria-Hungary would not be supported unless justified. While
Belgium, Serbia and Romania should all be restored, and consideration
given to an independent Poland, there should not be an automatic expansion of states in the Balkans despite the need to recognise self-determination
within the Austro-Hungarian and Ottoman Empires. Russia would be left to
its fate. Self-determination, of course, was a two-edged sword for the British
in view of the situation in Ireland. With great imperial proconsuls like Lords
Milner and Curzon in the War Cabinet, and many of Milner's disciples
within government, it was always evident that Turkey would be dismembered, and that British imperial interests would remain paramount. Lloyd
George's speech pre-empted but did not overshadow that of Wilson on
8 January.

Wilson had resolved that he must act unilaterally following the failure of
Lloyd George and Clemenceau to respond positively to the attempt by his
envoy, Colonel Edward M. House, to persuade them to adopt a general
declaration on war aims between 29 November and 3 December. It was
Wilson and House together who then worked on the statement Wilson
would make to Congress. They were assisted by the deliberations of
a wide-ranging academic study into a future peace settlement – the
Inquiry – established by House at Wilson's request in September 1917.
Wilson's subsequent expositions of his policy – the 'Four Principles' on 11
February 1918, the 'Four Additional Points' on 4 July 1918, and the 'Five
Particulars' on 27 September 1918 – were also issued unilaterally. Wilson
made little effort to coordinate policy with that of his allies.

A slender figure of just under 6 feet, with a high forehead, and now greying hair, the bespectacled Wilson was sixty-two in 1918. He was the son of a Presbyterian minister of 'Scotch-Irish' stock and an English mother whose family had emigrated to Canada when she was a child. He was born in Staunton, Virginia, in 1856, though the family soon moved to Georgia. Although he lived in Staunton for only four years, Wilson's birthplace was opened as a major museum and the centre for his 'Presidential Library' in 1990. Not to be outdone, his boyhood home at Augusta for the ten years between 1860 and 1870 became a museum in 1991 and a 'National Historic Landmark' in 2008. First in the field, although just as tenuous, is Wilson's last home in Washington's Embassy Row, in which he lived for just three years after leaving the presidency in 1921: that became a 'National Historic Landmark' in 1964.

Educated at Princeton and the University of Virginia, Wilson briefly prac-tised law in Atlanta before teaching history, jurisprudence and political economy at a number of institutions, returning to Princeton as its president in 1902. Apart from a five-volume history of the American people, Wilson also penned an influential book on congressional government. At Princeton he clashed with faculty and students, resigning in 1910 to contest the gover-norship of New Jersey. As a new and seemingly disinterested candidate, Wilson won the nomination, triumphing over Democrat Party bosses. A successful gubernatorial term saw Wilson go on to win the party's nomina-tion as presidential candidate in 1912, albeit it was only on the 46th ballot at the party convention. Seen as more moderate than William Jennings Bryan, who had unsuccessfully contested the presidency in the previous three elections, Wilson secured an overwhelming victory in the Electoral College. His 6.2 million popular votes, however, were fewer than the combined 7.6 million votes polled by the two former presidents, Theodore Roosevelt and William Howard Taft, who split the Republican vote. Wilson positioned himself as a progressive, breaking monopolies and restoring economic competition. He did rather better in securing re-election in 1916, winning 2.8 million more votes than four years previously, and having a clear lead in the popular vote over his Republican opponent, Charles Evans Hughes, a former governor of New York.

A shy and diffident young man – he did not learn to read until he was twelve – Wilson was imbued from the beginning with a strong Calvinist faith that gave structure to his life and also meaning to his rather simplistic view of right and wrong. Sentimental towards the 'Lost Cause' of the Confederacy, Wilson took a paternal view of black Americans, whom he felt unsuited for citizenship. Nor did his sense of morality prevent him from having a brief affair with a woollen manufacturer's wife in 1909–10. Wilson's first wife, Ellen, whom he had married in 1885, died in 1914. He then married a widow, Edith Galt, in 1915.

Lloyd George found Wilson agreeable on some occasions but also intensely suspicious on others. Wilson also struck him as humourless, stiff, unbending and uncommunicative, and a curious blend of 'the noble visionary, the implacable and unscrupulous partisan, the exalted idealist and the man of rather petty personal rancour'. Lloyd George was astonished at Wilson's outburst of 'acid detestation' when Lloyd George mentioned his own sorrow at the death of Theodore Roosevelt.[3] Others also found Wilson cold and impersonal. He tended to take an instant dislike to some he met. There was no doubt that Wilson bore grudges to an extraordinary degree. One who knew him at Princeton recalled, 'If you agreed with him you were perfect, if you disagreed, you were guilty of a personal insult.' Not surprisingly, Wilson's first Secretary of War, Lindley Garrison, felt Wilson 'a man of high ideals, but no principles'.[4]

Wilson believed that it was important to discern the public mood before taking major decisions. Equally, he judged that mood on the basis of his intuition, and assumed he could win the argument by the power of his not inconsiderable oratorical skills. Henry Cabot Lodge, who was to lead the campaign in the Senate against ratification of the Treaty of Versailles, rather nicely characterised the trait: 'When the President is approaching a new subject the first thing he does is to make up his mind, and when his mind is made up the thoughts which in more ordinary mortals are apt to precede the decision or determination of a great question are excluded; information upon the new subject is looked on as a mere impertinence.' Similarly, Robert Lansing, Bryan's successor as Secretary of State, noted in November 1921 that Wilson fitted the facts to his prejudged position: 'His judgements were always right in his own mind, because he knew that they were right. How did he know they were right? Why he knew it, and that was the best reason in the world. No other was necessary.'[5] Certainly, Wilson took poorly to Congressional scrutiny of his presidency though, paradoxically, he was usually prepared to allow his cabinet to run their own departments without excessive interference.

Wilson had only a small personal staff to advise him, principally Colonel House. The president had met the fifty-four-year-old House, a liberally minded Texan businessman, in 1911. The title was a purely honorary one confirmed on House by a Texas governor, and calling to mind an old saying in the American Southwest that a man without a title 'either didn't have any friends or any imagination'.[6] Short, with a receding chin and large ears, House shared some of Wilson's utopian views. He did not seek preferment as such and received no salary, but set out to make himself a useful friend. Amiable and unpretentious, House was no intellectual but he was fairly shrewd. House acted primarily as a kind of gatekeeper, *Harper's Weekly* describing him as Assistant President House in April 1913. It suited Wilson's need for some buffer between himself and others, Wilson once admitting that 'I have a sense of power in dealing with men collectively, which I do not feel always in dealing with them singly'.[7] Wilson's secretary, Joseph Tumulty, a lawyer of Irish-American extraction, was jealous of House, while Bryan disliked House intensely. House was also to find his access to Wilson resented by Edith.

A significant factor was Wilson's health. In the midst of the struggles at Princeton, Wilson suffered a stroke in May 1906 that left him with recurring blindness in the left eye. It was a sign of the progressive cerebral vascular disease that he had developed from about 1896 onwards. It would appear that Wilson also had a series of psychosomatic illnesses in his childhood. In 1913 he suffered a bad bout of neuritis and he also had constant digestive problems. It is generally suggested that the 1906 stroke made Wilson hypersensitive and far more intolerant and suspicious of others. His stamina and his memory were both fading by 1918.

Wilson's world view is best characterised as that of a 'progressive internationalist'. He believed that the United States should aspire to moral leadership in international affairs in a kind of 'missionary' diplomacy. He also felt that he was almost divinely ordained to provide such global leadership. Carried away by the occasion – he explained to Edith that his heart was in a 'whirl' because she had just asked what his intentions were towards her – Wilson proclaimed in a speech at Philadelphia in May 1915 that America was 'too proud to fight' for there was 'such a thing as a nation being so right that it does not need to convince others by force that it is right'.[8] Similarly, in calling on Congress to declare war on 2 April 1917, Wilson not only claimed that the world must be made 'safe for democracy'. He also indicated that the US sought no gains, indemnities or compensation in ensuring that the 'rights' of mankind 'have been made as secure as the faith and the freedom of nations can make them'.[9] Precisely the same sentiments underlined his speech on the Fourteen Points on 8 January 1918, namely that the world should be 'fit and safe to live in', that all peoples 'are in effect partners in this interest', and that the US saw 'very clearly that unless justice be done to others it will not be done to us'.[10] Wilson, though, was quite prepared to resort to force in what he rationalised as American national interests, intervening in Haiti in 1915, the Dominican Republic in 1916, and in Mexico in both 1914 and 1916.

In a speech Wilson composed in 1916 but never went on to deliver, he conceived the aim of a 'far-sighted statesman' should be to use the destruction and suffering of the war as an 'object less for the future', thereby demonstrating that war could not be 'a means of attaining national ambitions'. In May that same year he also set down some principles for the State Department as a basis for peace, namely mutual guarantees of political independence, territorial integrity, economic freedoms and limitation of armaments.[11] In his annual message to Congress on 4 December 1917, Wilson suggested that the US would talk peace with a government that truly represented the German people, and that there should be no vindictive action, no annexations, no contributions and no punitive indemnities.

In the light of the events in Russia in November 1917, Wilson crystallised his thoughts through conversations with the Serbian minister in Washington, Milento Vesnić, and the British naval attaché, William Wiseman. He valued Wiseman's views rather more than those of the British ambassador, Sir Cecil Spring Rice, whom Wilson felt to be too close to the Republicans. House brought the report of the Inquiry – 'The Present Situation: The War Aims and Peace Terms It Suggests' – on 4 January 1918. Walter Lippmann, a journalist who was acting as an assistant to the Secretary of War, had been the principal author of the report. House urged Wilson to take the initiative and demonstrate that the US was prepared to state its war aims as a means of encouraging progressives in Britain and France, and uniting Americans who wanted an idealistic settlement. House and Wilson talked until 2230 hours, Wilson continuing to work on the speech after House left. They resumed next morning and, using his portable typewriter, Wilson prepared a summary of the points he wished to make. House grouped them and numbered them.

Most attention was paid to the statement on Russia. Both men knew from a discussion with the Provisional Government's former Washington ambassador, Boris Bakhmetiev, that if the Bolshevik call for peace was simply ignored, it would strengthen the Bolsheviks. Alsace-Lorraine was also a delicate issue, House initially suggesting it not be mentioned at all, but they agreed on a formula. Wilson's call for freedom of the seas was another point of difficulty but, at House's urging, Wilson made it a strong statement irrespective of what British views might be. In all, the drafting took two hours before lunch.

Wilson decided to contact the British Foreign Secretary, Arthur Balfour, indicating that he felt compelled to issue a statement, and trusting no British statement would conflict with his views. Before this could be sent, news arrived of Lloyd George's Caxton Hall speech, of which Wilson had not received prior notice. Wilson felt initially that he could not now make his statement, but House argued that Lloyd George had cleared the air. His speech bore general comparison to Wilson's ideas. Wilson therefore proceeded, working on the final draft on the morning of 6 January. He discussed it with House that afternoon and they slept on some possible amendments, especially on freedom of the seas. After lunch on Monday, 7 January, they added a few qualifications on freedom of the seas and Alsace-Lorraine. For the first time the Secretary of State, Lansing, was called in at 1500 hours and he suggested minor changes to the wording. A new version was prepared by a stenographer, which Wilson checked, and the speech was sent off to the Government Printing Office for a reading copy. Tumulty hastily arranged a joint session of Congress for 1230 hours on 8 January, so hastily indeed that three cabinet members and several foreign diplomats did not hear of it. Wilson had been adamant that the press should not learn of his speech in advance.

Wilson's speech, received with frequent applause and a standing ovation at the end, came on the very day the Kaiser formally ordered preparations for the German spring offensives. The speech was delivered in the expectation that the negotiations at Brest Litovsk had broken down, and that the

Bolsheviks would remain in the war. It was aimed, therefore, as much at the Bolsheviks as at the Germans, as well as at what might be characterised as liberal progressive opinion within the Entente. The first half of the speech concentrated on Russia and Wilson's own denunciation of 'secret diplomacy', before he turned to his fourteen points. Austria-Hungary would not be dismembered. Germany would not be deprived of its status as a great power, though occupied territory would need to be evacuated including the two provinces of Alsace-Lorraine taken from the French in 1871. Equally, Britain and France would not be able to realise their economic and territorial aims, and Wilson's general principles would impact more on Britain than Germany.

The first four of Wilson's principles were general in nature. Rejecting 'secret' diplomacy, Wilson endorsed freedom of navigation on the seas, free trade and reduction of armaments. He believed that secret diplomatic deals had caused the war and that such a prohibition would prevent another. Wilson principally meant lower tariffs rather than free trade as such, hoping thereby to meet some of the French demands that German trade be carefully controlled after the war. Freedom of the seas, however the wording had been qualified, would never be acceptable in time of war to a maritime power such as Britain.

The fifth point – the adjustment of colonial claims in the interests of the populations concerned – was anathema to Britain, France and Japan. It could only be effectively applied to German overseas colonies, thus giving recognition to allied territorial claims. Restoration of occupied territory formed the basis for points six to eight, though, again, Belgium claimed territory that would secure it a better strategic frontier line for future defence. The restoration of Alsace-Lorraine to France also implied that there would be no plebiscite on self-determination here irrespective of its real identity after over forty years of German colonisation. Alsace was largely German speaking. Russia, over which Wilson could have little influence, would be left alone once the German presence had been removed, with the exception of the territory to be given to an independent Poland.

The thorny issue of self-determination underpinned points nine to thirteen. In effect, Wilson promised only autonomy for those within Austria-Hungary at this stage, though he did endorse an independent

Poland. Similarly, only autonomous development was envisaged for the subjects of the Ottoman Empire. Romania, Serbia and Montenegro would be restored and relationships in the Balkans determined by 'friendly counsel along historically established lines of allegiance and nationality'. Nothing was said with respect to French ambitions for possession of the Rhineland. It was Italian claims that were most challenged by Wilson's insistence on the frontier being determined along recognisable lines of nationality. By so doing, Wilson effectively rejected the wider Italian territorial claims enshrined in the 1915 Treaty of London.

Wilson's fourteenth and last point was the establishment of a post-war League of Nations. He ended with the rhetorical flourish that the American people were ready for justice and freedom so that, 'The moral climax of this the culminating and final war for human liberty has come, and they are ready to put their own strength, their own highest purpose, their own integrity and devotion to the test.'[12]

In the United States the speech was welcomed even by parts of the Republican press. On 10 January, a joint statement in Britain by the Labour Party, TUC and the Co-operative Parliamentary Representation Committee endorsed it, as did the French Left. In Russia, Lenin had it printed in *Izvestiya*. Where it mattered, the reception was more disappointing. The British and French press were less enthusiastic, and much of the Italian press was hostile. In France, *L'École de Paris* commented that the fourteen points were 'in those blissful realms where all the friends of humanity have tried to build the Salento of their dreams'.[13] Lloyd George and Clemenceau gave the speech only a lukewarm welcome. Lloyd George told the Italian prime minister, Vittorio Orlando, that his own speech at Caxton Hall did not affect the provisions of the Treaty of London. Curiously, perhaps, Wilson had greater impact in Germany and Austria-Hungary. Czernin responded by accepting the general principles but refused the possibility of making territorial concessions to Italy, Serbia, Romania and Montenegro, though Emperor Karl conceded the need for internal autonomy.

In Germany, the chancellor, Georg von Hertling, was more grudging, recognising that acceptance would require too great a territorial sacrifice to make the proposals acceptable to the military leadership. Consequently, he rejected them in a speech to the Reichstag Central Committee on 24 January, while contriving somehow to accept those principles that were most favourable to Germany. He suggested, for example, that Britain should give up Aden, the Falklands, Gibraltar, Hong Kong and Malta. As far as he was concerned, the ongoing negotiations with the Bolsheviks were of no concern to the western allies. Hertling also claimed that the annexation of Belgian and French territory was not part of any German war-aims programme, though no territory would be surrendered. Hertling's response dismayed the German Left, and contributed to the upsurge in strikes in January 1918.

On 11 February 1918 Wilson outlined 'Four Principles', repeating his Fourteen Points in general form, in an attempt to exploit the apparent divisions between Czernin and Hertling. Czernin's speech was welcomed but Hertling's condemned as contrary to the Reichstag Peace Resolution. Nonetheless, Wilson also explicitly warned his allies that territorial settlements had to be in the interests of the populations concerned. All 'well-defined aspirations' needed to be satisfied as far as possible, though this left room for manoeuvre.[14] In response, in the Reichstag on 25 February, Hertling signalled acceptance of an independent Poland but that it would need to offer territorial compensation to Germany. He also suggested, bizarrely, that the continuing advance of German forces on the Eastern Front represented 'rescue operations undertaken in the name of humanity'.[15] Karl accepted the Four Principles on 18 February but rejected the Fourteen Points, rendering the response largely meaningless. Ultimately, negotiations with Vienna conducted through King Alfonso XIII of Spain led nowhere. The dialogue ended with the Treaty of Brest Litovsk signed between Germany, Austria-Hungary and the Bolsheviks on 4 March, by which Germany achieved sweeping territorial gains. Ironically, the terms of Brest Litovsk did considerably more than Wilson's Fourteen Points to win the support of the political Left in the West for continuing the war.

With the start of the German spring offensive on 21 March 1918, Wilson's despair was expressed in an address at Baltimore on 6 April. Only force would now suffice to end the war: 'There is, therefore, but one response possible from us: Force, Force to the utmost. Force without stint or limit, the righteous and triumphant Force which shall make Right the law of the world, and cast every selfish dominion down in the dust.'[16] At Mount Vernon on 4 July, Wilson's 'Four Additional Points' emphasised that the necessary victory must be used for the higher purpose of destroying arbitrary power, settling territorial claims according to the wishes of peoples, respecting international law, and establishing an international organisation. There was a final summing up in New York on 27 September in which Wilson proclaimed 'Five Particulars' for a peace settlement: equal justice, no special interests overriding the common good, no secret treaties, no selfish economic combinations, and free disclosure of international agreements.

It has been suggested rightly of the Fourteen Points that the 'long-term repercussions exceeded their immediate effects'.[17] Nonetheless, when the Germans first applied for an armistice in October 1918, they did so on the basis of the Fourteen Points. Receiving the initial German request on 3 October 1918, Wilson demanded clarification. He did not consult his allies in doing so. Entente political leaders drew up a brief list of eight conditions intended to prevent the Germans using an armistice as a temporary breathing period. The terms included German evacuation of occupied French and Belgian territory, and retirement behind the Rhine, thus also vacating Alsace-Lorraine and the Rhineland. The allied Supreme War Council then formulated suitable terms on 8 October, a process not completed until 4 November largely through the desire of the allied supreme commander, Ferdinand Foch, and the British Admiralty to impose more severe conditions. As it was, Clemenceau and Lloyd George were wary of an armistice on the basis of Wilson's Fourteen Points, and Wilson conceded a French occupation of the Rhineland to achieve agreement on the broad principles. The South African member of the British War Cabinet, Jan Smuts, also convinced his colleagues that an armistice now would forestall greater American dominance of the peace process if the war continued into 1919.

In the meantime, Wilson hardened his position on Germany in response to the possibility of strong gains by the Republicans in the upcoming mid-term congressional elections, and to the loss of the liner Leinster to a German submarine on 12 October. Wilson's second note on 14 October was something of a shock for the German leadership in demanding absolute guarantees to maintain the present military supremacy of the allies. A third note on 23 October also made it clear that an armistice must make resumption of the war by Germany impossible, and that peace terms must bring about the end of Prussian militarism. Emperor Karl also appealed to Wilson for peace on the basis of the Fourteen Points, but Wilson replied only through Berlin. In any case, Wilson had indicated on 19 October that his tenth point, concerning Austria-Hungary, had already been superseded by events within the empire. With the exception of accepting freedom of the seas or a minimum level of reparations, Lloyd George and Clemenceau agreed to Wilson's armistice terms. They did so, however, only when House arrived in London for talks between 29 October and 4 November, in which he threatened that Wilson was prepared to consider negotiating a separate peace.

While the armistice terms of 11 November 1918 were far harsher than the Germans had anticipated, it is important to emphasise that they had not surrendered unconditionally. So far as they were concerned, they had accepted a military armistice on the basis of the Fourteen Points. Since Entente troops only occupied the Rhineland, and they did not parade through Berlin as German troops had through Paris in 1871, it was never brought fully home to the German people that they had been defeated. Hence the subsequent shock in Germany at the terms imposed in the Paris peace conference, which convened on 18 January 1919.

Much was already beyond the control of the victorious allied powers. The 'Big Four' of Wilson, Lloyd George, Clemenceau and Orlando could not enforce their collective will over some parts of Europe. The break-up of Austria-Hungary and of Tsarist Russia was established fact before the conference convened. The situation created thereby was irreversible. Poland, Czechoslovakia and Yugoslavia were all already in effective existence, and Finland, Estonia, Latvia, Lithuania, Georgia, Armenia and Azerbaijan had all declared independence from Russia. Despite his better judgement, Wilson had been persuaded to commit American troops against the Bolsheviks in August 1918, though they performed a limited role in protecting allied bases at Vladivostock, Murmansk and Archangel: he ordered them out in 1919. In most cases achieving economic and strategic frontiers was simply incompatible with the geographical spread of nationalities on the ground, rendering self-determination all but impossible. The negotiations were also to bring into play Clemenceau's desire for a punitive settlement, Lloyd George's desire for stability, and Wilson's desire for what he had articulated in January 1917 as a 'peace without victory'.[18] Wilson envisaged creating a better world based on principles of internationalism, arbitration, collective security, democracy and self-determination.

With the exception of freedom of the seas, Lloyd George considered the Fourteen Points sufficiently vague to allow of several interpretations. The Entente had also made widely contradictory wartime promises to allies or potential allies that were frequently incompatible with the underlying principles. Each Entente delegation at Paris also had to satisfy a public still imbued with the promises made them in return for their sacrifices. Despite American financial muscle, Wilson's position was weaker than it appeared. It was the first occasion any serving president had been absent from the United States during his term of office, and Wilson was widely feted on his appearance in London and then Paris. Wilson and his team, however, were inexperienced in the business of international politics compared with such accomplished and wily operators as Lloyd George and Clemenceau. Consequently, by humouring Wilson's overwhelming desire for the League of Nations, the Europeans wrested concessions on other Wilsonian principles. German collapse had also robbed him of a degree of leverage since the British and French were no longer dependent on US military and financial aid for survival, albeit the financial debt to the US was considerable. Wilson's absence from Paris between 14 February and 14 March 1919 was to prove unhelpful to his cause, though Lloyd George was also elsewhere for much of the same time. In Wilson's absence, House conceded more than Wilson would have liked, to try and speed agreement. More damaging, however, was a stroke Wilson suffered on 3 April 1919 following an attack of influenza, since the stroke appeared to exacerbate his inflexibility.

It followed a bruising series of confrontations between Wilson and Clemenceau over French demands to dismember Germany, Wilson at one point threatening to leave Paris altogether. There were many ways in which Wilson's interpretation of a suitable peace settlement contradicted that of his allies. He interpreted the issue of reparations only as compensating for 'unlawful' wartime action, such as the invasion of neutral Belgium. He did not anticipate that it would include reimbursement of war expenditure. The Fourteen Points had suggested that only Belgium and France could exact 'restoration' for civilian damages. Others, however, interpreted reparations rather more broadly. They were mindful of those the Germans had imposed upon Russia at Brest Litovsk and, even earlier, on the French in 1871. In addition, they bore in mind the Americans' own refusal to maintain economic measures that would have generated funds for reconstruction, and the US refusal to write off allied debts. In order to achieve the League, however, Wilson was forced during the course of April to concede Germany's 'war guilt', wider reparations, and French occupation of the Saar and Rhineland for fifteen years.

Wilson had also intended that there should be 'free, open-minded, and absolutely impartial adjustment' of colonial claims based upon the interests of indigenous populations. Resenting Wilson's interference, neither the British, the British dominions nor the French were willing to forego their colonial claims: all favoured outright annexation of German and Turkish colonial possessions. Annexation, however, would have been politically embarrassing. The solution that presented itself as a means of placating anti-imperial sentiment was the mandate, an idea owing much to Smuts.

Further afield, the Chinese had assumed that Wilson's support for them would sway the other powers, but their case was undermined by promises already made to the Japanese, and wartime agreements between the Chinese and Japanese governments. Many in the American delegation felt Wilson had gone too far in appeasing the Japanese; the concessions being another factor in the opposition to the League being generated in the United States that was to humble Wilson's vision for future American influence in world affairs. That vision, however, had a particular resonance not just for indigenous intellectuals in China but also for those in Egypt, India and Korea. Those such as the Indian poet Rabindranath Tagore, the founder of the Egyptian nationalist Wafd party, Sa'd Zaghlul, and a later co-founder of the Chinese Communist Party, Chen DuXiu, all co-opted the Wilsonian rhetoric of self-determination in the cause of indigenous nationalism. Versions of Wilson's speeches were published by the *Commercial Press* in Shanghai and by the nationalist Ganesh Press in India. His ideals suffused movements such as the disorders in Egypt following Zaghlul's arrest in March 1919; the protests in India against the Rowlatt Public Order Act after March 1919; the Fourth of May Movement in China protesting against the cession of the Shantung peninsula to Japan as a result of the Versailles Treaty in May 1919; and the First of March uprising and aborted declaration of independence, which the Japanese ruthlessly suppressed in Korea in March 1919. The Vietnamese nationalist, Nguyen Ai Quoc, later to be known as Ho Chi Minh, failed to gain access to Wilson in Paris to press the claims of Indochina for concessions from the French.

It has been argued persuasively that disillusionment with the failure of Wilson to effect real change was to turn many indigenous nationalists towards communism.

The details of the League of Nations had not been discussed while the United States was at war, leaving the Republicans to win domestic support for German unconditional surrender. Moreover, the mid-term elections in November 1918 had given the Republicans control of Congress, with a solid majority in the House of Representatives and a two-vote majority in the Senate. Wilson was not particularly influenced by domestic public opinion or interest groups, but he did have a developed sense of retributive justice which, in the short term, required appropriate punishment before Germany could be reintegrated into the new world order. Thus, the more the Germans resisted the idea of their 'war guilt', the more Wilson was convinced it was true. That at least accorded with American public opinion. But, in view of the Republican electoral success, Theodore Roosevelt ominously declared that Wilson and the Fourteen Points 'have ceased to have any shadow of right to be accepted as expressive of the will of the American people'.[19] Wilson also erred in not inviting a major Republican figure onto the Paris delegation, the choice falling on Henry White, a former ambassador to Paris with little influence in the party.

The League, under whose covenant signatories abjured recourse to war, was not something in which many Europeans had much confidence. They yielded, however, to Wilson's wishes to incorporate his vision of the League's covenant into the first twenty-six articles of the Versailles Treaty. Wilson hoped that the existence of the League would enable future adjustment of any faults in the peace treaties. He had to make some concessions to opposition in the Senate. Thus, he stated that the application of the Monroe Doctrine (1823) – by which the United States had long repudiated any European interference in the Americas – lay beyond the League's jurisdiction, and that it would not intervene in internal matters such as tariffs and immigration. It was not enough. Irish, Italian and German Americans all felt alienated by the settlement. Trying to convince Americans of the merit of the settlement, Wilson travelled 8,000 miles in twenty-two days in the course of September 1919, making thirty-two major speeches. The effort resulted in a physical collapse on 25 September 1918. He then suffered a serious stroke on 2 October 1919, which disabled him for a month, and from which he never really recovered. In its aftermath, Wilson declined to compromise further. He utterly rejected, therefore, Cabot Lodge's 'fourteen reservations' that implied some limited acceptance of Wilsonian principles. Wilson failed to build any consensus in the Senate, assuming that he held the moral high ground and that 'the people' would support him. The Republican-dominated Senate declined by fifty-three votes to thirty-eight on 19 November 1919 to ratify either the Treaty of Versailles or American participation in the League, on the grounds that the League infringed national sovereignty by compelling the United States to defend other nations against aggression. The League's General Assembly was thus convened for the first time in November 1920 without the Americans, the Senate having again voted against the treaty on 19 March 1920 by a majority of seven.

Relatively little of the Fourteen Points had survived in the peace settlement in the way Wilson had intended. Only lip service was paid to the four general principles. Arms control was to be attempted unsuccessfully on a limited scale after the war, but free trade was to fall in the face of economic depression. Open diplomacy and freedom of the seas were never likely to recommend themselves to the great powers. Alsace-Lorraine was returned to France, Belgium freed and Poland given independence. On the other hand, the unrealistic aspiration of self-determination had led to the Italians gaining German-speaking areas, and substantial (and exploitable) German and other minorities in all the new states of central and Eastern Europe that emerged from the break-up of Austria-Hungary, including Poland. Through Wilson's inability to carry Americans with him, the League of Nations was doomed to failure. Arguably, the peace settlement was the best that could have been achieved in the circumstances. The idealism of the Fourteen Points, however, had fallen in the face of realpolitik, with damaging consequences for the future.

Despite his obvious incapacity, which Edith and Wilson's doctor, Cary Grayson, tried to conceal, Wilson still sought a third presidential nomination. He was rebuffed and his last public duty was to attend the inauguration of his Republican successor, Warren Harding, on 4 March 1921. Wilson died on 3 February 1924.

CHAPTER 12

THE LAST THROW

The Opening of the German Lys Offensive,
9 April 1918

IN EXPLAINING why Germany lost the First World War, historians have made much of the allied military victories in the 'Hundred Days', starting at Amiens on 8 August 1918. The allies had endured a painful 'learning curve' on the Western Front. The British in particular had improved immeasurably in operational techniques by 1918, although the degree to which improvement had occurred uniformly is hotly debated. Yet, how much was due to German strategic failures in their five successive offensives in the spring of 1918, a 'covert military strike' on the part of German soldiers, the allied blockade, or the collapse of Germany's allies? The real turning point was the strategic failures of Germany's First Quartermaster General, Erich Ludendorff, within a series of offensives beginning on 21 March 1918. Each successive offensive – there were to be five – diluted the opportunity for overall strategic success, with Ludendorff switching operational priorities between (and within) offensives with bewildering speed. Arguably, it was the significant shift in priorities between the first offensive on the Somme in March and the second, Operation Georgette, opening on the Lys on 9 April 1918, that did most to destroy the chance of a breakthrough. Accordingly, Churchill identified the opening of the Lys offensive as 'the climax of the war'.[1] It was a decision that raises the question of Ludendorff's fragile state of mind and his ultimate psychological breakdown in the autumn of 1918.

By the spring of 1918 Ludendorff's authority was unquestioned within Germany. Hindenburg and Ludendorff had assumed the supreme direction of German policy in August 1916 following the dismissal of Erich Falkenhayn as Chief of the General Staff. Hindenburg had replaced Falkenhayn at General Headquarters (OHL). Ludendorff had become First Quartermaster General. Chancellor Bethmann-Hollweg believed that Falkenhayn's removal would end military interference in policy-making. In reality, the appointment of Hindenburg and Ludendorff dramatically increased OHL's interference in all aspects of policy. Its domination of strategic policy was epitomised by the reintroduction of unrestricted submarine warfare. Bethmann-Hollweg was dismissed on the threat of resignation by Hindenburg and Ludendorff on 13 July 1917 following a Reichstag Peace Resolution. OHL found his successor, Georg Michaelis, conveniently pliable. When Michaelis proved incapable of providing any degree of political leadership, the Kaiser replaced him on 1 November 1917 with a Bavarian Catholic from the Centre Party, Count Georg von Hertling. Hertling was more resistant, but OHL still increased its hold over foreign policy. Hindenburg and Ludendorff again used the threat of their own resignations to remove, first, the chief of the Kaiser's civil cabinet, Rudolf von Valentini, in January 1918, and then the Foreign Minister, Richard von Kühlmann, in June 1918. The latter had proclaimed that the war could not be won by military means alone.

Any negotiated peace was unacceptable to Hindenburg and Ludendorff, especially given the increasing turmoil in Russia. OHL's true ambition was well illustrated by the draconian annexation policies imposed on Russia at Brest Litovsk on 3 March 1918. The Bolsheviks yielded 90 per cent of Russia's coalmines, 54 per cent of its industry, 33 per cent of its railways, 32 per cent of its agricultural land and 34 per cent of its population. Similarly harsh terms were imposed on Romania in the Treaty of Bucharest on 7 May 1918, which, among other provisions, ceded Romania's oil fields to German and Austro-Hungarian control for ninety-nine years. These treaties did not exhaust OHL's territorial ambitions. At the time of the armistice in November 1918, OHL was pursuing ideas of a German sponsored puppet state in the Ukraine, enhanced German influence in Transcaucasia, and expansion into the Baltic provinces and Finland. At Spa on 2–3 July 1918, in a pause between the fourth and fifth German spring offensives, the German leadership effectively restated all of its long-standing war aims.

Hindenburg and Ludendorff were equally dominant domestically. Invocation of the Prussian Law of Siege in 1914 placed considerable local authority in the hands of twenty-four Deputy Commanding Generals responsible only to the Kaiser. They retained much of their independence until October 1918. They could imprison individuals without trial and acted as press censors. Military censorship soon metamorphosed into political censorship. The army became involved increasingly in key policy areas such as the provision of raw materials, food supplies and manpower. The War Food Office was established in May 1916 under the direction of Wilhelm Groener, former head of the General Staff's railways section. Military intervention was characterised by new agencies such as the Weapons and Munitions Procurement Office, established in September 1916. All such agencies were then incorporated into a new Supreme War Office under Groener on 1 November 1916. The creation of the Supreme War Office itself reflected the determination of Hindenburg and Ludendorff to raise war production dramatically through the so-called Hindenburg Programme of 31 August 1916, intended to increase artillery and machine guns by a third, and to double ammunition and mortar production.

In pursuit of its production goals, OHL attempted to introduce total labour conscription through the Auxiliary Service Law of 5 December 1916. The price of getting the law through the Reichstag was some concession to organised labour. In February 1917, however, Groener issued a decree prohibiting workers in key industries from leaving on penalty of conscription and, in March, many exemptions were cancelled. As industrial unrest grew, Groener branded strikers 'curs' in April 1917. In the light of the continuing disturbances, Bethmann-Hollweg promised post-war reform of the Prussian franchise in February 1917. The Kaiser was also persuaded to make the same commitment in April, but a suffrage bill failed to reach the final stage for approval until October 1918 as OHL delayed it. Strikes in January and February 1918 were ruthlessly suppressed by force. In March 1918, Ludendorff proposed reducing wages and, in June, Hindenburg demanded that all workers be placed under direct military supervision. Not surprisingly, Bethmann-Hollweg's former secretary, Kurt

Riezler, recorded in April 1918 that Hindenburg and Ludendorff ran Germany as a 'barely veiled military dictatorship'.[2]

Before the war it would have seemed unlikely that Paul von Beneckendorff und von Hindenburg and Erich Ludendorff would have reached such heights of power: Hindenburg had retired in 1911, and Ludendorff had been sidelined in 1913. The choice of Hindenburg to command the German Eighth Army in East Prussia on 22 August 1914 following the dismissal of General Max von Prittwitz und Gaffron had an element of chance. After a routine career, Hindenburg had been sounded out as a possible future Chief of the General Staff in 1903 but had indicated that he did not feel equipped to deal with a position at court. He had been briefly considered as Prussian war minister in 1909. Though he had retired after commanding IV Corps, he was considered for a possible wartime field command in 1912. Nonetheless, it was fortuitous that Hindenburg was living at Hanover on a direct rail line to East Prussia, and that his steadiness seemed better suited than the characters of other potential candidates to work with the man appointed earlier that day to take over as Eighth Army's Chief of Staff. The sudden call left Hindenburg time 'only to buy some woollen under-clothing and to make my old uniform presentable again',[3] so that he arrived in East Prussia in Prussian blue rather than field uniform. The individual already appointed to restore the military situation was Ludendorff. As head of the General Staff's Operations Section, Ludendorff had pressed so hard for an increase in army size, and trod on so many toes in the process, that he had been sent off to a regimental command at Düsseldorf in January 1913. In 1914 Ludendorff had been recalled and led the improvised task force that captured the key Belgian fortress of Liège on 7–8 August. The two men met for the first time at 0400 hours on 23 August on the railway platform at Hanover station as the train stopped to collect Hindenburg.

Russian mobilisation had occurred faster than anticipated. Von Prittwitz, thoroughly alarmed as his forces were pushed back, had proposed to abandon East Prussia, and was dismissed. Arriving at their new headquarters on 23 August, Hindenburg and Ludendorff found that Eighth Army's able head of operations, Lieutenant Colonel Max Hoffmann, had already worked out a scheme for a counter-attack. This they promptly adopted, using strategic railways to concentrate against the Russian Second Army. It was defeated in a spectacular double envelopment at Tannenberg between

27 and 29 August 1914. The Russian First Army was then shattered around the Masurian lakes on 9 and 10 September. Tannenberg had actually been fought around Frögenau, but the nearby Tannenberg was deliberately chosen as the battle's name because it symbolised the reversal of the defeat there of the Teutonic Knights by the Poles and Lithuanians in 1410.

Tannenberg was not a crippling blow for the Russians, but the propaganda value was such that Hindenburg and Ludendorff became instant national heroes. Later, Hoffmann is said to have remarked sourly to visitors to OHL of Hindenburg that, 'This is where the Field Marshal slept *before* the battle, that is where he slept *after* the battle, and that, my friends, is where he slept *during* the battle.' Hindenburg in particular became almost a 'wartime cottage industry'.[4] Widely promoted as a symbolic figure, Hindenburg had the Silesian town of Zabrze renamed after him. A series of wooden statues of him was erected in many cities, into which nails could be hammered upon donation to war charities or bonds: that in Berlin had space for two million nails. After the war, a huge commemorative monument was unveiled at Tannenberg in September 1927, under which Hindenburg was buried when he died in August 1934. His body was removed and the monument destroyed in January 1945 rather than allow it to be destroyed by the advancing Russians.

Falkenhayn believed that France and, especially, Britain posed the greatest threat to German interests. In order to concentrate in the West, he was prepared to countenance seeking terms with Russia. By contrast, Hindenburg and Ludendorff were convinced 'easterners', believing that decisive victory was still possible in the East. Weakened by criticism of the failure to break through at Ypres in October 1914 and aware of the danger posed him by Hindenburg and Ludendorff, Falkenhayn attempted to have Ludendorff transferred to the Carpathians in January 1915. Hindenburg persuaded Kaiser Wilhelm to allow Ludendorff to remain. Falkenhayn survived an attempt, in turn, by Hindenburg to have him dismissed. The Kaiser took umbrage at Hindenburg's open challenge to his own authority and came close to having him cashiered for insubordination, but Hindenburg was already too popular to be removed. Ultimately, the failure of the Verdun offensive, and Romanian entry to the war against Germany in August 1916, brought about Falkenhayn's dismissal, the Kaiser reluctantly accepting the elevation of two men whom he disliked and whose ambition he feared. It was rumoured that the Kaiser had never forgiven Hindenburg for refusing to allow him to 'win' the annual manoeuvres in 1908. Hindenburg had remarked, 'Had this been for real, Your Majesty would now be my prisoner.'[5] Wilhelm equally loathed Ludendorff because he was a 'dubious character, eaten away by personal ambition'. As suggested in an earlier chapter, one of the aides in the Kaiser's Military Cabinet, Colonel von Marschall had predicted that Ludendorff would destroy Germany and, with it, the Hohenzollern dynasty.[6] To the aristocratic officers around the Kaiser, Ludendorff was an uncouth technocrat.

Born in 1848 the aristocratic Hindenburg was a veteran of the Austro-Prussian and Franco-Prussian Wars. An imposing figure, thick set, impressively moustachioed, and over 6 feet tall, he appeared stolid, digni-fied, and wedded to duty. As a result, some thought him unimaginative and unintelligent. He was sufficiently astute to recognise the power vacuum that had opened through the Kaiser's incapacity to exercise authority, even if he maintained an outward appearance of traditional deference towards the monarch. He also recognised his own limitations, giving Ludendorff 'free scope for his intellectual powers' and 'superhuman' capacity for work.[7] Just as Hindenburg and Ludendorff preferred to operate behind the political shield of pliable politicians, Ludendorff equally recognised his need to work behind Hindenburg's popularity. In turn, Hindenburg provided that sense of calmness that Ludendorff so conspicuously lacked.

Both Hindenburg and Ludendorff had been born in Posen (Poznán) in West Prussia, but there the similarity ended. Ludendorff, seventeen years Hindenburg's junior, had little respect for tradition or position. Of middle-class merchant stock, Ludendorff was the supreme technocrat, ruthlessly ambitious and fanatically addicted to his work. His military outlook was a radical one, subordinating everything to the drive for perceived efficiency. He was to argue after the war, when he dabbled briefly with Nazism, that Germany's failure had been one of insufficient totality of political and socio-economic mobilisation, for war was 'the highest expression of the racial will of life'.[8] Ludendorff's narrow military outlook made him dependent for political and socio-economic ideas on the even more radical artillery expert, Colonel Max Bauer. As head of OHL's Section II, the ambi-tious Bauer, a consummate intriguer, was to become the architect of the

Hindenburg Programme. As events would prove, while exceptionally talented as a tactician, Ludendorff had little strategic insight.

There was certainly a glacial quality to Ludendorff, who often appeared arrogant, vain and rigidly humourless. An artist once told Ludendorff's first wife, Margarethe, that her husband gave him 'cold shivers down my back'.[9] Some meeting him for the first time, however, found him more agreeable than anticipated. In his private life, Ludendorff was undoubtedly devoted to the vivacious Margarethe, and the three sons and a daughter she brought to the marriage. Two of his stepsons were to be killed in the war, the youngest shot down over allied lines on 23 March 1918. He had met Margarethe when sharing an umbrella in a rainstorm, and she had divorced her businessman husband to marry Ludendorff in 1909. There were times, though, when even his family 'knew that grim countenance' and were suitably wary.[10] What many also noted was the restless energy and an underlying nervous tension. He had the habit, for example, of rolling breadcrumbs at the table when concentrating or worrying. By the start of the spring offensives in March 1918, Ludendorff had taken only four days' leave in two and a half years, and was also suffering from an exophthalmic goitre that had only increased his irritability. By mid-July he was also drinking heavily.

The separation of the military and civilian spheres of government, the lack of administrative mechanism for the long-term discussion of strategic policy and the underestimation of the resources of Britain and the United States all contributed to the incapacity of Hindenburg and Ludendorff to weigh the balance between short-term gain and long-term strategic risk. They sought only operational solutions to strategic problems. That marked not only the decision on unrestricted submarine warfare but also the attempt to win the war in the West before the United States could intervene in force. Germany did not need to launch offensives in 1918 for negotiations were still entirely possible, but Ludendorff wished to attack because he feared the consequences of delay given the likely build-up of American forces by 1919. As Ludendorff wrote later, 'The offensive is the most effective means of making war; it alone is decisive. Military history proves it on every page. It is the symbol of superiority.' He also believed that the army shared his view for 'they thought with horror of fresh defensive battles and longed for a war of movement'.[11]

The decision to launch a spring offensive was taken on 11 November 1917 at a conference at the Mons headquarters of Crown Prince Rupprecht of Bavaria. Present were Rupprecht's chief of staff, Hermann von Kuhl; the chief of staff of Crown Prince Wilhelm's army group, Friedrich von der Schulenberg; Lieutenant Colonel Georg Wetzell, the head of OHL's Operations Section; Bauer; and Ludendorff. Earlier in October, Crown Prince Wilhelm, Rupprecht and Kuhl had all agreed that only a limited offensive in the West was possible. Ludendorff had seemingly concurred, suggesting such an operation in Flanders would 'deflect the impact of the Americans'. Subsequently, Wetzell argued that 'an annihilating blow' could be struck before the Americans arrived in strength.[12] Ludendorff readily agreed. A victory would solve all problems, but precisely where such an offensive should be launched and with what specific operational objectives was left unresolved. Ludendorff favoured attacking the British on the Somme, but Kuhl suggested attacking on the Lys in Flanders. His expectation was that this might forestall a British offensive, though the area was liable to flooding until at least April. Schulenberg favoured attacking Verdun. As staff studies continued, Kuhl and Wetzell concluded that an offensive towards either Verdun or Hazebrouck might offer better opportunities, Wetzell now proposing that a series of offensives should be mounted. On 27 December Ludendorff directed that planning be undertaken for a number of potential operations including an offensive on the Somme around St Quentin (code-named *Michael* from St Michael), at Arras (*Mars*), and towards Hazebrouck (*Georg I* from St George) and Ypres (*Georg II*), as well as diversionary operations at Verdun and in the Vosges. He still favoured the Somme, which Kuhl and Wetzell felt too ambitious. Moreover, despite initially implying there were enough resources for only one offensive, Ludendorff now seemed to believe that *Georg* would be necessary if *Michael* failed. Kuhl told the postwar Reichstag Committee of Inquiry into the Causes of the German Collapse that, in view of the lack of both horse and vehicle transport, he doubted whether the German army 'was still sufficiently mobile to be fit, as it was hoped, for larger operations in the open after breaking through the enemy lines'.[13] Discussions continued until Ludendorff eventually settled on *Michael* on 21 January 1918. Final orders were issued on 10 March.

What was abundantly clear was that strategic considerations were being sacrificed to tactical considerations. Ludendorff saw the possibility of breaking through the allied lines in certain sectors as more important than the potential strategic objectives that could be achieved. It was a fantasy that a tactical breakthrough could lead to the complete collapse of the allied armies, albeit there was some basis for optimism in the collapse of the Italians at Caporetto in November 1917. Influenced by his experience on the Eastern Front, where 'we always merely set a near goal and then discovered where to go next', Ludendorff remarked that he would simply punch a hole in the allied lines and, 'For the rest, we shall see.'[14]

In opting for the Somme (*Michael*) Ludendorff hoped to deal the British a decisive blow though he was later to pursue the idea of separating the British from the French, with the possibility of a more general advance in conjunction with the subsidiary supporting offensive around Arras (*Mars*). The British would be forced back on the Channel ports and the French on Paris, leaving both armies' exposed flanks vulnerable. But the allied defence was weakest on the Somme precisely because it had less strategic significance, albeit Amiens was a rather more important allied north–south communications centre than the Germans realised. The Lys was a far more sensitive area for the British because any German success there immediately threatened the Channel ports and the British lines of communications. Accordingly, a local German success on the Somme would not necessarily fulfil any higher objective. Significantly, too, the three participating German armies in *Michael* – the Second, Seventeenth and Eighteenth Armies – had different axes of advance.

In theory, the resources of the Eastern Front were to be directed towards the breakthrough in the West. Yet, the continued expansion eastwards never actually resulted in sufficient troops being made available to secure such a victory on the Western Front. A total of 48 divisions was sent west from Russia, Romania and Italy between November 1917 and March 1918, leaving 47 divisions in the East. The result was a balance in the West in favour of Germany of 191 divisions to 178.[15] The Germans' most successful commanders were also brought to the West: Oskar von Hutier, victor at Riga in the East in September 1917, took over Eighteenth Army; Otto von Below, who had won the major victory over the Italians at Caporetto, took command of Seventeenth Army; and Georg von Marwitz, whose counter-attack had wiped out British gains at Cambrai in November 1917, took over Second Army.

The German army seemed well equipped for the coming offensive. It had adapted more quickly to the changing nature of warfare than the allies. If there was a British 'learning curve' on the Western Front, it was a distinctly uneven one. The Germans had learned most from the battles of the Somme and Verdun in 1916. The impact of the British artillery bombardment on the Somme in July 1916 led to the development of what has been characterised as 'elastic defence in depth' in the winter of 1916–17. This thinned front-line manpower but considerably deepened the defensive zone. It opened up the possibility of surrendering ground in order to render the attackers vulnerable to a mobile counter-attack by specially designated counter-attack divisions. Following the British success on 7 June 1917, when the British Second Army took the Messines ridge by detonating huge mines placed under the German line, yet further defensive lines were hastily prepared with an emphasis upon concrete pillboxes as strongpoints. The Germans also greatly refined infantry tactics in 1917, in the belief that it was not possible to hold a forward zone against the combination of artillery and tanks, and that a successful defence depended upon resourceful infantry counter-attack.

Experimentation with new infantry tactics had begun as early as March 1915, with the creation of a Storm Detachment of pioneers supporting a new 37 mm light-artillery piece, which was intended to neutralise obstacles to an advance by bringing direct fire to bear at close range. In October 1916 eighteen Storm Battalions were formed, each including pioneers, machine gunners, light artillery and mortar crews, and flame-throwers. Specially located Stormtrooper formations featured in the German counter-attack at Cambrai on 30 November 1917. Stormtroopers were formed into small self-sufficient groups, lightly equipped but heavily armed with mobile mortars and Bergmann sub-machine guns. Infiltrating between strongpoints they were to effect a break-in and to achieve maximum penetration at least as far as the defending artillery lines. Control of reserves was vested in the forward elements so that they would reinforce success rather than failure.

Allied to this was the artillery method devised by Colonel Georg Bruchmüller – partly in response to falling levels of shell production – to support the advance with rapid and accurate fire in a short hurricane bombardment. A liberal mix of high-explosive and gas shells added to the disorienting effect, paralysing and disrupting the opposing command structure. Bruchmüller's methods had been used at Riga, Caporetto and Cambrai. The overall operational concept was enshrined in a new manual, *The Attack in Position Warfare*, that began to be distributed on 1 January 1918.

At the same time, however, weaknesses were becoming apparent. Casualties, and the evolution of a war economy, had resulted in manpower problems. After the launching of the Hindenburg Programme, industrial requirements had a greater priority and skilled men frequently had to be returned from army to industry. Thus, it became largely a question of pressing convalescents back into service early as well as mortgaging the future by calling up ever-younger men. The defeat of Russia had enabled men to be transferred to the West, but it has been estimated that at least 10 per cent deserted en route. There was also little confidence on the part of German commanders in those who had been repatriated after being prisoners of the Russians. Consequently, there was an attempt to claw back men from industry. It has also been claimed that as many as a million German soldiers were effectively 'shirkers', participating in a so-called 'undercover military strike' in rear areas during the last few months of the war as men either went missing or declined to take any more risks at the front. This is now disputed, and there seems no real evidence of large numbers wandering the rear areas before October 1918. Real disintegration only occurred once the army returned to the east bank of the Rhine after the armistice. Nonetheless, there were divisions between officers and men, the post-war Reichstag inquiry paying particular attention to 'abuses' of officers' privileges and the sense of grievance among ordinary soldiers.

Once the United States came into the war in April 1917, the economic blockade of Germany had become far more effective since restrictions could be enforced on remaining neutrals without diplomatic repercussions. Progressively, therefore, the blockade had an impact on Germany, especially when coupled with the poor harvests of 1916 and 1917. Soldiers on leave or in transit between western and eastern fronts could not be isolated from civilian privation. It was in the rear echelons of the army that collapse was most apparent. The plundering of army food stocks and their redistribution to civilians by soldiers was a particular sign of collapse. In the rear, tensions arising from supply problems and other difficulties, as

Hew Strachan has put it, 'could simmer and seethe . . . without the direct pressure of the enemy to suppress them'.[16]

At best, there was a kind of stoicism, in the expectation of peace, in the German army. A programme of 'patriotic instruction', originally started in March 1917, was stepped up in September 1917 in preparation for the spring offensives. German army trench newspapers had always had far more rhetoric of comradeship, and of justification for the war, than those of the British or French. Now they also presented the image of an idealised soldier, peddling the idea that a 'victorious peace' was the only viable one. The refusal of Hindenburg and Ludendorff to embrace any form of political and social reform undermined the propaganda effort among troops. In addition, morale was affected by poor rations and a lack of transport disrupting leave arrangements. Influenza also took its toll of the German troops to a greater extent than in the British and French armies, with at least 630,000 men being affected by July 1918. Reputedly, when informed of the outbreak, Ludendorff simply remarked that 'he knew of no influenza'.[17]

At 0440 hours on 21 March 1918, at the opening of *Michael*, Bruchmüller used 6,608 guns in just under six hours' preliminary bombardment against the British Fifth Army. A total of 3.2 million rounds – a third of them gas rounds – were fired in seven carefully prepared phases. The Germans also committed 52 of their 70 specially created mobile attack divisions, 40 of which were fully equipped. The British had tried to recreate a German-style defence in depth over the winter of 1917–18. Rather than matching the flexibility of the German system, the British tended to rely upon static defensive points with minimal counterstroke capability. Matters were not assisted by the need to extend the Fifth Army's line by 28 miles just six weeks before the German spring offensive began. The result was that the 'rear zone', in which the relatively few available reserves were to be held, hardly existed.

In 1916 the allies had painfully won 98 square miles on the Somme in 140 days at a cost of 1.5 million casualties: assisted by mist and fog, the Germans now seized 140 square miles of the same area in just twenty-four hours at a cost of only 39,000 casualties. Nonetheless, there was weakness in the failure to maintain the infiltration tactics after the initial break-through. British prisoners of war later reported that there was considerable disorganisation behind the German lines. German troops were soon exhausted by their exertions, often slowing their advance to loot British food-supply depots. They were also advancing into areas devastated by war – not least by their own strategic retreat to the Siegfried line in April 1917 – and devoid of communications. They were critically short of horses to bring forward their artillery, heavy machine guns and mortars.

Hutier's Eighteenth Army had made the greatest gains in the south. Arguably, there was little purpose in reinforcing this success, where resistance was least, when the supposed aim was to drive the British to the northwest. Initially Ludendorff allocated half the available reserves to the Eighteenth Army but then chose on 23 March to maintain pressure across the front as a whole. Rupprecht argued that success was still possible if resources were devoted to continuing the advance to the northwest against the British. But, on 25 March, Ludendorff decided to implement a scaled-down version of *Mars* aimed at Arras, to help the Seventeenth Army on the right of the existing offensive, as well as continuing south of the Somme. At the time the Germans were only 12 miles from Amiens. *Mars*, however, failed to break through the British Third Army on 28 March, and the southern axis of advance ground to a halt at Noyon on 29 March. Increasingly, the British front was stabilising. In meetings at Doullens on 26 March, and at Beauvais on 3 April, the allies established unity of command at the strategic level with Ferdinand Foch as supreme allied commander, though tactical control of the British and French armies remained respectively with Haig and Pétain. *Michael* had cost the allies 254,000 casualties, but the Germans had suffered 239,000 casualties.

Ludendorff continued to look for purely tactical gains, Rupprecht noting on 5 April that OHL was living 'from hand to mouth, without acknowledging a fixed purpose'.[18] Increasingly, Ludendorff was bypassing Rupprecht and issuing orders direct to his armies in notably abrupt telephone calls. On 1 April he had ordered a scaled-down version of *Georg* on the Lys, now to be codenamed *Georgette*. While Ludendorff's conduct of *Georgette* was to display the same vices as his planning for *Michael*, it was the first real indication as his utter bankruptcy of his strategic vision.

Opening on 9 April 1918 after a day's delay due to heavy rain, the offensive was entrusted to the German Fourth and Sixth Armies. These armies, however, were far weaker than those committed to *Michael*. The frontage was only 20 miles compared to the 50 miles covered by *Michael* and, of the

26 divisions allocated, only 12 were the specially trained stormtroop formations. Moreover, there was not sufficient artillery available to support both armies simultaneously, so the attack of the Fourth Army was postponed until 10 April. Bruchmüller had been seconded to the Sixth Army and there was another hurricane bombardment of four and a half hours, though mounted after only nine days' preparation compared to the seven weeks available for *Michael*. Fortunately for the Germans, Haig had been compelled to commit 46 of his 58 divisions on the Somme, leaving few reserves available in Flanders. Two under-strength divisions of the Portuguese Expeditionary Force held part of the British First Army's front and they immediately collapsed as the Sixth Army pushed towards Hazebrouck.

When the German Fourth Army began its attack towards Mount Kemmel on 10 April it faced tired divisions sent north to recuperate from the battle on the Somme. Gains so painfully made by the British during the Passchendaele offensive in 1917 were swiftly erased as the British pulled back between 12 and 14 April. On 11 April Haig issued his 'backs to the wall' Order of the Day: 'There is no other course open to us but to fight it out. Every position must be held to the last man. There must be no retirement. With our backs to the wall, and believing in the justice of our cause, each one of us must fight on to the end.'[19] The Germans were within 5 miles of Hazebrouck, another key rail centre for allied supply lines, when Ludendorff changed the direction of the attack to the north, and away from the town on 12 April. The same day, Kuhl urged that all efforts should now be concentrated against the British and that *Georgette* should take priority over attacks anywhere else. Ludendorff only partially acknowledged Kuhl's pleas. In any case, little progress was being made in the new direction of the offensive towards Ypres. By 19 April it appeared little more could be achieved, though Mount Kemmel was taken from its French defenders on 28 April to improve the tactical position. Ludendorff blamed the troops and, especially, the Sixth Army's chief of staff, Lieutenant Colonel Hermann, Ritter von Lenz, for the lack of further progress. He also complained that, as on the Somme, troops had stopped to plunder food depots, and officers had not exercised sufficient control to prevent it. By 29 April it was clear that the offensive had failed. *Georgette* had cost the Germans another 86,000 casualties. March and April had proved the costliest months for German casualties on the Western Front of the entire war, with 232,000 casualties sustained in March and 244,000 in April.[20]

The fatal flaw evident in *Georgette* was to be repeated, with three more offensives launched in quick succession to exploit fleeting short-term advantages. *Blücher* (and its subsidiary *Yorck*, both named for Prussian generals of the Napoleonic Wars) on the Chemin des Dames on 27 May was intended to draw French reserves south from Flanders and enable a *Neu Georg* to be mounted. Once more, Ludendorff was seduced by its early progress to convert what had been intended only as a limited tactical operation into a thrust towards Paris. It was German reserves who ended up being brought from the north. Consequently, *Gneisenau* (another hero of the wars against Napoleon) followed on the Aisne between Montdidier and Noyon on 9 June. It petered out three days later with no appreciable gains, and with Paris still 37 miles distant. The Kaiser came forward to witness *Friedensturm* ('peace offensive') in the Champagne-Marne region on 15 July, although precisely what it was intended to achieve was unclear. The pace of German advance achieved – amounting to 35 miles in just four days on the Aisne in May where the French were caught by surprise – was prodigious by previous standards. But it still did not impart sufficient psychological paralysis to create strategic success. Moreover, the Germans merely created vulnerable salients for themselves – the German front had increased from 242 miles on 20 March to 316 miles by 25 June – while the stormtroop divisions suffered very heavy casualties. The allies were capable of replacing their losses, but the Germans were not. Coupled with the heavy losses, the failure of the offensives damaged morale. Conceivably, elasticity in attack and defence encouraged the belief among German troops that ground was of little value once the allies began to counter-attack in July and August 1918.

The allied counter-attack began on the Marne on 18 July, frustrating Ludendorff's hopes of a sixth thrust of his own in Flanders. This was *Neu Georg*, now codenamed *Hagen* for the Wagnerian character who stabbed the hero, Siegfried, in the back. The main counter-offensive by the British came at Amiens on 8 August 1918 assisted by the extraordinary amount of materiel resources now available. The successful British assault on the Hindenburg line on 29 September 1918, for example, saw a bombardment that delivered 126 shells per 500 yards of German line per minute for eight hours. The British rate of advance in the 'Hundred Days' of 1918 – approximately 28 miles a month – was greater than that of the allies during the Italian campaign of 1943–45. In part, it reflected a massive improvement in logistical support. What needs to be emphasised, however, is that the technical means to completely break through an opposing defensive system was never available on the Western Front for all the developments in artillery and communications. The Germans were forced back but the line was still continuous on 11 November 1918. By this time, the allies' own advance had slowed due to determined German rearguard actions, and with the difficulties experienced in supplying their armies across previously devastated battlefields. As late as 19 October 1918, therefore, Haig believed the Germans quite capable of retiring to their own frontiers and holding them so that the war would continue into 1919.

By November 1918, the Germans had sustained 1.7 million casualties since 21 March. Those losses had been among the best of Germany's remaining troops and those who had the highest morale. Ludendorff's hope of holding the line of the Meuse began to look ever more doubtful as the British Third and Fourth Armies forced the canalised river Sambre on 4 November. In effect, the German army had lost the belief that it could achieve victory. That applied, too, to Ludendorff, whose power began to wane when the spring offensives manifestly failed to bring victory. Younger German staff officers were increasingly aghast at the lack of overall strategic direction, the future Field Marshal Wilhelm, Ritter von Leeb, then a major on Rupprecht's staff, concluding on 31 March that not only did Ludendorff have no operational vision but also that he had 'totally lost his nerve'.[21] News of the French offensive on the Marne on 18 July came as Ludendorff and Hindenburg were discussing the prospects for *Hagen* at Ludendorff's advanced headquarters at Avesnes. Over lunch, Hindenburg suggested using all available reserves for a counter-attack north of Soissons, but Ludendorff angrily dismissed the idea. According to an OHL staff officer, Colonel Hermann, Ritter Merz von Quirnheim, Hindenburg immediately left the room 'clearly annoyed and scarlet in the face'. After dinner, Hindenburg again raised the idea, only for Ludendorff 'with an expression of rage on his face' to turn to leave, 'letting out one or two words like "madness!" in profound irritation'. Hindenburg demanded 'a word' with Ludendorff and they retired to the latter's study out of von Quirnheim's hearing. Hindenburg, who never forgave Ludendorff's open insubordination, reminded him 'to remember his place'.[22] According to Quirnheim, Ludendorff was close to nervous collapse. When summoned to discuss *Hagen* on 20 July, Fritz von Lossberg, the Fourth Army's chief of staff, was equally appalled to find Ludendorff blaming Wetzell for the setback on the Marne. Ludendorff threatened to resign when Lossberg urged a retreat to the Siegfried line to shorten the German front.

Ludendorff had recovered his confidence sufficiently by early August to be predicting success for *Hagen*. When the British attacked at Amiens on 8 August, however, Ludendorff showed distinct signs of nervous panic: he was later to call it the 'black day' of the German army. He tried to micromanage the response, Kuhl writing that Ludendorff was 'continually insisting on having a say in all the particulars, talking to all the armies and their chiefs, arranging details often quite contrary to his orders to me'.[23] His confidence broken by the British success, Ludendorff tendered his resignation on 13 August only for the Kaiser to reject it. The alternating moods of recognition of defeat and confidence in ultimate victory continued. On the following day at a Crown Council at Spa, Hindenburg and Ludendorff seemed confident that the allied will to fight could now be broken by a 'strategic defensive', still enabling Germany to attain its aims. Worn out by overwork, Ludendorff refused to contemplate replacing Wetzell as head of the Operations Section with a more experienced officer, who would be able to bear more of the detailed staff work, primarily because he feared that this might be a precursor to his own removal. In the end, Colonel Wilhelm von Heye succeeded Wetzell in September. Many felt Heye too junior to have much of an impact, but he emerged as an important voice of realism. There was now sufficient concern about Ludendorff's condition for a staff psychologist from Imperial Headquarters, Dr Hochheimer, to be called in on 4 September to treat Ludendorff's nerves. Hochheimer counselled rest, singing German folk songs on waking each morning, and enjoying the roses in the garden of Ludendorff's quarters.

Bauer, for long an unqualified supporter, was manoeuvring to survive Ludendorff's likely fall, encouraging those such as Heye who believed the military situation critical. Ludendorff now appeared to pin his hopes on influenza having broken out in the French army. On 28 September

1918, with the news that Bulgaria had sought an armistice, Ludendorff had a nervous collapse. Believing him to be out of touch with reality, Heye, Quirnheim and the head of OHL's Political Section, Colonel Paul von Bartenwerffer, took it upon themselves to inform the German Foreign Office that peace negotiations were urgently required. On being informed, Ludendorff decided unexpectedly to urge Hindenburg to seek an armistice, though his intention was merely to win time in order to continue the war.

Accompanied by Heye, Hindenburg and the Foreign Secretary, Admiral Paul von Hintze, Ludendorff informed the Kaiser of the need for an armistice on 29 September. While the Kaiser and Hintze assumed Hindenburg and Ludendorff wished to appeal for an eventual armistice, they were surprised when Ludendorff demanded it immediately. All were agreed, however, on the need for a new 'liberal' government to secure agreement with Woodrow Wilson on the basis of the Fourteen Points, though Hindenburg and Ludendorff had never actually read them. Ludendorff began laying the foundations of the post-war 'stab in the back' myth by announcing to his staff on 1 October that 'those circles which we have above all to thank for having brought us to this point' could now 'eat the broth they have cooked for us'.[24] Having arrived at Spa after the decision had been taken, Hertling, who had suffered a heart attack in June, resigned as chancellor. Hintze also resigned. Prince Max of Baden was brought in as chancellor on 3 October to handle the negotiations. Max initially demurred from approaching Wilson, but was pointedly told he had not been brought in to create difficulties.

Max had no illusions that the price of peace would be high. Max requested that Wilson arrange an armistice on 3 October 1918 on the basis of the Fourteen Points, to which Wilson responded by asking for clarification. Wilson's second and third notes on 14 and 23 October made it clear that an armistice must make any German resumption of the war impossible. Ludendorff had now recovered his nerve and, with Hindenburg, proposed to renew the war, only to find that his position had been undermined. Without permission to do so, Hindenburg and Ludendorff journeyed to Berlin to meet the Kaiser on 27 October 1918, Ludendorff intending to demand rejection of Wilson's notes. Wilhelm pointedly complained that Ludendorff had first demanded an armistice and now, a month later, demanded negotiations be broken off. Knowing that Max had threatened to resign if Ludendorff remained, the Kaiser accepted Ludendorff's proffered resignation while refusing that of Hindenburg. Furious that Hindenburg had remained in office, Ludendorff stormed from the room and refused even to share a car with him. Groener became First Quartermaster General in succession to Ludendorff on 29 October. Groener concluded that Germany could not continue the war once that continuation had been called into question. The scene was thus set for the negotiations leading to the armistice.

As Germany dissolved into chaos, Ludendorff went into exile in Sweden. Military victory had been intended to compensate for wartime privations and the lack of political reform. When it was not forthcoming, political tensions simply increased with no authoritative political figure to counter them. Ludendorff's own mystique as a military saviour had been destroyed. Hindenburg became president of the Weimar Republic in 1925, one of his opponents in the presidential election being Ludendorff. Ludendorff had been involved in the so-called Kapp putsch against the republic five years earlier and, flirting with fascism, he had also participated in Hitler's abortive Munich beer hall putsch in 1923. He had grown distant from Margarethe, and become increasingly influenced by the extreme views of the widowed Dr Mathilde von Kemnitz, whom he divorced Margarethe to marry in 1926. In the end Ludendorff broke with Hitler. On Hindenburg's death in 1934, Hitler declared himself both president and chancellor as Führer. When Ludendorff died three years later, the one time 'silent dictator' was given a Nazi state funeral against his express wishes.

CONCLUSION

IT WAS the seventeenth-century French mathematician, scientist and philosopher, Blaise Pascal, who mused that had Cleopatra's nose been shorter, the whole face of the world would have been changed. As outlined in the introduction, the intention behind this volume was to identify seminal events during the First World War that could be characterised as meaningful turning points in military, political, socio-economic or cultural terms, which had significant consequences in the longer term. Some would be familiar but others had gone generally unrecognised. It was not intended to speculate on counter-factual 'what ifs'.

Yet, by way of conclusion, it is appropriate briefly to consider the alternative course of events but for the pivotal points suggested. Of course, a major war will throw up countless alternative possibilities if this or that decision had or had not been taken. Such questions can be posed onwards from the fateful decision of Archduke Franz Ferdinand's chauffeur to bring the car to a halt at the very corner in Sarajevo where Gavrilo Princip was standing on 28 June 1914.

In terms of the flooding of the Yser, the German invasion of France and Belgium had already been thoroughly disorganised by the allied counter-attack on the Marne. Yet there was still the real possibility that the renewed offensive in Flanders could have broken through to the Channel ports but for the British defence of Ypres and, crucially, the Belgians unleashing the floodwaters. Had Turkey not entered the war, there would have been no new fronts in the Middle East with all that was implied for the post-war settlement of the region. The Balfour Declaration might never have been issued. Instead of Gallipoli, Australians would remember more a blooding on the Western Front. Ironically, the first significant Australian action there – at Fromelles in July 1916 – has only recently escaped the shadow of Gallipoli through the discovery and excavation of 250 (mostly Australian) bodies from German burial pits in 2009. This was followed by the opening at Fromelles in 2010 of the first new Commonwealth War Graves Commission cemetery since the end of the Second World War.

Had the Ministry of Munitions not been created in 1915, Britain might not have sufficiently grasped the nettle of the mobilisation of all of its resources. Had the documentary film on the battle of the Somme not been made then, the powerful imagery of the Western Front might not have had such an impact on public consciousness then and since. In the same way, had the Germans not deployed heavy bombers against London, the subsequent fear of aerial bombardment might not have evolved in the way it did during the interwar period.

Had Emperor Franz Joseph died earlier than towards the end of 1916, his successor, Karl, might have found the means of saving the Austro-Hungarian Empire. Alternatively, if the old emperor had survived longer, residual loyalties might also have saved his empire. Equally, but for the war, the Tsarist system might well have survived far longer, since it was the challenge of the war that interrupted reforms which were beginning to make a difference. Had it not attempted to continue the war, the Provisional Government might not have succumbed to the Bolsheviks.

German decisions in particular played a crucial role in shaping the war and its outcome, starting with the decision to plunge Europe into conflict in the first place. Had the decision on unrestricted submarine warfare not been taken, it is conceivable that the United States would have remained a neutral, albeit one generally more inclined towards the Entente. Had Ludendorff been a better strategist, his 1918 spring offensives might yet have forced the Entente to negotiate. That would have implied a very different outcome even from the one the Germans thought they had achieved through requesting an armistice on the basis of Woodrow Wilson's 'Fourteen Points'. Had Wilson been less of an idealist, his mediation might have had less disastrous results, and the United States might have remained engaged in international politics.

But in the last analysis, the case studies that have been presented as the pivotal points of the First World War deal with the reality of the war and its impact. I quoted in the introduction some lines from John Dryden. Let me conclude with some lines from Charles Dickens's *A Christmas Carol*:

'I told you these were shadows of the things that have been,' said the Ghost. 'That they are what they are, do not blame me!'

NOTES

Introduction

1. Charles Lehautcourt [General Palat], *La Ruée vers Calais* (Paris, 1922), p. 23.
2. Charles Carlton, *This Seat of Mars: War and the British Isles, 1485–1746* (New Haven and London, CT, 2011), p. 150.
3. See, for example, Arthur Marwick, *The Deluge: British Society and the First World War*, 2nd edn (London, 1991), pp. 16–17; idem, *Total War and Social Change* (London, 1988), pp. xiv–xv; Roger Chickering and Stig Förster, eds, *Great War, Total War: Combat and Mobilisation on the Western Front, 1914–18* (Cambridge, 2000), passim.
4. Sir Edward Creasy, *Fifteen Decisive Battles of the World* (London, 1851).
5. Compare the optimistic view of Gary Sheffield, *The Somme* (London, 2003), with the more realistic assessment of Robin Prior and Trevor Wilson, *The Somme* (New Haven and London, CT, 2005).
6. See Brian Bond, *The Unquiet Western Front: Britain's Role in Literature and History* (Cambridge, 2002); and Dan Todman, *The First World War: Myth and Memory* (London, 2005).
7. See J. Paul Harris and Niall Barr, *Amiens to the Armistice: The BEF in the Hundred Days Campaign, 8 August to 11 November 1918* (London, 1998).
8. Hew Strachan, *The First World War: To Arms* (Oxford, 2001), p. 729. See also W. E. D. Allen and Paul Muratoff, *Caucasian Battlefields: A History of the Wars on the Trans-Caucasian Border, 1828–1921* (Cambridge, 1953).
9. Ian F. W. Beckett, *Ypres: The First Battle, 1914* (Harlow, 2004), pp. 227, 240.
10. Fritz von Lossberg, *Meine Tätigkeit im Weltkriege, 1914–18* (Berlin, 1939), p. 351; Seventh Army War Diary, 18 July 1918, quoted in Michael Neiberg, *The Second Battle of the Marne* (Bloomington, IN, 2008), p. 131. See also Lawrence Sondhaus, *World War One* (Cambridge, 2011), p. 412.
11. Trevor Wilson, *The Myriad Faces of War* (Cambridge, 1986), p. 564. See also Charles Messenger, *The Day We Won the War: Turning Point at Amiens, 8 August 1918* (London, 2010).
12. See Tim Cook, *No Place to Run: The Canadian Corps and Gas Warfare in the First World War* (Vancouver, 1999).
13. See J. Paul Harris, *Men, Ideas and Tanks: British Military Thought and Armoured Forces, 1903–39* (Manchester, 1996); Tim Travers, *How the War Was Won: Command and Technology in the British Army on the Western Front, 1917–18* (London, 1992).

14. See Mark Clodfelter, *The Limits of Air Power: The American Bombing of North Vietnam* (New York, 1989).
15. Matthew Hughes and Matthew Seligmann, eds, *Leadership in Conflict, 1914–18* (Barnsley, 2000), pp. 1–10.
16. Arthur Link, *Wilson the Diplomatist*, 2nd edn (Chicago, 1965), p. 61.

Chapter 1 The Silent Conqueror

1. Charles Lehautcourt [General Palat], *La Ruée vers Calais* (Paris, 1922), p. 23.
2. T. Bentley Mott, trans., *The Personal Memoirs of Joffre*, 2 vols (New York, 1932), I, p. 37.
3. Paul van Pul, *In Flanders Flooded Fields* (Barnsley, 2006), p. 6.
4. Martin Gilbert, *Winston S. Churchill: Volume III Companion, Part 1, 1914–15* (London, 1972), p. 122.
5. Michael and Eleanor Brock, eds, *H.H. Asquith: Letters to Venetia Stanley* (Oxford, 1982), pp. 257–58, 275–76.
6. Ibid., pp. 262–63.
7. Charles Le Goffre, *Dixmude* (Philadelphia, PA, 1916), p. 48.
8. Jean Stengers, 'Belgium', in Keith Wilson, ed., *Decisions for War, 1914* (London, 1995), p. 155.
9. Christopher Duffy, 'The Siege of Antwerp', *Purnell's History of the First World War*, 1:14 (1970), p. 378.
10. Ibid., p. 380.
11. Jean Ratinaud, *La Course à La Mer* (Paris, 1967), p. 294.
12. *Ypres, 1914: An Official Account Published by Order of the German General Staff* (London, 1919), pp. 47–48.
13. Marie-Rose Thielemans and Emile Vandewoude, eds, *Le Roi Albert: Au Travers de ses lettres inédites, 1882–1916* (Brussels, 1982), pp. 535–36.
14. Emile Cammaerts, *Albert of Belgium: Defender of Right* (New York, 1935), p. 197.
15. Léon Van der Essen, *The Invasion and the War in Belgium from Liège to the Yser* (London, 1917), p. 336.
16. *Ypres, 1914*, p. 51.

Chapter 2 The Widening of the War

1. Mary Soames, ed., *Speaking for Themselves: The Personal Letters of Winston and Clementine Churchill* (London, 1998), p. 31.
2. Henry Morgenthau, *Ambassador Morgenthau's Story* (New York, 1919), pp. 31–32, 114–15.
3. Lewis Einstein, *Inside Constantinople: A Diplomat's Diary during the Dardanelles Expedition, April–September 1915* (London, 1917), p. 1.
4. Ibid., p. 18.
5. Morgenthau, *Ambassador's Story*, pp. 21–23.
6. *The Times*, 16 March 1921, p. 11; idem, 17 March 1921, p. 11.
7. Margaret FitzHerbert, *The Man Who Was Greenmantle: A Biography of Aubrey Herbert* (London, 1983), p. 83.
8. Morgenthau, *Ambassador's Story*, p. 173.
9. Hew Strachan, *The First World War: To Arms* (Oxford, 2001), p. 680.
10. Einstein, *Inside Constantinople*, p. 25. See also Morgenthau, *Ambassador's Story*, pp. 5, 17.
11. Richard Wright, 'Goeben and Breslau', *Purnell's History of the First World War* 1:13 (1969), p. 342.
12. Brock and Brock, eds, *Asquith: Letters to Venetia Stanley*, p. 168.
13. Morgenthau, *Ambassador's Story*, p. 106.
14. Mustafa Aksakal, *The Ottoman Road to War in 1914* (Cambridge, 2008), p. 177.

Chapter 3 The Making of a Nation

1. General Sir Ian Hamilton, *Gallipoli Diary*, 2 vols (London, 1920), I, p. 28.
2. Tonie and Valmai Holt, *Major and Mrs Holt's Battlefield Guide to Gallipoli* (Barnsley, 2000), p. 244.
3. *Daily Telegraph*, 7 May 1915.
4. C. E. W. Bean, *The Story of Anzac: From the Outbreak of War to the End of the First Phase of the Gallipoli Campaign* (Sydney, 1921), pp. 248–52. Bean's diary noted the sound of continuous rifle fire reaching the ships offshore at 4.43 a.m.: see Australian War Memorial, C. E. W. Bean MSS, AWM38, 2DRLL606/4/1.
5. John Robertson, *Anzac and Empire* (London, 1990), pp. 68–69, 71.
6. Ibid., p. 73.
7. The National Archives (hereafter TNA), CAB 19/31, Cable 881.
8. John Lee, *A Soldier's Life: General Sir Ian Hamilton* (London, 2000), p. 162.
9. Henry Nevinson, *Last Changes, Last Chances* (London, 1928), p. 35.
10. Compton Mackenzie, *Gallipoli Memories* (London, 1929), p. 200.
11. Ellis Ashmead-Bartlett, *Ashmead-Bartlett's Despatches from the Dardanelles* (London, 1915), pp. 49, 77–78.
12. Dudley McCarthy, *Gallipoli to the Somme: The Story of C. E. W. Bean* (London, 1983), p. 128.
13. Philip Schuler, *Australia in Arms: A Narrative of the Australasian Imperial Force and Their Achievements at Anzac* (London, 1916), p. 291.
14. Kevin Fewster, ed., *Gallipoli Correspondent: The Frontline Diary of C. E. W. Bean* (Sydney, 1983), p. 155. See also C. E. W. Bean, 'Sidelights of the War on Australian Character', *Journal of the Royal Australian Historical Society* 13 (1927), pp. 211–21, in which Bean contrasts the Anzacs with the 'dregs of England's cities'.
15. Bean, *Story of Anzac*, pp. 4–5.
16. Fewster, *Gallipoli Correspondent*, pp. 156–59.
17. Jenny Macleod, *Reconsidering Gallipoli* (Manchester, 2004), p. 67.
18. Christopher Pugsley, *The Anzac Experience: New Zealand, Australia and Empire in the First World War* (Auckland, 2004), pp. 303–04.
19. *The Times*, 29 September, 1915; Robertson, *Anzac and Empire*, p. 130.
20. Bruce Scates, *Return to Gallipoli: Walking the Battlefields of the Great War* (Cambridge, 2006), p. 215.

Chapter 4 The Man and the Hour

1. Lord Beaverbrook, *Politicians and the War, 1914–16* (London, 1928), p. 95.
2. *The Times*, 7 April 1915 and 10 April 1915.
3. Winston S. Churchill, *The World Crisis* (London, 1931), abridged edn, p. 255.
4. TNA, CAB 37/128/19, Asquith to Cabinet, 17 May 1915.
5. TNA, T 170/55, Minutes of Conference between Lloyd George and Representatives of Bankers and Traders.
6. TNA, WO 159/15, Robertson to von Donop, 16 November 1914.
7. Sir George Arthur, *Life of Lord Kitchener*, 3 vols (London, 1920), III, pp. 244, 326–42.
8. TNA, CAB 22/2, Report of Cabinet meeting, 20 August 1915; ibid., CAB 41/36/40.
9. David Lloyd George, *War Memoirs*, 6 vols (London, 1933–36), II, p. 751; Leo Amery, *My Political Life*, 3 vols (London, 1953–55), II, p. 23.
10. Lord Hankey, *The Supreme Command, 1914–18*, 2 vols (London, 1961), I, p. 221; Beaverbrook, *Politicians and the War*, p. 69.
11. Brock and Brock, eds, *Asquith*, p. 488.
12. Mark Bonham Carter, ed., *The Autobiography of Margot Asquith* (London, 1962), p. xxxv.
13. National Library of Wales, Lloyd George MSS, 20,404.

14. Lord Riddell, *War Diary, 1914–18* (London, 1933), p. 294.
15. Martin Gilbert, ed., *Winston S. Churchill*, vol. III Companion, Pt II, Documents, 1915–16 (London 1972), pp. 1,016–17.
16. Lloyd George, *War Memoirs*, I, p. 238.
17. *History of the Ministry of Munitions*, 12 vols (London, 1922), VII, Pt 1, p. 16.
18. *The Manchester Guardian History of the War* (Manchester, 1920), IX, p. 159.
19. *Forward*, 1 January 1916.
20. Hansard 5th series, 10 March 1915, col. 1460.

Chapter 5 The Power of Image

1. Stephen Badsey, 'The Battle of the Somme (1916): The Film of the Battle', in Stephen Badsey, *The British Army in Battle and Its Image, 1914–18* (London, 2009), p. 119.
2. W. K.-L. Dickson, *The Biograph in Battle: Its Story in the South African War* (London, 1901), pp. 145–46.
3. *The Optical Magic Lantern Journal and Photographic Enlarger*, January 1900, p. 4
4. Cate Haste, *Keep the Home Fires Burning: Propaganda in the First World War* (London, 1977), p. 45.
5. Lucy Masterman, *C. F. G. Masterman* (London, 1939), p. 283.
6. TNA, MEPO 2/1691.
7. Masterman, *Masterman*, p. 368.
8. Geoffrey Malins, *How I Filmed the War* (London, 1920), pp. 303–04.
9. Roger Smither, ed., *The Battle of the Somme, and The Battle of the Ancre and the Advance of the Tanks* (Imperial War Museum, 1993), p. 35.
10. Malins, *How I Filmed the War*, p. 162.
11. *Bioscope*, 17 August 1916, p. 627.
12. Ibid., p. 576.
13. Roger Smither, '"A Wonderful Idea of the Fighting": The Question of Fakes in "The Battle of the Somme"', *Historical Journal of Film, Radio, and Television* 13 (1993), pp. 149–68.
14. *Manchester Guardian*, 11 August 1916, p. 9; *Daily Mirror*, 11 August 1916, p. 10; *Spectator*, 26 August 1916, p. 227; *The Times*, 11 August 1916, p. 10; *Bioscope*, 17 August 1916, p. 577.
15. D. S. Higges, ed., *The Private Diaries of Sir Henry Rider Haggard* (London, 1980), p. 84.
16. Rowland Feilding, *War Letters to a Wife: France and Flanders, 1915–19* (London, 1929), reprint edn (2001), pp. 65–66.
17. *The Times*, 2 September 1916, p. 3.
18. A. J. P. Taylor, ed., *Lloyd George: A Diary by Frances Stevenson* (London, 1971), p. 112.
19. Nicholas Reeves, 'Through the Eye of the Camera: Contemporary Cinema Audiences and their "Experience" of War in the Film, Battle of the Somme', in Hugh Cecil and Peter Liddle, eds, *Facing Armageddon* (Barnsley, 1996), p. 793.

Chapter 6 The Death of Kings

1. Alan Palmer, *Twilight of the Habsburgs* (London, 1994), p. 349.
2. Count Ottokar von Czernin und Chudenitz, *In the World War* (London, 1919), p. 33.
3. Palmer, *Twilight of Habsburgs*, p. 285.
4. Max Hoffmann, *War Diaries and Other Papers*, 2 vols (London, 1929), I, p. 201.
5. Holger Afflerbach, *Falkenhayn: Politisches Denken und Handeln im Kaiserreich* (Munich, 1994), pp. 196–97; Erich Ludendorff, *Ludendorff's Own Story*, 2 vols (New York, 1920), I, pp. 138–39.
6. R. A. Kahn, *The Multinational Empire: Nationalism and National Reform in the Habsburg Monarchy, 1848–1918*, 2 vols (New York, 1983), II, p. 231.
7. Nellie Ryan, *My Years at the Austrian Court* (London, 1915), pp. 12–13.

8. Joseph Redlich, *Emperor Francis Joseph of Austria: A Biography* (London, 1929), p. 524.
9. Fritz Fellner, 'Austria-Hungary', in Keith Wilson, ed., *Decisions for War, 1914* (London, 1995), p. 16; Gordon Tunstall, 'Austria-Hungary', in Richard Hamilton and Holger Herwig, eds, *The Origins of World War I* (Cambridge, 2003), p. 134.
10. Palmer, *Twilight of Habsburgs*, p. 224; Steven Beller, *Francis Joseph* (London, 1996), p. 136.
11. Beller, *Francis Joseph*, pp. 215, 218; Albert von Margutti, *Kaiser Franz Joseph: Persönliche Erinnerungen* (Vienna, 1924), p. 414.
12. Palmer, *Twilight of Habsburgs*, pp. 147, 334.
13. Lawrence Sondhaus, *Franz Conrad von Hötzendorf: Architect of the Apocalypse* (Boston, 2000), p. 133.
14. Gina Conrad von Hötzendorf, *Mein Leben mit Conrad von Hötzendorf* (Leipzig, 1935), pp. 113–14.
15. Winston S. Churchill, *The Unknown War: The Eastern Front* (New York, 1931), p. 132.
16. Josef Stürgkh, *Im Grossen Deutschen Hauptquartier* (Leipzig, 1921), p. 116.
17. Albert von Margutti, *The Emperor Franz Joseph and His Times* (London, 1921), p. 362.
18. John Elliot, *Fall of Eagles* (London, 1974), p. 177; Redlich, *Emperor Francis Joseph*, pp. 533–34.
19. Czernin, *In the World War*, pp. 27, 217.
20. Elliot, *Fall of Eagles*, p. 208.
21. A. J. P. Taylor, *The Habsburg Monarchy, 1809–1918* (1948; Harmondsworth, 1990), p. 259.

Chapter 7 The Ungentlemanly Weapon

1. *Bucks Advertiser and Aylesbury News*, 3 October 1914.
2. Richard Hough, *The Great War at Sea, 1914–18* (Oxford, 1986), p. 169.
3. Churchill College, Fisher MSS, FISR1/14/763, Churchill to Fisher, 1 January 1914; ibid., FISR5/18/4290, Note by Jellicoe; A. J. Marder, *Fear God and Dread Nought*, 3 vols (London, 1952 and 1956), I, p. 333.
4. Walter Görlitz, *The Kaiser and his Court* (London, 1961), pp. 125–26.
5. Paul König, *Voyage of the Deutschland* (New York, 1917), p. 115.
6. Arthur Mee, *Adventure of the Island* (London, 1919), p. 40.
7. Holger Herwig, 'The Dynamics of Necessity: German Military Policy during the First World War', in Allan Millett and Williamson Murray, eds, *Military Effectiveness* (Boston, 1988), pp. 89–92.
8. National Maritime Museum, Duff Diary, 11 February 1915.
9. State of the Union Address, 8 December 1914.
10. Görlitz, *Kaiser and Court*, p. 153.
11. Gerhard Ritter, *The Sword and the Sceptre*, 4 vols (Coral Gables, FL, 1972), III, p. 205.
12. Wilhelm Deist, 'Strategy and Unlimited War in Germany', in Roger Chickering and Jürgen Förster, eds, *Great War, Total War* (Cambridge, 2000), pp. 265–79, at pp. 275–76.
13. Michael Hadley, *Count Not the Dead* (Montreal, 1995), p. 28.
14. Hough, *Great War at Sea*, p. 302.
15. Reinhard Scheer, *Germany's High Seas Fleet in the World War* (London, 1920), p. 248.
16. Ibid., pp. 248–52.
17. Ritter, *Sword and Sceptre*, III, pp. 305–06.
18. Holger Herwig, *The First World War: Germany and Austria-Hungary, 1914–18* (London, 1997), p. 315.
19. Fritz Fischer, *Griff nach der Weltmacht* (Dusseldorf, 1961), p. 400. It is rendered slightly differently in Fritz Fischer, *Germany's Aims in the First World War* (London, 1967), p. 308.
20. Joachim Schröder, *Die U-Boote des Kaisers* (Lauf an der Pegnitz, 2001), p. 304.
21. Görlitz, *Kaiser and Court*, pp. 228–29.

22. *Official German Documents Relating to the World War* (New York, 1923), II, pp. 1320–21.
23. Gaddis Smith, 'Unrestricted U-Boat War', *Purnell's History of the First World War* 5, 1, 1971, p. 1,808; Konrad Jarausch, *The Enigmatic Chancellor* (New Haven, CT, 1973), p. 300; Görlitz, *Kaiser and Court*, pp. 230–31; Helmut Otto and Karl Schmiedel, eds, *Der Erste Weltkrieg: Dokumente* (East Berlin, 1977), pp. 222–24.
24. David Welch, *Germany, Propaganda and Total War, 1914–18* (New Brunswick, NJ, 2000), p. 129.
25. 65 Cong., 1st Sess. Senate Doc. 5, Ser. 7264 (Washington, 1917), pp. 3–8.
26. Alfred Brown was my great-uncle, and Fred, therefore, would have been my second cousin.

Chapter 8 The Path to Revolution

1. IWM, Q81828.
2. J. A. S. Grenville, *A World History of the Twentieth Century, 1900–45*, 2 vols (London, 1980), I, pp. 218–19.
3. Major General Sir John Hanbury-Williams, *The Emperor Nicholas II as I Knew Him* (London, 1922), p. 15.
4. Sir George Buchanan, *My Mission to Russia and Other Diplomatic Memories*, 2 vols (London, 1923), II, p. 76.
5. Meriel Buchanan, *Petrograd: The City of Trouble, 1914–18* (London, 1918), p. 87.
6. Bernard Pares, *The Fall of the Russian Monarchy* (London, 1939), p. 57.
7. Joseph Fuhrmann, ed., *The Complete Wartime Correspondence of Tsar Nicholas II and the Empress Alexandra, 1914–17* (Westport, CT, 1999), p. 676.
8. Ibid., p. 177.
9. Ibid., p. 166.
10. Buchanan, *Mission to Russia*, II, p. 46.
11. Norman Stone, *The Eastern Front, 1914–17* (London, 1975), p. 159.
12. Peter Gatrell, *A Whole Empire Walking: Refugees in Russia during World War I* (Bloomington, IN, 1999), pp. 211–15.
13. Stone, *Eastern Front*, p. 299.
14. Allan K. Wildman, *The End of the Imperial Russian Army*, 2 vols (Princeton, NJ, 1980 and 1987), I, pp. 106–07.
15. Buchanan, *Petrograd*, pp. 95–96.
16. Maurice Paléologue, *An Ambassador's Memoirs*, 3 vols (London, 1923), III, p. 221.
17. Sir Alfred Knox, *With the Russian Army, 1914–17* (New York, 1921), p. 553.
18. Stella Arbenina, *Through Terror to Freedom* (London, 1928), p. 37.
19. Fuhrmann, ed., *Wartime Correspondence*, pp. 690–94, 698–702.
20. Pares, *Fall of Russian Monarchy*, p. 443.
21. Princess Catherine Radziwill, *Nicholas II: The Last of the Tsars* (London, 1931), p. 293.
22. Mark Steinberg and Vladimir Khrustalëv, *The Fall of the Romanovs* (New Haven and London, CT, 1995), p. 81.
23. Ibid., p. 59.
24. Fuhrmann, ed., *Wartime Correspondence*, p. 697.
25. Ibid., pp. 695–97.
26. Steinberg and Khrustalëv, *Fall of the Romanovs*, p. 97.

Chapter 9 The Shadow of the Bomber

1. *The Times*, 16 June 1917, p. 4, 'A Gallant Constable'; idem, 16 June 1917, p. 7, 'Air Attack Warnings'.
2. Clive diary, 15 October 1917, quoted in David French, 'A One-Man Show? Civil-Military Relations in Britain during the First World War', in Paul Smith, ed., *Government and the Armed Forces in Britain, 1856–1990* (London, 1996), pp. 75–108, at p. 82.
3. *Living Age*, 15 January 1928.

4. Sylvia Pankhurst, *The Home Front* (London, 1932), p. 114.
5. TNA, AIR 1/577/16/15/167.
6. *The Times*, 21 December 1914, p. 8.
7. *The Times*, 21 January 1915, p. 11, 'The Spirit of Yarmouth: Courage and Pride'.
8. Pankhurst, *Home Front*, p. 193.
9. TNA, SUPP 5/1052, 'Personal Record of Air Raid Alarms at Woolwich Arsenal', by F. Blythe, p. 10.
10. Ibid., p. 14; Mrs C. S. Peel, *How We Lived Then* (London, 1929), p. 145.
11. IWM, MISC 276/3728, Account by G. Davies.
12. J. B. Firth, *Dover and the Great War* (Dover, 1919), p. 91.
13. TNA, AIR 1/589/16/15/199, Pt 1.
14. Peel, *How We Lived*, pp. 147-49.
15. Ian Castle, *London 1917-18: The Bomber Blitz* (Oxford, 2010), p. 21.
16. *The Times*, 16 June 1917, p. 7, 'Air Raid Warnings'.
17. *The Times*, 16 June 1917, p. 4, 'Child Victims of the Enemy'.
18. *The Times*, 10 July 1917, p. 7, 'Parliament and the Air Raid'.
19. TNA, MEPO 2/1657.
20. Joseph Morris, *The German Air Raids on Great Britain, 1914-18* (London, 1925), p. 244; *Daily Mail*, 25 September 1917.
21. A. D. Harvey, *Collision of Empires: Britain in Three World Wars, 1793-1945* (London, 1992), p. 398.
22. *The Times*, 18 July 1917, p. 2, 'Home Resorts, Spas and Hotels for Change and Rest'.
23. Michael Paris, *Winged Warfare* (Manchester 1992), p. 176.
24. TNA, CAB 24/22, Second Report of the War Cabinet Committee on Air Organisation and Home Defence against Air Raids', 9 August 1917.
25. TNA, BT 102/27; E. B. Ashmore, *Air Defence* (London, 1929), pp. 106, 130.

Chapter 10 The Promised Land

1. Keith Jeffery, *The British Army and the Crisis of Empire, 1918-22* (Manchester, 1984), p. 122.
2. David Fromkin, *A Peace to End All Peace*, 2nd edn (New York, 2001), p. 103.
3. TNA, FO 371/1973, quoted in Jonathan Schneer, *The Balfour Declaration* (London, 2010), p. 39.
4. Sir Ronald Storrs, *The Memoirs of Sir Ronald Storrs* (New York, 1937), p. 168; T. E. Lawrence, *Seven Pillars of Wisdom*, 5th edn (London, 1976), p. 41.
5. Elie Kedourie, *Into the Anglo-Arab Labyrinth: The McMahon-Hussayn Correspondence and Its Interpretation*, 2nd edn (London, 2000), p. 108.
6. David French, *The Strategy of the Lloyd George Coalition, 1916-18* (Oxford, 1995), p. 135.
7. Chaim Weizmann, *Trial and Error* (New York, 1949), pp. 109-10.
8. Ruddock Mackay, *Balfour: Intellectual Statesman* (Oxford, 1985), p. 41.
9. Leonard Stein, *The Balfour Declaration* (London, 1961), p. 152.
10. Max Egremont, *Balfour* (London, 1980), p. 295; Blanche Dugdale, *A. J. Balfour*, 2 vols (London, 1936), II, p. 160.
11. Dugdale, *Balfour*, II, p. 173.
12. TNA, CAB 23/245.
13. William Mathew, 'War-time Contingency and the Balfour Declaration of 1917: An Improbable Regression', *Journal of Palestine Studies* 40(2011), pp. 26-42, at pp. 27 and 38.
14. Weizmann, *Trial and Error*, pp. 152-53.
15. Stein, *Balfour Declaration*, p. 428.
16. Ibid., pp. 470, 664.
17. Barnet Litvinoff, *Weizmann* (London, 1976), p. 109.

248   NOTES to pp. 195–224

18. David Lloyd George, *The Truth about the Peace Treaties*, 2 vols (London, 1938), II, p. 1,133.
19. Fromkin, *Peace to End All Peace*, p. 295; David Vidal, *Zionism: The Crucial Phase* (Oxford, 1987), p. 371.
20. TNA, CAB 21/58, Mins, War Cabinet, 4 October 1917.
21. Weizmann, *Trial and Error*, p. 108.
22. Stein, *Balfour Declaration*, pp. 548–49, 664.
23. Dugdale, *Balfour*, II, p. 301.

Chapter 11 The Moral Imperative

1. State Department, *Papers Relating to the Foreign Relations of the United States: The Lansing Papers, 1914–20* (Washington, DC, 1939–40), I, p. 421.
2. Arthur Link, *Woodrow Wilson: Revolution, War, and Peace* (Arlington Heights, IL, 1979), p. 80.
3. David Lloyd George, *The Truth about the Peace Treaties*, 2 vols (London, 1928), I, pp. 230, 232.
4. W. S. Myers, ed., *Woodrow Wilson: Some Princeton Memories* (Princeton, NJ, 1946), pp. 42–44; Arthur Link, *Wilson: The New Freedom* (Princeton, NJ, 1956), p. 121.
5. William Widenor, *Henry Cabot Lodge and the Search for an American Foreign Policy* (Berkeley, CA, 1980), p. 208; John Braeman, ed., *Wilson* (Englewood Cliffs, NJ, 1972), p. 87.
6. John M. Myers, *The Alamo*, 2nd edn (Lincoln, NB, 1973), p. 189.
7. J. M. Blum, *Woodrow Wilson and the Politics of Morality* (Boston, MA, 1956), p. 19.
8. Arthur Link, ed., *The Papers of Woodrow Wilson*, 63 vols (Princeton, NJ, 1966–90), 33, p. 149.
9. Congressional Record, Special Session and 65th Congress, 1st Sess., LV, 1917, Pt 1, pp. 102–04.
10. Ibid., 2nd Sess. LVI (1917–18), Pt 1, pp. 680–81.
11. Link, *Wilson: Revolution, War, and Peace*, pp. 26–27, 76–77.
12. For the speech as a whole, see R. S. Baker and W. E. Dodd, eds, *The Public Papers of Woodrow Wilson*, 2 vols (New York, 1927), I, pp. 155–62.
13. J. J. Huthmacher and W. I. Susman, eds, *Wilson's Diplomacy: An International Symposium* (Cambridge, MA, 1973), p. 25.
14. Link, *Wilson: Revolution, War, and Peace*, p. 85.
15. Fritz Fischer, *Germany's Aims in the First World War* (London, 1967), p. 616.
16. Link, *Wilson: Revolution, War, and Peace*, p. 85.
17. David Stevenson, *The First World War and International Politics* (Oxford, 1988), p. 195.
18. August Heckscher, *Woodrow Wilson: A Biography* (New York, 1991), p. 425.
19. Louis Auchincloss, *Woodrow Wilson* (New York, 2000), p. 89.

Chapter 12 The Last Throw

1. Winston Churchill, *The World Crisis*, 6 vols (London, 1923–31), IV (1916–18, pt II), p. 433.
2. Kurt Riezler, *Tagebücher, Aufsätze, Dokumente*, ed. K. D. Erdmann (Göttingen, 1972), pp. 459–60.
3. A. G. Gardiner, *The War Lords* (London, 1915), p. 194.
4. Denis Showalter, *Tannenberg: Clash of Empires* (Washington, DC, 2004), pp. 330–31.
5. Holger Herwig, *The First World War: Germany and Austria–Hungary, 1914–18* (London, 1997), p. 121, fn. 22.
6. Holger Afflerbach, *Falkenhayn: Politisches Denken und Handeln im Kaiserreich* (Munich, 1994), pp. 222–23; Gerald Feldman, *Army, Industry and Labour in Germany, 1914–18*, 2nd edn (Providence, RI, 1992), p. 142.

7. Paul von Hindenburg, *Out of My Life* (London, 1920), p. 84.
8. Erich Ludendorff, *Der Totale Krieg* (Munich, 1935), p. 10.
9. Margarethe Ludendorff, *My Married Life with Ludendorff* (London, 1930), p. 26.
10. Ibid., p. 19.
11. Erich Ludendorff, *My War Memoirs, 1914-18* (London, 1919), pp. 541-43.
12. Herwig, *First World War*, pp. 393-94.
13. R. H. Lutz, *The Causes of the German Collapse* (Stanford, CA, 1934), p. 73.
14. Crown Prince Rupprecht, *Mein Kriegstagebuch*, 3 vols (Berlin, 1929), II, pp. 322, 372; Trevor Wilson, *The Myriad Faces of War* (Cambridge, 1986), p. 556.
15. 'The Movement of German Divisions to the Western Front, Winter 1917-18' by, respectively, John Hussey, Tim Travers and Giordan Fong, in *War in History* 4 (1997), pp. 213-20; 5 (1998), pp. 367-70; and 7 (2000), pp. 225-35.
16. Hew Strachan, 'The Morale of the German Army, 1917-18', in Hugh Cecil and Peter Liddle, eds, *Facing Armageddon: The First World War Experienced* (London, 1996), pp. 383-98, at p. 394.
17. Reichsarchiv, *Der Weltkrieg 1914-1918*, 14 vols (Berlin, 1925-44), XIV, p. 445.
18. Rupprecht, *Kriegstagebuch*, II, p. 372.
19. TNA, WO 95/18.
20. James McRandle and James Quirk, 'The Blood Test Revisited: A New Look at German Casualty Costs in World War I', *Journal of Military History* 70(2006), pp. 667-701, at p. 603.
21. Herwig, *First World War*, p. 409.
22. Wolfgang Foerster, *Der Feldherr Ludendorff im Unglück* (Wiesbaden, 1952), pp. 18-19; William Astore and Denis Showalter, *Hindenburg: Icon of German Militarism* (Dulles, VA, 2005), p. 66.
23. Foerster, *Feldherr Ludendorff*, p. 45.
24. Martin Kitchen, *The Silent Dictatorship* (London, 1976), pp. 256-57; Albrecht von Thaer, *Generalstabsdienst an der Front und in der OHL* (Göttingen, 1958), pp. 234-35.

FURTHER READING

Chapter 1 The Silent Conqueror

Key sources for King Albert of the Belgians are two edited collections of his correspond-ence, Marie-Rose Thielemans and Emile Vandewoude, eds, *Le Roi Albert: Au Travers de ses lettres inédites, 1882–1916* (Brussels, 1982), and Marie-Rose Thielemans, ed., *Albert Ier: Carnets et correspondance de guerre, 1914–18* (Paris and Louvain, 1991). There is also a useful, if laudatory, biography, Emile Cammaerts, *Albert of Belgium: Defender of the Right* (New York, 1935), and a similar memoir by Albert's military adviser, Emile Galet, *Albert, King of the Belgians in the Great War* (London, 1931). The Belgian experience of war gener-ally is covered in Sophie de Schaepdrijver, *La Belgique et la première guerre mondiale* (Brussels, 2004); and Serge Jaumain, Michaël Amara, Benoît Majerus and Antoon Vrints, eds, *Une Guerre Totale? La Belgique dans la première guerre mondiale* (Brussels, 2005), while the Belgian entry into the war is dealt with in Jean Stengers, 'Belgium', in Keith Wilson, ed., *Decisions for War, 1914* (London, 1995), pp. 151–76. For Belgian relations with the British and French, see William Philpott, *Anglo-French Relations and Strategy on the Western Front, 1914–18* (Basingstoke, 1996); and idem, 'Britain, France and the Belgian Army', in Brian Bond, ed., *Look to Your Front: Studies in the First World War* (Staplehurst, 1999), pp. 121–36. For the German perspective, see *Ypres, 1914: An Official Account Published by Order of the German General Staff* (London, 1919); Otto Schwink, *La Bataille de L'Yser* (Brussels, 1919); and Erich von Tschischwitz, *Antwerpen* (Berlin, 1924). For the French, see Jean Ratinaud, *La Course à la Mer* (Paris, 1967). The most recent overall account of First Ypres and the autumn campaigns in Flanders is Ian F. W. Beckett, *Ypres: The First Battle, 1914* (Harlow, 2004), while there is a brief overview of the Belgian army in 1914 in W. Labbeke, 'The First Three Months: The Campaign of the Belgian Army in 1914', *Stand To* 28 (1990), pp. 20–26. The most comprehensive treatment of the Belgian inunda-tion is Paul van Pul, *In Flanders Flooded Fields* (Barnsley, 2006), who has the considerable advantage of being a land surveyor specialising in surface water control.

Chapter 2 The Widening of the War

For the Young Turks, see Feroz Gred Ahmad, *The Young Turks: The Committee of Union and Progress in Turkish Politics, 1908–14* (Oxford, 1969); Erik Zürcher, *The Unionist Factor: The Role of the Committee of Union and Progress in the Turkish National Movement, 1905–26*

(Leiden, 1984); M.Naim Turfan, *The Rise of the Young Turks: Politics, the Military, and Ottoman Collapse* (New York, 2000); and M.Şauukrü Hanioğlu, *Preparation for a Revolution: The Young Turks, 1902–08* (New York, 2001). The Turkish decision for war is discussed in F.A.K. Yasamee, 'The Ottoman Empire', in Keith Wilson, ed., *Decisions for War, 1914* (London, 1995), pp. 229–68; Ulrich Trumpener, 'Turkey's Entry into World War I: An Assessment of Responsibilities', *Journal of Modern History* 34 (1962), pp. 369–80; idem., 'The Ottoman Empire', in Richard Hamilton and Holger Herwig, eds, *The Origins of World War I* (Cambridge, 2003), pp. 337–55; Y.T. Kurat, 'How Turkey Drifted into World War I', in Kenneth Bourne and Donald Cameron Watt, eds, *Studies in International History: Essays presented to W. Norton Medlicott* (London, 1967), pp. 291–315; and Feroz Gred Ahmad, 'Ottoman Armed Neutrality and Intervention, August–November 1914', in Sinan Kuneralp, ed., *Studies on Diplomatic History* (Istanbul, 1990), IV, pp. 41–69. The most recent revisionist assessment is that of Mustafa Aksakal, *The Ottoman Road to War in 1914* (Cambridge, 2008), who has also examined the proclamation of jihad in 'Holy War Made in Germany? Ottoman Origins of the 1914 Jihad', *War in History* 18 (2011), pp. 184–99. Relations between Turkey and Germany are covered in H.S. Corrigan, 'German-Turkish Relations and the Outbreak of War in 1914: A Reassessment', *Past & Present* 36 (1967), pp. 144–52; Frank Weber, *Eagles on the Crescent: Germany, Austria and the Diplomacy of the Turkish Alliance, 1914–18* (Ithaca, NY, 1970); Ulrich Trumpener, *Germany and the Ottoman Empire, 1914–1918* (Lexington, KY, 1970); and idem, 'Suez, Baku, Gallipoli: The Military Dimensions of the German-Ottoman Coalition, 1914–18', in Keith Neilson and Roy Prete, eds, *Coalition Warfare: An Uneasy Accord* (Waterloo, ON, 1983), pp. 31–51. Apart from discussing Turkish entry, Hew Strachan also covers the Turkish contribution to the German strategy of subversion in Hew Strachan, *The First World War: To Arms* (Oxford, 2001), pp. 644–814. A useful recent overview is Hamit Bozarslan, 'The Ottoman Empire', in John Horne, ed., *A Companion to World War I* (Chichester, 2010), pp. 494–507.

Chapter 3 The Making of a Nation

The literature on the Anzacs, and on Gallipoli, is enormous, much of it popular in nature, highly coloured and excessively partisan. Two popular accounts penned by academic historians for the general reader are Bill Gammage, *The Broken Years: Australian Soldiers in the Great War*, 2nd edn (Ringwood, 1975); and John Robertson, *Anzac and Empire: The Tragedy and Glory of Gallipoli* (London, 1990). Both lack a critical perspective. More balanced academic studies of the Australian experience are to be found in Lloyd Robson, *The First AIF: A Study of its Recruitment* (Melbourne, 1970); Michael McKernan, *The Australian People and the Great War* (Melbourne, 1980); E. M. Andrews, *The Anzac Illusion: Anglo-Australian Relations during World War I* (Cambridge, 1993); Joan Beaumont, ed., *Australia's War, 1914–18* (St Leonards, 1995); and Christopher Pugsley, *The Anzac Experience: New Zealand, Australia and Empire in the First World War* (Auckland, 2004). For Gallipoli itself, see Tim Travers, *Gallipoli, 1915* (Stroud, 2002); Jenny Macleod, ed., *Gallipoli: Making History* (London, 2004); idem, *Reconsidering Gallipoli* (Manchester, 2004); Nigel Steel and Peter Hart, *Defeat at Gallipoli* (London, 1994); Robin Prior, *Gallipoli: The End of the Myth* (New Haven, CT and London, 2009); and Nigel Steel's important article, 'A Tough Job: The Gallipoli Landings of 25 April 1915', *Sandhurst Journal of Military Studies* 2 (1991), pp. 29–40. Macleod's work touches on commemoration, on which there is also a significant literature. Much of the important work of Ken Inglis is collected in John Lack, ed., *Anzac Remembered: Selected Writings of K. S. Inglis* (Melbourne, 1998). See also Michael McKernan, *Here is Their Spirit: A History of the Australian War Memorial, 1917–90* (St Lucia, 1991); Alistair Thomson, *Anzac Memories: Living with a Legend* (Melbourne, 1994); J. F. Williams, *Anzacs, the Media and the Great War* (Sydney, 1999); Bruce Scates, *Return to Gallipoli: Walking the Battlefields of the Great War* (Cambridge, 2006); and J. G. Pavils, *Anzac Day: The Undying Debt* (Adelaide, 2007). For Charles Bean, see Dudley

McCarthy, *Gallipoli to the Somme: The Story of C. E. W. Bean* (London, 1983); Kevin D. A. Kent, 'The Anzac Book and the Anzac Legend: C. E. W. Bean as Editor and Image-maker', *Historical Studies* 21 (1985), pp. 376–90; Alistair Thomson, 'Steadfast unto Death? C. E. W. Bean and the Representation of Australian Military Manhood', *Australian Historical Studies* 23, (1989), pp. 462–78; Ken Inglis, 'C. E. W. Bean: Australian Historian', in Lack, ed., *Anzac Remembered*, pp. 63–96; and Kevin Fewster, ed., *Gallipoli Correspondent: The Frontline Diary of C. E. W. Bean* (Sydney, 1983). For Ashmead-Bartlett, see Kevin Fewster, 'Ellis Ashmead-Bartlett and the Making of the Anzac Legend', *Journal of Australian Studies* 6 (1982), pp. 17–30. The story of the Australian Light Horse is covered in Peter Burness, *The Nek: The Tragic Charge of the Light Horse at Gallipoli* (Kenthurst, 1996).

Chapter 4 The Man and the Hour

Apart from the official history, the principal modern sources for the Ministry of Munitions are Chris Wrigley, 'The Ministry of Munitions: An Innovatory Department', in Kathleen Burk, ed., *War and the State: The Transformation of British Government, 1914–1918* (London, 1982), pp. 32–56; and R. J. Q. Adams, *Arms and the Wizard: Lloyd George and the Ministry of Munitions, 1915–16* (London, 1978). The military and political background are traced in David French, *British Economic and Strategic Planning, 1905–15* (London, 1982), idem, 'The Military Background to the Shell Crisis of May 1915', *Journal of Strategic Studies* 2 (1979), pp. 192–205; idem, *British Strategy and War Aims, 1914–16* (London, 1986); Clive Trebilcock, 'War and the Failure of Industrial Mobilisation, 1899 and 1914', in Jay Winter, ed., *War and Economic Development: Essays in Memory of David Joslin* (Cambridge, 1975), pp. 139–64; John Turner, *British Politics and the Great War: Coalition and Conflict, 1915–18* (New Haven, CT, 1992); M. D. Pugh, 'Asquith, Bonar Law and the First Coalition', *Historical Journal* 17 (1974), pp. 813–36; and Cameron Hazlehurst, *Politicians at War, July 1914 to May 1915* (London, 1971). From an extensive literature on businessmen in government, see Keith Grieves, *Sir Eric Geddes: Business and Government in War and Peace* (Manchester, 1989); John Turner, ed., *Businessmen and Politics* (London, 1984); and John McDermott, ' "A Needless Sacrifice": British Businessmen and Business as Usual in the First World War', *Albion* 21 (1989), pp. 263–82. There is an even more extensive literature on labour relations, including Gerry R. Rubin, *War, Law and Labour: The Munitions Acts, State Regulation and the Unions* (Oxford, 1987); and Alistair Reid, 'Dilution, Trade Unionism and the State in Britain during the First World War', in S. Tolliday and J. Zeitlin, eds, *Shop Floor Bargaining and the State* (Cambridge, 1985), pp. 46–74. For women, see Arthur Marwick, *Women at War, 1914–18* (London, 1977); Gail Braybon, *Women Workers in the First World War* (London, 1981); Angela Woollacott, *On Her Their Lives Depend: Munition Workers in the Great War* (Berkeley, CA, 1994); and Deborah Thom, *Nice Girls and Rude Girls: Women Workers in World War I* (London, 1998).

Chapter 5 The Power of Image

For the *Battle of the Somme*, see Nicholas Reeves, *Official British Film Propaganda during the First World War* (London, 1986); idem, 'Film Propaganda and its Audience: The Example of Britain's Official Films during the First World War', *Journal of Contemporary History* 18 (1983), pp. 463–94; idem, 'Cinema, Spectatorship and Propaganda: The Battle of the Somme and its Contemporary Audience', *Historical Journal of Film, Radio, and Television* 17 (1996), pp. 5–28; idem, ' "The Real Thing at Last": The Battle of the Somme and the Domestic Cinema Audience in the Autumn of 1916', *Historian* 51 (1996), pp. 4–8; idem, 'Through the Eye of the Camera: Contemporary Cinema Audiences and their "Experience" of War in the Film, Battle of the Somme', in Hugh Cecil and Peter Liddle, eds, *Facing Armageddon* (Barnsley, 1996), pp. 780–98; Roger Smither, ' "A Wonderful Idea of the Fighting": The Question of Fakes in "The Battle of the Somme" ', *Historical Journal of*

Film, Radio, and Television 13 (1993), pp. 149–68; idem, 'Watch the picture carefully and see if you can identify anyone', *Film History* 14 (2002), pp. 390–404; Stephen Badsey, 'Battle of the Somme: British War Propaganda', *Historical Journal of Film, Radio, and Television* 3 (1983), pp. 99–115, revised as 'The Battle of the Somme (1916): The Film of the Battle', in Stephen Badsey, ed., *The British Army in Battle and Its Image, 1914–18* (London, 2009), pp. 107–36; Toby Haggith, 'Reconstructing the Musical Arrangement for The Battle of the Somme', *Film History* 14 (2002), pp. 11–24; Luke McKernan, 'Propaganda, Patriotism and Profit: Charles Urban and British Official War Films in America during the First World War', *Film History* 14 (2002), pp. 369–89; Nick Hiley, 'Hilton DeWitt Girdwood and the Origins of British Official Filming', *Historical Journal of Film, Radio, and Television* 13 (1993), pp. 129–48; J. Hodgkins, 'Hearts and Minds and Bodies: Reconsidering the Cinematic Language of the Battle of the Somme', *Film and History* 38 (2008), pp. 9–19; and Alastair Fraser, Andrew Robertshaw and Steve Roberts, *Ghosts on the Somme: Filming the Battle, June–July 1916* (Barnsley, 2009). For British propaganda generally, see Cate Haste, *Keep the Home Fires Burning: Propaganda in the First World War* (London, 1977); Michael Sanders and Philip Taylor, *British Propaganda during the First World War, 1914–18* (London, 1982); and Gary Messinger, *British Propaganda and the State in the First World War* (Manchester, 1992). For the cinema, see Leslie Midkiff DeBauche, *Reel Patriotism: The Movies and World War I* (Madison, WI, 1997); Michael Paris, ed., *The First World War and Popular Cinema: 1914 to the Present* (Edinburgh, 1999); Karel Dibbets and Bert Hogenkamp, eds, *Film and the First World War* (Amsterdam, 1995); Andrew Kelly, *Cinema and the Great War* (London, 1997); and Kevin Brownlow, *The War, the West and the Wilderness* (London, 1979). On photography, see Jane Carmichael, *First World War Photographers* (London, 1989).

Chapter 6 The Death of Kings

Among older works, A. J. P. Taylor, *The Habsburg Monarchy, 1809–1918* (London, 1948) is still useful while, from the perspective of the dynasty, Edward Crankshaw, *The Fall of the House of Habsburg* (London, 1963), can be updated with Alan Palmer, *Twilight of the Habsburgs* (London, 1994), and Steven Beller, *Francis Joseph* (London, 1996). The wider problems of the empire are covered in R. A. Kahn, *The Multinational Empire: Nationalism and National Reform in the Habsburg Monarchy, 1848–1918*, 2 vols (New York, 1983), and Alan Sked, *The Decline and Fall of the Habsburg Empire, 1815–1918* (London, 1989). Austria-Hungary's part in the outbreak of war is covered in Samuel Williamson, *Austria-Hungary and the Origins of the First World War* (London, 1991), while Lawrence Sondhaus, *Franz Conrad von Hötzendorf: Architect of the Apocalypse* (Boston, 2000), deals with that central figure. For the general war effort see Holger Herwig, *The First World War: Germany and Austria-Hungary* (London, 1997); Robert Kann, Béla Király and Paula Fichter, eds, *The Habsburg Empire in World War I* (Ithaca, NY, 1977); and Manfred Rauchensteiner, *Der Tod des Doppeladlers* (Graz, 1994). The endgame is traced in Mark Cornwall, ed., *The Last Years of Austria-Hungary: Essays in Political and Military History, 1908–18* (Exeter, 1990), and Mark Cornwall, *The Undermining of Austria-Hungary* (Basingstoke, 2000). Maureen Healy, *Vienna and the Fall of the Hapsburg Empire* (Cambridge 2004), provides a vivid picture of increasing tensions, while the difficulties of the alliance with Germany are dealt with in Gerard Silberstein, *The Troubled Alliance: German-Austrian Relations, 1914–17* (Lexington, KY, 1970), and G. W. Shanafelt, *The Secret Enemy: Austria-Hungary and the German Alliance, 1914–18* (Boulder, CO, 1985).

Chapter 7 The Ungentlemanly Weapon

The best overviews of Germany's war experience are Roger Chickering, *Imperial Germany and the Great War, 1914–18* (Cambridge, 1998), and Holger Herwig, *The First World War:*

Germany and Austria-Hungary, 1914–18 (London, 1997). For German naval policy, see Rolf Hobson, *Imperialism at Sea* (Boston, 2002), and Gary Weir, 'Tirpitz, Technology and Building U-boats', *International History Review* 6 (1984), pp. 174–90. British attitudes are covered in Christopher Martin, 'The Complexity of Strategy: Jackie Fisher and the Trouble with Submarines', *Journal of Military History* 75 (2011), pp. 441–70; and Christopher Bell, 'Sir John Fisher's Naval Revolution Reconsidered', *War in History* 18 (2011), pp. 333–56. The best guide to the evolution of maritime law with respect to Anglo-American relations is John W. Coogan, *The End of Neutrality: The United States, Britain and Maritime Rights, 1899–1915* (Ithaca, NY, 1981). More specialist studies of the submarine decision include Holger Herwig and David F. Trask, 'The Failure of Imperial Germany's Undersea Offensive against World Shipping, February 1917-October 1918', *Historian* 33 (1971), pp. 611–36; Holger Herwig, 'Total Rhetoric, Limited War: Germany's U-boat Campaign, 1917–18', in Roger Chickering and Jurgen Förster, eds, *Great War, Total War* (Cambridge, 2000), pp. 265–79. Cultural aspects of submarine warfare are covered in Duncan Redford, *The Submarine: A Cultural History from the Great War to Nuclear Conflict* (London, 2010); and Michael Hadley, *Count Not the Dead: The Popular Image of the German Submarine* (Montreal, 1995).

Chapter 8 The Path to Revolution

Norman Stone, *The Eastern Front, 1914–17* (London, 1975) remains indispensable for the Russian conduct of the war, while the collapse of the Russian army is traced comprehensively in Allan Wildman, *The End of the Russian Imperial Army*, 2 vols (Princeton, NJ, 1980–1987). Lewis Siegelbaum, *The Politics of Industrial Mobilisation in Russia, 1914–17: A Study of the War-Industries Committee* (London, 1984) deals with one aspect of wartime mobilisation. R. B. McKean, *The Russian Constitutional Monarchy, 1907–17* (London, 1977), sets wartime events in context while the most recent, and best, overview of Russia's war experience is Peter Gatrell, *Russia's First World War: A Social and Economic History* (Harlow, 2005). The wartime role of Nicholas and Alexandra is best analysed from their wartime correspondence, now fully available through Joseph Fuhrmann, ed., *The Complete Wartime Correspondence of Tsar Nicholas II and the Empress Alexandra, 1914–17* (Westport, CT, 1999). Their correspondence and other documents for the period from March 1917 onwards are also reproduced in Mark Steinberg and Vladimir Khrustalëv, *The Fall of the Romanovs* (New Haven, CT, 1995). Of the many studies of the Russian Revolution, a useful guide is Edward Acton, *Rethinking the Russian Revolution* (London, 1990), while there is a sweeping overview in Orlando Figes, *A People's Tragedy: The Russian Revolution, 1891–1924* (1996). One particular aspect of revolutionary evolution is traced by both Norman Saul, *Sailors in Revolt: the Russian Baltic Fleet in 1917* (Lawrence, KS, 1978), and Evan Mawdsley, *The Russian Revolution and the Baltic Fleet: War and Politics, 1917–18* (London, 1978). The best overview of the resulting civil war between 1917 and 1921 is Evan Mawdsley, *The Russian Civil War* (London, 1987).

Chapter 9 The Shadow of the Bomber

The German bombing campaign has been the subject of a number of popular accounts including H. G. Castle, *Fire Over England* (London, 1982), A. P. Hyde, *The First Blitz* (Barnsley, 2002); C. M. White, *The Gotha Summer* (London, 1986); and N. Hanson, *First Blitz* (London, 2008). Each and every raid is catalogued in Christopher Cole and E. F. Chessman, *The Air Defence of Britain, 1914–18* (London, 1984). Ian Castle has produced two especially well-illustrated accounts for the general reader, *London, 1914–17: The Zeppelin Menace* (Oxford, 2008), and *London 1917–18: The Bomber Blitz* (Oxford, 2010). For pre-war fears of air attack, see Michael Paris, *Winged Warfare: The Literature and Theory of Aerial Warfare in Britain, 1859–1917* (Manchester, 1992). The evolution of air defences is covered in Alfred Gollin, 'A Flawed Strategy: Early British Air Defence

Arrangements', in R. J. Q. Adams, ed., *The Great War: Essays on the Military, Political and Social History of the First World War* (London, 1990), pp. 31–37; Marian C. McKenna, 'The Development of Air Raid Precautions in World War I', in Tim Travers and C. Archer, eds, *Men at War: Politics, Technology and Innovation in the Twentieth Century* (Chicago, 1982), pp. 173–95; and John Ferris, '"Airbandit": C3I and Strategic Air Defence during the First Battle of Britain, 1915–18', in Michael Dockrill and David French, eds, *Strategy and Intelligence: British Policy during the First World War* (London, 1996), pp. 23–66. For the Smuts Report, see John Sweetman, 'The Smuts Report of 1917: Merely Political Window Dressing?', *Journal of Strategic Studies* 4 (1981), pp. 152–74; and Malcolm Cooper, *The Birth of Independent Airpower: British Air Policy in the First World War* (London, 1986). British retaliation is covered in S. F. Wise, 'The Royal Air Force and the Origins of Strategic Bombing', in Travers and Archer, eds, *Men at War*, pp. 151–8; Christian Geinitz, 'The First Air War against Non-combatants: Strategic Bombing of German Cities in World War I', in Roger Chickering and Stig Förster, eds, *Great War, Total War* (Cambridge, 2000), pp. 207–25; and George Williams, *Biplanes and Bombsights: British Bombing in World War I* (Maxwell, AL, 1999).

Chapter 10 The Promised Land

General accounts of British policy in the Middle East include David Fromkin, *A Peace to End All Peace: The Fall of the Ottoman Empire and the Creation of the Modern Middle East*, 2nd edn (New York, 2001). The classic account of the Balfour Declaration is Leonard Stein, *The Balfour Declaration* (London, 1961), but Stein should now be supplemented by Ronald Sanders, *The High Walls of Jerusalem* (New York, 1983), and Jonathan Schneer, *The Balfour Declaration: The Origins of the Arab-Israeli Conflict* (London, 2010). Contrasting views are expressed in Mayir Vereté, 'The Balfour Declaration and Its Makers', *Middle Eastern Studies* 6 (1970), pp. 48–76; Jehuda Reinharz, 'The Balfour Declaration and Its Maker: A Reassessment', *Journal of Modern History* 64 (1992), pp. 455–92; Mark Levene, 'The Balfour Declaration: A Case of Mistaken Identity', *English Historical Review* 108 (1992), pp. 54–77; James Renton, 'The Historiography of the Balfour Declaration: Toward a Multi-causal Framework', *Journal of Israeli History* 19 (1998), pp. 109–28; and William Mathew, 'War-time Contingency and the Balfour Declaration of 1917: An Improbable Regression', *Journal of Palestine Studies* 40 (2011), pp. 26–42. Its relationship to Anglo-Jewry is traced in Stuart Cohen, *English Zionists and British Jews: The Communal Politics of Anglo-Jewry, 1895–1920* (Princeton, NJ, 1982), and David Vital, *Zionism: The Crucial Phase* (Oxford, 1987). The wider issues of Palestine are covered in Isaiah Friedman, *The Question of Palestine, 1914–18* (London, 1973), and the same author's *Palestine: A Twice-promised Land* (New Brunswick, 2000).

Chapter 11 The Moral Imperative

There are many studies of American wartime diplomacy including David Trask, *The United States in the Supreme War Council: American War Aims and Inter-allied Strategy, 1917–18* (Middletown, CT, 1961); Patrick Devlin, *Too Proud to Fight* (Oxford, 1974); Robert Ferrell, *Woodrow Wilson and World War I* (New York, 1985); Kendrick Clements, *Woodrow Wilson: World Statesman* (Boston, 1987); idem, *The Presidency of Woodrow Wilson* (Lawrence, KS, 1992); Lloyd E. Ambrosius, *Wilsonian Statecraft: Theory and Practice of Liberal Internationalism during World War I* (Wilmington, DE, 1991); and David Esposito, *The Legacy of Woodrow Wilson: American War Aims in World War I* (Westport, CT, 1996). Inevitably, several studies cover Wilson's aims at the Paris peace conferences, and the failure of the US to ratify the Versailles Treaty, including Victor S. Mamatey, *The United States and East Central Europe, 1914–18: A Study in Wilsonian Diplomacy and Propaganda* (Princeton, NJ, 1957); Arthur Walworth, *Wilson and His Peacemakers: American Diplomacy at the Paris*

Peace Conference, 1919 (New York, 1986); Lloyd E. Ambrosius, *Woodrow Wilson and the American Diplomatic Tradition: The Treaty Fight in Perspective* (Cambridge, 1987); and John M. Cooper, *Breaking the Heart of the World: Woodrow Wilson and the Fight for the League of Nations* (Cambridge, MA, 2001). The most recent interpretation of the impact of Wilsonian rhetoric in the Middle East and Far East is to be found in Erez Manela, *The Wilsonian Moment: Self-determination and the International Origins of Anti-colonial Nationalism* (Oxford, 2007). The most detailed biography of Wilson is Arthur Link, *Wilson*, 5 vols (Princeton, NJ, 1947–65). As in his *Woodrow Wilson: Revolution, War, and Peace* (Arlington Heights, IL, 1979), Link remains a dedicated defender of Wilson's record.

Chapter 12 The Last Throw

On German strategy and civil-military relations, see Martin Kitchen, *The Silent Dictatorship: The Politics of the German High Command under Hindenburg and Ludendorff, 1916–18* (London, 1976), and Robert Asprey, *The German High Command at War: Hindenburg and Ludendorff and the First World War* (London, 1994). The 1918 offensives are covered in Martin Kitchen, *The German Offensives of 1918* (Stroud, 2001), and David Zabecki, *The German 1918 Offensives: A Case Study in the Operational Level of War* (London, 2006); and that on the Lys in Chris Baker, *The Battle for Flanders: German Defeat on the Lys, 1918* (Barnsley, 2011). The evolution of German operational and tactical methods is covered by Bruce Gudmundsson, *Stormtroop Tactics: Innovation in the German Army, 1914–18* (New York, 1989); Timothy Lupfer, *The Dynamics of Doctrine: The Change in German Tactical Doctrine during the First World War* (Leavenworth, KS, 1981); Martin Samuels, *Command and Control? Command, Training and Tactics in the British and German Armies, 1888–1918* (London, 1995); David Zabecki, *Steel Wind: Colonel Georg Bruchmüller and the Birth of Modern Artillery* (Westport, CT, 1994); and the classic G. C. Wynne, *If Germany Attacks: The Battle in Depth in the West* (London, 1940), now available in an unexpurgated edition (Brighton, 2010). There is now a great deal of contrasting material on German military morale, including Wilhelm Deist, 'The German Army, the Authoritarian Nation-state and Total War', in John Horne, ed., *State, Society and Mobilisation in Europe during the First World War* (Cambridge, 1997), pp. 160–72; idem, 'The Military Collapse of the German Empire: The Reality Behind the Stab-in-the-Back Myth', *War in History* 3 (1996), pp. 186–207; Alex Watson, *Enduring the Great War: Combat, Morale and Collapse in the German and British Armies, 1914–18* (Cambridge, 2008); Hew Strachan, 'The Morale of the German Army, 1917–18', in Hugh Cecil and Peter Liddle, eds, *Facing Armageddon: The First World War Experienced* (London, 1996), pp. 383–98; Robert Nelson, *German Soldier Newspapers of the First World War* (Cambridge, 2011); and Scott Stephenson, *The Final Battle: Soldiers of the Western Front and the German Revolution of 1918* (Cambridge, 2009).

INDEX